ECONOMIC PHILOSOPHY OF JAWAHARLAL NEHRU

ECONOMIC PHILOSOPHY OF JAWAHARLAL NEHRU

Edited by

ANIL KUMAR THAKUR

and

DEBES MUKHOPADHAYAY

Published on behalf of
THE INDIAN ECONOMIC ASSOCIATION

DEEP & DEEP PUBLICATIONS PVT. LTD.
F-159, Rajouri Garden, New Delhi-110027

ECONOMIC PHILOSOPHY OF JAWAHARLAL NEHRU

ISBN 978-81-8450-272-5

Typeset by S.S. COMPOSERS
3190, Mohindra Park, Shakur Basti, Delhi-110034.

Printed in India at MAYUR ENTERPRISES
WZ Plot No. 3, Gujjar Market, Tihar Village, New Delhi-110018.

Published by DEEP & DEEP PUBLICATIONS PVT. LTD.
F-159, Rajouri Garden, New Delhi-110027.
Phones: 25435369, 25440916
E-mail: ddpbooks@yahoo.co.in • ddpubs@gmail.com
Showroom:
2/13, Ansari Road, Daryaganj, New Delhi-110002 • Telefax: 23245122

Contents

Preface

The year 1947 brought an end of the imperialist power and at the stroke of the midnight hour on August 14 the entire nation awoke 'to life and freedom', as the first guardian of this independence, Jawaharlal Nehru, declared in his classic and celebrated 'Tryst with Destiny' speech. A free independent India was thus born. The country celebrated its 62nd anniversary of independence in 2009. The route that Nehru charted out during 1947-64 as the first Prime Minister of this one of the largest democracies of the world had now been reversed at the behest of the IMF-World Bank. Against this background, the present volume on "Economic Philosophy of Jawaharlal Nehru" is an outcome of the papers selected for technical session in the 91st Annual Conference of the IEA held at Mohanlal Sukhadia University, Udaipur, Rajasthan during 27-29 December, 2008.

For this volume, we are indebted to many of our friends and colleagues who offered their constructive comments as well as positive encouragement while editing the book.

We must also acknowledge the co-operation from all the people associated with the printing of the edited book. We are afraid that we would be remiss if we do not mention the contribution of Sri G.S. Bhatia, Managing Director, Deep & Deep Publications Pvt. Ltd. for the publication of this edited volume in the quickest possible time.

ANIL KUMAR THAKUR
DEBES MUKHOPADHAYAY

From the Editors' Desk

Jawaharlal Nehru (1889-1964) was one of the leading international citizens of the world in the twentieth century. His political mentor, Gandhi, made him the first Prime Minister of India at the age of 58, though his political career started in the mid-1920s against the backdrop of Indian nationalist movement directed towards the British imperial power. It is not at all an exaggeration that his life was largely dominated by politics. This great statesman, undaunted by the grim sight of new-born crises like the truncated India consequent upon the Partition and the attendant tribulations, experimented with the planning mechanism within the democratic frame so as to fulfil the high hopes and aspirations of the 360 million Indian people. This great political man had no basic training of Economics. But he ventured in this discipline with plenty of guts. His economic policy, often christened as "Nehruvian economic policy", was nothing but state-directed development and central planning in a mixed economy frame. The Nehruvian legacy continued till mid-1991 when market-led development was given a warm welcome by the then guardians of the Indian economy. Nehru's economic policy is now judged in the light of the present state of development. Revaluation of economic philosophy of Jawaharlal Nehru is now the subject of study. Very rightly, the Indian Economic Association decided in 2007 to have discussions on Nehru's economic policy so as to bring out an edited volume of the IEA 91st Annual Conference to be held in 2008.

The present volume on "Economic Philosophy of Jawaharlal Nehru" is the product of the 91st Annual Conference of the IEA held at Mohanlal Sukhadia University,

Udaipur, Rajasthan in December 2008. It should contain a collection of papers that are supposed to be arranged in accordance with the *guidelines set for the paper-writers*. Indeed, what transpired at the time of editing the volume is that many of the authors did not trek within the straight-jacket of the set guidelines and travelled all over the sub-themes. Again, a few of the authors adroitly crossed over the porous boundaries of the sub-themes. Thus the stitching of all these papers in accordance with the set *guidelines* is really a difficult task since cross-border movement of these "goods" definitely with some kind of rationale cannot be ruled out. In fact, such 'movements' are required to be respected. Above all, most of the writers had shown their proclivities towards Nehruvian economic policies encircling mainly 'Nehru's Ideas about Planning', 'Nehru on Mixed Economy', and 'Nehru on Industrialization'. Other sub-themes like 'Neo-classical Criticism of Nehru', 'Land Reforms' and 'Science and Technology' thus remained virtually unfocused in this volume. Some contributors of this volume endeavored to locate Nehru in the current phase of globalization. Another group of writers concentrated on Nehru's foreign policy with special reference to Africa—a new chapter on South-South relations.

Editors had to encounter practical problems of accommodating these papers and that too in a proper place, given the set design of the present project. Anyway, the volume is expected to stimulate readers' judgment and belief in right perspective concerning the country's longest-serving (17 years) first Prime Minister so far.

ANIL KUMAR THAKUR
(Secretary and Hon'y Treasurer,
Indian Economic Association)
DEBES MUKHOPADHAYAY
(Former Teacher-in-charge,
St. Paul's C.M. College, Kolkata,
Former Guest Faculty,
Presidency College, Kolkata)

List of Contributors

A. Ranga Reddy, Professor, Department of Economics, Sri Venkateswara University, Tirupati.

A.K. Jha, University Professor, Deptartment of Economics, B.N.M. University (W.C.), Saharsa.

Ambrish Kumar Jha, Dept. of Economics, M.L.S.M. College, Darbhanga, Bihar.

Arun Kumar, Professor and Head, Department of Economics, P.G. Centre, College of Commerce, Patna.

Ashish N. Pandya, Lecturer in Economics, S.P.B. English Medium College of Commerce, Surat, Gujarat.

Asim K. Karmakar, Lecturer, Department of Economics, Jadavpur University, Kolkata.

Bhavna Jha, Lecturer in I.R.P.M., M.A.M. College, Naugachia, T.M. Bhagalpur University, Bhagalpur.

Debdas Ganguly, Campus Director, Alphia Institute of Business Management, Salt Lake City, Kolkata, West Bengal.

Debes Mukhopadhayay, Teacher-in-charge (Former), St. Paul's CM College, Kolkata; Former Guest Faculty, Presidency College, Kolkata

G.S. Bhalla, Professor Emeritus, Center for the Study of Regional Development, School of Social Sciences, JNU, New Delhi.

Girish Chandra Mishra, Dept of History, T.N.B. Law College, Bhagalpur.

Hemant Kumar Sharma, Girija Prashad ka Ahata, Main Road Tundla (UP).

Kapil Sharma, Indra Colony, Near P.W.D. Inspection House, Aligarh Road, Hathras (U.P.).

L.S.N. Prasad, Lecturer, Department of Economics, Hindu College, Guntur.

M.M. Goel, Professor and Chairman, Department of Economics, Kurukshetra University, Kurukshetra, Haryana.

Madhulika, Ph.D. Scholar, B.R.A. Bihar University, Muzaffarpur.

Mrinal Kumar Dasgupta, Former Reader and Head, Department of Economics, B.N. College (B.U.).

Naresh Jha, Director, Jan Shikshan Sansthan, Gaya.

Neeraj Sharma, Research Scholar, K.A. College, Kasganj (U.P.).

Nilima Sahay, Head, Department of Economics, S.G.G.S. College, Patna City.

P. Vasudeva Rao, Sr. Lecturer, Department of Economics, Hindu College, Guntur.

Pankaj Basu, Former Lecturer, Department of Commerce, Kanchrapara College, West Bengal.

Poonam, Department of Economics, College of Commerce, Patna.

Radha Raman Singh, Professor and Head, Department of Economics, B.R.A. Bihar University, Muzaffarpur (Bihar).

Raghubansh Singh, Former Principal, S.S. College, Jehanabad, Bihar.

Rajan Kumar Sahoo, Lecturer in Economics, U.N.S. Mahavidyalaya, Khairabad, Mugpal, Jajpur, Orissa.

Rajesh Kumar, Department of Economics, L.S.W. College, Magadh University, Bodh Gaya.

S.K. Karimulla, Ph.D. Scholar in Economics, Sri Venkateswara University, Tirupati.

Smriti Mukherjee, Reader, Gokhale Institute of Politics and Economics, Pune.

Subodh Kumar Sinha, Department of Economics, S.N.S. College, B.R.A.B.U. Muzaffarpur (Bihar).

Swami Prakash Srivastava, Reader, Department of Economics, Faculty of Social Sciences, Dayalbagh Educational Institute, Agra.

T.G. Gite, Reader and HOD, Chairman of BOS, Business Economics, University of Pune, H.R. College, Rajgurunagar.

Ugra Mohan Jha, Former Prof. and Head, University Dept. of Rural Economics and Cooperation and Former Director, Agro-Economic, Research Centre for Bihar and Jharkhand, TM Bhagalpur University, Bhagalpur.

Introduction

I

NEHRUVIAN ECONOMICS: AN INTRODUCTION

Of the Nehru-Gandhi family—"first family" of Indian politics—Jawaharlal (1889-1964) was made the first Prime Minister of India between 14 August and 15 August 1947, as Bapuji wanted.

Indian people, without any qualms, can take legitimate pride in having the most eminent founders of modern India—the father of the nation, the Bapuji and J.L. Nehru, the latter was the "apprentice" of the former in politics in the 1920s. Attracted by his charm, agnostic vision for the country's freedom and future development, passion for humanism, modern science and technology, organizational capability of becoming a mass leader, commitment to secularism, Gandhi thought Nehru as his political successor. Gandhi experienced the realization of his dream on 15 August 1947 not from Delhi as he was then travelling different affected pockets of the country following communal orgy and the holocaust of Partition.

Although an aristocrat, western educated elite, Nehru was the darling of the Indian crowd. After all, in spite of the presence of Gandhi in the Congress Party, Nehru became the leader of the left-wing of the INC. An Indian version of socialism that is, "an Englishman in Indian clothing" or in the words of Nehru, "the socialistic pattern of society" was presented to the Indian people by Nehru.

Nehru began conceptualizing his vision for a free, liberated and politically independent India in the 1920s when he spent some best years of his life (five and half years) in prison. After independence proper management of the Indian economy through economic planning was his forte. Nehru immediately after independence, said in Calcutta, 15 December, 1947 that although the struggle for political independence was over, but he reminded another 'an equally important struggle, namely the economic well-being of the masses, is far from being over.' Over the years, his economic maturity was then increasing at an exponential rate. His vision for India's economic problems and policies had never been tangential or shaped and designed by bureaucrats and experts, though he was not professional economist. His economic maturity may be summed up as he said in 1955: "I am fed up of politics, my entire life has been spent in politics and even now I have to give most of my time to it. But I do not want to waste my time in entire politics or international affairs. My mind is full of our economic problems and the need to make economic progress, to make the people better-off, and so on...the real problem before us is the economic progress of India." This kind of economic perception of Pandit Nehru helped to devise economic agenda to be followed for the uplift of the Indian economy.

Nehru, being an institution-builder, mixed up 'development' and 'democracy'. He built up the parliamentary form of democracy where elected representatives would be designated as the rulers of the country. Meanwhile, the first General Election was held in 1951-52, and thus Nehru's Prime Ministership was endorsed by the people's choice in 1952. Thus democratic system and institutions were born. Indeed, India's experiment with the parliamentary democracy against the backdrop of a backward, an almost illiterate economy owes more to Nehru than anyone else. However, some critics like Rajani Kothari strongly made a plea that the democratic governance could not be pursued because of the rise of 'extra-constitutional' individuals and groups.

For the management of the Indian economy Nehru revelled in economic planning as he viewed planning in a somewhat different perspective: "Behind the plan lies the conception of India's unity and of a mighty cooperative effort of all the people of India...The more we think of this balanced picture of the whole of India...the less we are likely to go astray in the crooked paths of provincialism, communalism, casteism and all other disruptive and disintegrating tendencies." Nehru would have wailed today if he had escaped death in May 1964.

It is indeed true that the keystone of 'Nehruvian' economic policy is planning. In Nehru's scheme of economic policies there are as many as three main elements: (i) modernization of the economy through industrialization; (ii) self-reliance; and (iii) socialism or to be more specific "socialistic pattern of society" (adopted at the *Avadi* session in 1955) and not a rigid textbook doctrinaire.

Nehruvian Industrialization

To Nehru, modernization of the Indian economy is synonymous with industrialization. Since industrialization is 'a conduit of technology and the scientific spirit,' the word 'modernization' then gets fraternized with industrialization. As rapid economic growth was to be achieved industrialization was needed. The strategy that was mapped out was the establishment of basic, critical heavy industries, mainly in the public sector. However, Nehru was not averse to private enterprise and foreign capital and technology, as well as foreign assistance to finance the massive investment, but not at the expense of the country's economic independence. Obviously 'the aim will be the good of India.' But Nehru did not visualize the alternative industrialization paradigm of 'small is beautiful'. But rapid industrialization necessitates rapid agricultural development. In his broadcast to the nation on the New Year's Eve 31 December 1952, Nehru said: "Greater production is essential, both through agriculture and industries if we are to fight poverty and raise standards, as we must." This means that Nehru was talking about the balanced growth approach. On another occasion, he asserted: "In India we have to develop, we have to consider many things and one is the balance between rural and urban economy." But as far as policies and programs are concerned, interdependence as well as the balance between agriculture or rural and industry or urban economy had not been endorsed with all seriousness. Agriculture has the potentially of bringing about a higher growth rate. The early green revolution years bear testimony to this fact. The era of Nehruvian industrialization indeed dates back to the Second and Third Plan periods (1956-66). In the First Plan, as the objective was to stabilize the economy, larger allocations were made in favor of agriculture and not industry, as such.

Self-reliance and Import Substitution

Self-reliance refers to independence from foreign capital and foreign assistance. But Nehru wanted industrialization particularly heavy and basic industries with foreign capital, or to be more specific foreign aid. Planners under the direction of Nehru-Mahalanobis opted for the policy of Import Substituting Industrialization (ISI)—the foundation stone of the Indian planning.

In the 1950s, 60s and 70s, the dominant strategy of economic development of the third world countries was the ISI strategy under which anti-trade attitudes prevailed. The strategy demanded tariff barriers were to be erected with the aim of fostering domestic industries. In simple words, it referred to the so-called "infant industry" logic for protection. The rationale for the adoption of this strategy in India could be traced to the goal of self-reliance and reduction of external dependence so as to deepen and widen her industrial base. This strategy yielded encouraging results in some East Asian countries, often called the East Asian Miracle. Such did not happen in India. Some critics say that this prescription was a disaster. The strategy is often criticized for creating inefficiencies in Indian industries, including public sector industries. Sheltering of domestic market brought havoc in the export sector. In brief, the "inefficient" nature of ISI policy fostered the development of (i) high cost industrial structure, (ii) industrial sickness, (iii) elimination of competition and consolidation of monopoly, (iv) low productivity, (v) interplay of propertied classes in cornering state resources in the policy-making, and (vi) distortion in industrial structure, etc.

Socialism

Nehru was not a Marxist but had deep regard for Marxism. Thus Nehru's socialism could not be identified with the complete public ownership and state planning. In fact, he had his own version. Nehru articulated, "Planning will be no planning if it does not cover all our activities, public or private. The public sector will necessarily be more precise and definite." Thus he had his own sketch of socialism—an ideal not for 'any single party or group lout of India as a whole'. This *â la* version of socialism has been christened as the "socialistic pattern of society", 'where the principal means of production are progressively speeded up and there is equitable distribution of the national wealth'.

Nehruvian socialism is often associated with public enterprises which had been focused largely 'as an instrument of planning for industrialization and growth'. Nehruvian legacy no longer holds as public sector enterprises are now described as failed institutions. Never had it functioned as efficient tools of management of government policies.

Nehru on Science and Technology

Nehru's thrust in science and technology could be traced to the early months of 1938 when his message was read in the Indian Science Congress. He said that science alone could solve India's endemic problems of hunger and poverty, insanitation and illiteracy and so on. After becoming the Prime Minister, he planned to construct 'temples of science' in the country through which the country would be able to promote self-sustaining scientific and technological growth. The 'brain drain' of our scientists across the globe in the late 1950s could be traced to the vision that Nehru had in mind relating to science and technology.

But as far as primary education was concerned, strangely Nehru gave primary education the brush-off!

Nehru's Foreign Policy

India's foreign policy was marked by non-aggression and non-interference as soon as Nehru assumed power. The essence of such foreign policy was the preservation of peace. The policy that he founded came to be known as the policy of non-alignment under which 'free exchange of ideas and trade and other contacts between different nations' would prosper. There is no iota of doubt that Nehru contributed to the lessening of the international tensions and conflicts between different nations.

But the War with China in 1962 inflicted upon a great blow to India's self-respect and Nehru's policy of friendship with China. This war cost him heavily as he contemplated that war or an even conflict with China was an 'historical impossibility'. First, China was not India's natural friend as was believed by Nehru. Secondly, India's lack of defense preparedness was exposed. Following the 'China factor', Nehru's popularity was on the wane. He had to assimilate uncharitable comments from many quarters. Some people say that his foreign policy was his 'greatest failure'.

Flustered by criticisms and threatened by leadership question by some political bigwigs, Nehru began to crumble. In the last years of his life, proliferation of both domestic and external problems thus brought immense mental stress and strain in January 1964 when Nehru suffered a stroke. However, the "gentle colossus" survived till 27 May 1964 when another stroke killed him. The Nehru age in India's history ended. As Nehru enjoyed some sort of centralization of power, he wanted Indira Gandhi—his only child—to enter India's political scene. She had to wait for two years more after Nehru's death so as to build up the Nehru-Gandhi dynasty in Indian politics.

A Peep into Nehru's Works

Nehru's flowering of literary genius needs to be told here rather in brief.

As far as book purchases were concerned, Nehru was indeed extravagant. The gift that he was used to make to his beloved ones including the little child Indira was books only on birthdays and other occasions.

One of the classics that he wrote in 1928 was the *"Letters from a Father to His Daughter"* (published by the Children's Book Trust). It is the collection of as many as 30 letters meant for 10-year old Indira Nehru—the only child. In a schoolmasterly tone, he taught natural history and the story of civilization. This simple book is considered as the 'encyclopedia for children of the world'. This book he gave to Indira as a 'birthday gift' from prison.

"Glimpses of World History" (1934) is again a collection of about 200 letters on world history of mankind. Nehru's world history starts from 6000 BC to the mid-1930s. Nehru gave a succinct account of the rise and fall of the great empires and civilizations of the world over the centuries. Indira proudly said in the *Foreword* of *"The Discovery of India"* that *'Glimpses'* was written for me. It remains the best introduction to the story of man for young and growing people in India and all over the world.'

If one is interested in knowing Nehru's literary genius, he should go through *"The Discovery of India"* (1946). He wrote this book during 1942-46. Nehru intended to discover India from the days of the Indus Valley Civilization to the end of the British Raj and himself through the medium of history.

Several editions of another great works of Nehru—*"An Autobiography"* (1936, 1949 and 1958)—were published during his lifetime. Regarding the *Autobiography,* Indira Gandhi mentioned that this book "has been acclaimed as not merely the quest of one individual for freedom, but as an insight into the making of the mind of new India."

Concluding Observations

Anyway, Nehruvian economic policies and the development strategies that had been rolled out in the poverty-stricken, predominantly agrarian backward Indian economy yielded moderate growth rates but higher than the pre-independent levels. However, her performance in the export sector was a pathetic one 'when the world economy was expanding rapidly in the 1950s and 1960s, and India's share of world markets fell.' All these have had a depressing effect on the overall economic growth rate consequent upon the terrific balance of payment crisis of the mid-1960s. However, some sort of economic stability through conservative but prudent monetary and fiscal management policies was maintained during the Nehru era. Sunil Khilnani observes: "Nehru's real failures in the economic sphere lay in his inability to establish an effective system of primary education and to alter the rural property order – two achievements that proved essential to the economic surge that enabled other Asian countries to leap past India in later decades. Yet it is still perhaps early days to come to a final judgment about his legacy. Were the Indian economy to move into a sustained high growth pattern in the twenty-first century, and if it is able to achieve a measure of redistribution, the choices made by Nehru, subject in recent years to much criticism, may ultimately be vindicated."

Let me conclude in the words of Bipan Chandra and Mukherjee: "The legacy he left behind is in many respects a sheet anchor for the Indian people who are today buffeted about in a sea of despair. What more could a people ask from a leader? Has any society, any people, the right to ask from a leader, however great, to solve all the problems once for all." In fact, it was Nehru who laid 'the foundation of a new India'.

ANIL KUMAR THAKUR
DEBES MUKHOPADHAYAY

References

S.Gopal and Uma Iyengar (eds), (2003), *The Essential Writings of Jawaharlal Nehru,* Vol. II; OUP

Jawaharlal Nehru (1946), *The Discovery of India,* Signet Press, Calcutta.

Akbar, M.J. (1988), *Nehru : The Making of India,* Viking, London.

Mukherjee, Hirendranath (1964), *The Gentle Colossus: A Study of Jawaharlal Nehru,* Manisha Granthalaya, Calcutta.

Brown Judith (2003), *Nehru: A Political Life,* OUP.

Judd, Denis (1993), *Jawaharlal Nehru,* GPC Books.

Bipan Chandra, (*et. al.*) (1999), *India Since Independence,* Penguin Books.

Hiranmay Karlekar (ed.) (1998) *Independent India: The First Fifty Years,* Indian Council for Cultural Relations.

John McLeod (2004), *The History of India,* Greenwood Press.

N.N. Vohra and Sabyasachi Bhattacharya (ed.) (2002), *Looking Back: India in the Twentieth Century,* National Book Trust.

Sunil Khilnani (1997), *The Idea of India;* Hamish Hamilton, London.

Kaushik Basu (ed.) (2007), *The Oxford Companion to Economics in India,* OUP.

Anne O. Krueger (ed.) (2002), *Economic Policy Reforms and the Indian Economy,* OUP.

II

OVERVIEW

G.S. Bhalla's paper entitled as *Economic Philosophy of Jawaharlal Nehru* covers all the sub-themes of the *Guidelines for the Paper-writers*. Bhalla links Nehru's economic philosophies with the country's freedom movement. Almost all the strategies based on the idea of Nehruvian socialism have been presented. The author offers an imprint of Nehru's thought on Science and Technology and higher education in shaping the future destiny of India in the right and meaningful direction. These are the foundations upon which the development of agriculture, industry and others of the then new-born child depended. One of the intentions of this paper is to silence the neo-classical critics of Nehru. In addition, Nehru's economic performance in terms of growth indicators is an attempt to vindicate his opinion: a higher growth trajectory could also be attained in a closed and planned economy. To the author, Nehru was not only a dreamer but also an achiever who needs to be remembered with reverence.

Radha Raman Singh and Madhulika's paper—*Economic Philosophy of Jawaharlal Nehru*—draws our attention to the fact that by innovating the concept of mixed economy, Nehru intended not to have class struggle in the Indian soil. But Nehru's endeavor in building several institutions as pillars of democracy, secularism, socialism, nationalism brought conflicts and contradictions. Instead of a pan-Indian socialistic pattern of society, the country during Nehru's regime could not come out from the quagmire of poverty, illiteracy, social inequalities as well as destructive activities and corruption. The irony is that a mass leader's philosophy turned out to be the ideology of the elite middle classes. They conclude that Nehru's philosophy was more prophetic without concrete operational support for which Nehru himself was responsible. Further, his economic philosophy was subject to irresponsible interpretations by many decision-makers and the inheritors who wanted to vilify him.

Smriti Mukherjee in her paper titled *Nehru and the*

Choice of Mixed Economy says that Nehru's brand of socialism comes closer to the New Economic Policy of the erstwhile USSR and not soviet-type socialism. Since welfare of the Indian masses was his greatest concern, he remained a firm believer of the mixed economy principle as a principle of governance throughout his life. But the experiment with the mixed economy caused huge embarrassments—like growing poverty and increasing inequality along with lower growth rates—to many Indians. To save from these embarrassments India had to wait till 1991 when the era of reform of the Nehruvian mixed economy was replaced by the free market principles—an anathema of the principle of state capitalism. Ms. Mukherjee strongly argues that being an international citizen, Nehru would have joined in the current bandwagon of liberalization, privatization, etc., for the sake of higher growth even by disowning his own 'baby'—the mixed economy principle—had he been alive.

Mrinal Kumar Dasgupta in his paper *Nehru: A Synthesizer of Two Extreme Economic Doctrines* has highlighted the fact that Nehru amalgamated the Gandhian doctrine with the neo-classical free market principles of growth, equity and justice. The process of amalgamation of the two opposite doctrines gave birth to the doctrine of mixed economy and ultimately state capitalism as the strategy for India's economic development. This synthesis, the author argues forcefully, produces an optimum solution in a feasible region as it incorporates the right qualities of the two economic institutions. Herein exists the essence of democratic socialism in India. But Nehru, being a dreamer, could not foresee any distortions that may creep in and thus the difficulties in the attainment of basic objectives of the society. In spite of this, the author believes that as a synthesizer Nehru's contribution can never be debunked.

Kapil, Neeraj and Hemant Kumar Sharma in their joint paper outline first how Nehru combined the prevailing two 'isms'—capitalism and socialism—and made a mixed economy principle as an economic system that still prevails in India even in this world of market economy. It could then be referred to as a "Specialism." Sharmas then argue that Nehru designed his foreign policy in the light of

India's the then state of economic development and conclude that the Nehruvian ideas could not be pushed behind the neo-liberal economic world as Nehru was not likely to be averse to (emotional) globalization.

Debes Mukhopadhayay's paper entitled *J.L. Nehru—A Model-maker of India's Democracy and Development* suggests that Nehru was not only the father of Indian economic planning but also his version of state planning was regarded as a model for Asian and African developments. Nehru's economic policies had been greatly influenced by the prevailing development theories like import substituting industrialization strategy coupled with a regime of protective walls and controls and regulations although Nehru had never been a rigid doctrinaire. Indeed, his agnostic vision was essentially a pan-Indian. Even then, the author mentions that the country experienced 'a distorted model of both democracy and development'. Institutional failure, crisis of governance, soft state, growth through exclusion, etc.,—the endemic crises that the country now sees—were then sprouting their heads.

Swami Prakash Srivastava in his paper *The Economic Ideas of Pandit Jawaharlal Nehru and their Relevance in the Changing Scenario* looks upon the best achievements of Nehru. Although Gandhi was responsible to make Nehru as the first prime minister of independent India, Nehru's dependence on Gandhiji was filial. Gandhi and Nehru differed on the issue of industrialization: former favored village and *khadi* industries and the latter favored industrialization for modernization of the country. The author emphasizes how Nehru employed Keynesian approach suited to the underdeveloped countries like India. Pleasure-hunting people criticize Nehru and Nehru's greatness and achievements bear testimony to the fact that he is remembered even today as a great political leader, a true democrat, and a great achiever in economic front.

Raghubansh Singh's paper on *Nehru's Economic Policy and Current Global Crisis* elaborates how Nehruvian concept of mixed economy as well as the philosophy of Nehruvian socialism was abandoned under the impact of New Economic Policy introduced by the people in power of the same Indian National Congress Party in 1991 that Nehru fostered throughout his life. The author argues that the current economic meltdown could be mitigated only by infrastructural spending by the government even against the backdrop of the poor state of public finance. The paper recommends the steps to be taken now to stem the rot inflicted upon the economy through global economic downturn.

The paper—*The Nehruvian Legacy: Its Impact on the Indian Economy* authored by **Asim K. Karmakar**—says that instead of "being a modernizer *par excellence*" (Sukhamay Chakraborty), Nehru sought the route of land reforms programme instead of technology-led agricultural development. Nehru's concept of self-reliance was something different but embedded in inward-looking ISI strategy. The author draws attention to the fact that in spite of self-reliance model of development, foreign exchange crisis that erupted during the mid-1950s caused great embarrassment to Nehruvian economic policy. This development enticed Western powers to perk their 'aid' and 'machineries' for India's industrialization effort. Karmakar concludes that Nehru's economic policy in a democratic polity suffered a lot under the edifice of state control resulting in throttling of the future growth of the country.

T.G. Gite in his paper *Pt. Nehru on Industrialization,* argues that Nehru did acknowledge the role of small scale and cottage industries in the country's development. But at the same time compulsive industrialization was his big agenda as the country's development could be made higher only through industrialization, especially the large scale one. All these are made known in the Industrial Policy Resolutions of 1948 and 1956. This resulted in higher allocation to heavy public sector industries. But the worst was to come after Nehru's death in 1964. The industrial economy of India since the mid-60s experienced underused and expensive capital goods capacity, that is, industrial stagnation. Author, for this quandary, finds fault with the Nehruvian socialistic policies and nothing else.

Ugra Mohan Jha and Naresh Jha in their long-sized joint paper *Relevance of Nehruvian Economics under Globalization Regime* have articulated Nehruvian philosophy of public sector-led industrialization strategy as the major 'engine of growth'. During his life time, public sector acquired the "commanding heights of the economy" as its power and potentials spread in almost all the strategic sectors of the economy. After Nehru's demise and particularly in the current reform era public sector has been losing its pre-eminence rapidly against the backdrop of disinvestment and globalization. Authors very strongly argue that the current globalization process rather gave a mortal blow to the Nehruvian views of state-led development and economic planning—a distinctive Nehruvian economic philosophy and a pan-Indian economic identity. This unfortunate development needs to be reversed so that India again makes a stand for 'welfare state' as conceived by Nehru.

While demonstrating the relevance of the Nehruvian economic thoughts, **M.M. Goel** in his paper *Relevance of the Economic Thoughts of Jawaharlal Nehru in Present Times* suggests that revisiting Nehru's economic thoughts is needed for making a room for 'continuous economic reforms'. He argues the essential sinews of green revolution in agriculture were laid by Pt. Nehru. Controls and regulations devised during this regime, however, brought failures in the execution of industrial policies. The so-called privatization move of the current period can even be traced to the Nehruvian control regime and its consequent evils. Today, marketists criticize Nehru for his state-sponsored development. But his beliefs and economic convictions—the idea of mixed economy, the terms of trade thesis and the emergence of the ISI strategy—were influenced by the then economic thinking. Nehru's achievements are then undeniable. As Nehru was not a rigid doctrinaire, he would have enfolded the current neo-classical economic policies had he been alive. As editors, we could not sectionalize Goel's paper as making of such sectional division of the paper is the task of the author himself. Further, no references and bibliography of the paper are available with the editors.

Rajan Kumar Sahoo in his paper *Socialism and Thoughts of Jawaharlal Nehru* begins with the famous speech of Nehru's "tryst with the destiny" when he assumed the charge of the country's first Prime Ministership on 15 August 1947. Nehru designed a roadmap for the socialistic pattern of society in a parliamentary form of democracy. Since socialization is an anathema in a class-based economy, Nehru coalesced planning in India with a socialistic stance. The author believes that the posterity will remember Nehru for ever as a builder of modern India.

Subodh Kumar Sinha and Rajesh Kumar in their joint paper entitled *Nehru and Indian Economic Planning with Special Reference to the Second Five Year Plan* elucidate Nehru's Second Five Year Plan, also known as Mahalanobis model. They have presented in a simple way the Mahalanobis 4-sector economy comprising investment goods sector, consumer goods sector, household industries and services sector. Run-of-the-mill comments over the said Plan have been made. The source of Table 1 (p. 165) is available on *The Review of Economics and Statistics,* Vol. XLI, No. 1, February 1959, instead of C.D. Wadhva's book as claimed by the authors. However, authors firmly believe that Nehru's ideas and strategies towards the country's socio-economic issues 'are more relevant than even in his time'.

In their joint paper entitled *An Assessment of Role of Economic Thoughts and Basic Philosophy* of *Jawaharlal Nehru over Growth and Development of India,* **Debdas Ganguly and Pankaj Basu** illustrate, in a nutshell, Nehru's basic economic philosophy. Economic planning and democratic socialism are the two great economic policies and actions that Nehru cherished till his death. Authors have tried to explain successfully that Nehru devised and implemented five year plans to give not only an economic lift of a backward country but also and more importantly to forge an emotional unity among the different regions of the country characterized by varied cultures, caste, creed, etc. The paper also emphasizes that the science and technology were not Nehru's passion as such; rather he was stubborn to its application because of 'its capacity to transform an economy of scarcity into abundance'. It is not fair enough to blame Nehru for all the shortcomings and failures of his policies.

A.K. Jha, Bhavna Jha and Girish Chandra Jha in their lengthy paper *Economic and Technological Co-operation with Resurgent Africa: An International Vision of Nehru* dwell upon mainly Nehru's foreign policy with respect to primarily Africa and other developing countries. Nehru indeed was more concerned with the South-South economic co-operation. Indeed as Nehru was a visionary, he sought for people-to-people cooperation between Africa and India so that the latter could follow India's model of development, exchange knowledge, and experiences. Such co-operation rose to an all-time high during Nehru's term of premiership. It is said that the co-operation between India and Africa rested on three main fulcrums of trade, technical assistance, and joint ventures. Authors have traveled very extensively all the areas of technical, academic, military co-operation—the hallmarks of the spirit of partnership between South-South without any ulterior motive.

The paper entitled *Economic Philosophy of Jawaharlal Nehru and its Implications: An Appraisal* of **Ambrish Kumar Jha** is another over-sized paper. Ambrish K. Jha mulls an idea that in addition to awarding political independence to the people of India from the British rule, Nehru gave economic freedom too to the nation through the means of planning, mixed economy, industrialization, etc. India is often criticized in the light of high growth performance of the reform era, of course, in a neo-liberal setting rather than from the scaffolding of the mixed economy. Such uncharitable criticisms are too difficult to digest, as is believed by the author. In fact, he finds the real causes of such malaise should be traced in our parliamentary form of democracy, work culture, implementation of policies, etc., and not Pt. Nehru's policies as such.

Nilima Sahay, Arun Kumar and Poonam in their joint paper *Economic Philosophy of Jawaharlal Nehru: An Agenda for Justice and Equality* carefully and very rightly point out that institution-building is essential for development of the independent India. Nehru deserves commendation for building up a slew of institutions that could not only act as agents of development but also act as bulwarks against inequity and injustice. Authors argue with greater conviction that the patronage politics with a wide network of patronage distribution catering to the poor, marginalized, sub-altern people for whom Nehru had deep regard indeed helped to empower these underdogs of the society. To be honest enough, Nehru made a preparatory stage for the institution-building in India.

L.S.N. Prasad and P. Vasudeva Rao in their joint paper *Nehru—the Builder of Indian Economic Empire* struggle to demonstrate that Nehru wanted more production and that too with a social motive is indeed a contradiction. Nehru batted for private big industrialists very deftly and a mammoth *private* sector (such as, agriculture, small and cottage industries and medium-sized industries, and big-sized industries of big businesses) was allowed to flourish. This kind of so-called Nehruvian socialism could be dubbed as 'un-Indian'. Above all, Nehru wanted to have a balance between agriculture and industry as a strategy of development, but in the process agriculture rather received a step-motherly treatment. However, authors very rightly make a strong plea that for any kinds of failure Nehru is not to be held responsible alone.

S.K. Karimulla and A. Ranga Reddy in their joint but concise paper *Nehru: A Visionary for Democracy and Development* start with the origin of the Parliamentary system. Like many, these authors believe that the foundation of democracy and development through economic planning that Nehru nurtured during his term of Prime Ministership (1947-1964) of the country must be more deep-rooted in India for the welfare of the Indian masses.

In his paper *Nehru and the Policy of Mixed Economy*, **Ashish N. Pandya** elaborates why Nehru opted for the mixed economy principle—the middle path of development—in the Indian economy. This paper attempts to justify the rationale of the ISI strategy for industrialization on the basis of the prevailing doctrines preached by Nurkse, Singer, Prebisch, etc. The author concludes that as this strategy resulted in huge accumulation of public debt, rethinking on mixed economy is needed.

ANIL KUMAR THAKUR
DEBES MUKHOPADHAYAY

1

Economic Philosophy of Jawaharlal Nehru

G.S. Bhalla

Nehru's penchant for Marxism and the real success of the Soviet Union built on pure socialist ideas enthralled Nehru so much that he designed radical economic programmes for the Congress Party. How did Nehru translate his economic thinking, policies, etc., that he cultivated during the pre-independent years into action after independence has been discussed in section I. Section II is inconcerned with land reforms while sections III and IV delineate state-led industrialization in tandem with the private sector but a controlled one. In sections V and VI, Nehru's attitude toward 'science and technology', and a brief idea about his foreign policy based on non-alignment movement have been addressed. Section VII is an attempt to challenge the neo-classical criticisms of Nehru. Being a planner in a true Indian sense, Nehru's policies yielded better results than the current one. The data summarized in Table 1 tend to substantiate this claim.

INTRODUCTION

Nehru's economic philosophy can be analysed by looking at and his intimate knowledge of Indian reality as a freedom fighter and peasant leader, his socialistic ideology, and later on his imprint on policy as the Prime Minister of India. From its earliest beginnings, Indian nationalism had a large element of economic thinking and social reform. This was, to some extent, an unusual feature for a national movement. As a leader of the Indian National Congress, along with Gandhi, Nehru was instrumental in gradually imparting economic content to national movement.

The Marxist background gave him an understanding of history and enabled him to understand the forces underlying change. As he writes in his Autobiography, "The Marxist interpretation threw a flood of light on it (history), and it became an unfolding drama with some order and purpose, howsoever unconscious, behind it....it was the essential freedom from dogma and the scientific outlook of Marxism that appealed to me."

Freedom was considered the indispensable means to overcome mass poverty, to protect the farmers and the artisans, to create modern industry, to remove privilege and injustice and to reconstruct the entire fabric of India's social and economic life. Beginning with Dadabhai Naoroji, whose paper on "The Poverty of India" (2 parts) was presented as far back as 1873-76, a long line of national leaders placed these aims in the forefront of the national struggle. With the coming of Mahatma Gandhi, the movement spread with remarkable rapidity to the peasantry and the workers of India. To Gandhiji freedom was not merely a political objective, but the raising of the masses of the people from their poverty and degradation. He aligned himself with the masses of the Indian people and as the Third Five Year Plan (1961) puts it: "In this way, as the political struggle for Independence developed and took shape in mighty movements, it was allied in some measure to India's basic social and economic problems, and more particularly the agrarian problem. The social and economic aims of the struggle for freedom became progressively more definite."

I. NEHRU'S EARLY IDEAS ABOUT PLANNING AND DEVELOPMENT STRATEGY

Hence, Nehru's economic philosophy can only be understood in the historical context of India's struggle for independence and his role as a leader of India's national movement which was in the forefront of freedom struggle. As a freedom fighter and as leader of national movement, Nehru along with Gandhi saw the political struggle for freedom as the only way to emancipate the lot of people from hunger and deprivation. Thus struggle for freedom got inextricably intertwined with economic and social policies for development and poverty eradication.

Keeping in mind the political realities, there was a gradual change in the ideological position of Nehru also. In this matter, it has been suggested that Nehru's stay in Europe for three years and his association with the Marxists and Communists in England and his participation in the Brussel's Conference in 1926, had profound impact on him. It has also been suggested that Nehru seems to have been transformed from a reformist Gandhian to a confirmed Marxist.[1] There is no doubt that he was profoundly impressed by the socialist experiment in Soviet Union when he visited there during the early 1927. But a much more important explanation for his gradual transformation is the fact that being a perceptive leader he was also able to comprehend the changing mood of the Indian national movement and was convinced of the need to give a progressive content to it.

By the time he came back to India, Nehru started advocating radical economic programme for the Congress. In his Presidential Address delivered to the Congress on 26th January, 1929 at Lahore, Nehru while pleading for Indian independence, also unfolded some of his thinking about the peasant question. He stated "It is the peasantry that cries loudly and piteously for relief and we must deal with their present condition. Real relief can only come by a great change in the land laws and the basis of the present system of land tenure."[2] His new ideological position was clearly contained in the programme of the Independence for India League which Nehru had organized as a pressure group within the Congress. The objective as stated by the league was both to achieve independence and to reconstruct Indian society by changing its capitalist and feudal base. "The League aims at the *socialist democratic state* in which every person has the fullest opportunities of development and the state control of the means of production and distribution." On the agrarian front, in UP, in particular, Nehru found no alternative to the abolition of landlordism, but this should be done with the payment of partial compensation and replaced by small holdings owed by individual peasant proprietors with no right of 'alienation'. There would not be nationalization but socialization of land and the most that the state would manage would be model farms. Agricultural debts should be written off but after part payments. The state should gradually acquire key industries, ensure a minimum living wage and impose sharply graduated taxes, an inheritance tax and a tax on agricultural incomes.[3]

A comprehensive economic programme was adopted in as early as 1931 and an agrarian programme in 1936. Towards the end of 1938, a National Planning Committee was constituted and, thus, the idea of planning came into prominence in India. The National Planning Committee could not carry on its work effectively because of the beginning of the Second World War, in the course of which many of its members found themselves in prison. But it considered nearly all aspects of planning and ultimately produced a series of studies containing social and economic policies and programmes, which formed the basis of a more organised attempt at planning after independence. These reports provide rich material that provides an insight into Nehru's ideology which was shaped by belief in socialism combined with an intimate knowledge of not only world history but also of Indian economic situation.

Nehru was able to translate his thinking about economic policies and planning soon after independence. Early in 1950, following the adoption of the new Constitution by the Constituent Assembly of India, the central government took the most important step of setting up the Planning Commission to assess the country's material, capital and human resources and to formulate a Plan for their most effective and balanced utilization. In the Constitution the basic objectives were set forth as "The Directive Principles of State Policy." Among those 'Directive Principles' were that:

"The State shall strive to promote the welfare of the people by securing and protecting, as effectively as it may, a social order in which justice, social, economic and political, shall inform all the institutions of national life."

Further that:

> "The State shall, in particular, direct its policy towards securing:
> (a) that the citizens, men and women equally, have the right to an adequate means of livelihood;
> (b) that the ownership and control of the material resources of the community are so distributed as best to subserve the common good;
> (c) that the operation of the economic system does not result in the concentration of wealth and means of production to the common detriment."

These general principles were given a more precise direction in December, 1954, when Parliament adopted the 'socialist pattern of society' as the objective of social and economic policy.

The planned development of the Indian economy commenced with the launching of the First Five Year Plan in the beginning of the fifties. But before launching the First Five Year Plan in 1951, the government under the leadership of Nehru had already laid down the broad contours of land reforms and the land reform legislation had been passed in most of the states in the early 1950s.

Nehru drew up the *First Five-Year Plan* in 1951. This was essentially a Plan for government's investments in industries and agriculture. Increasing business and income taxes, Nehru envisaged a *mixed economy* in which the government would manage strategic industries such as mining, electricity and heavy industries, serving public interest and a check to private enterprise.

As noted earlier, the national movement was committed to carrying radical land reforms to emancipate the vast sections of peasantry. Thus, in the early years two main objectives have dominated the thinking of the leaders of Indian national movement. These are land reforms and rapid industrialization for rapid growth of the economy. Nehru's main ideas about these two aspects are discussed below.

II. NEHRU'S VIEWS ABOUT LAND REFORMS

Nehru's experience as a political leader and intimate interaction with the peasantry as the leader enabled him to clearly understand the stranglehold of feudal exploitation. He saw first hand the extreme poverty of rural masses and this convinced him of the need to bring in land reforms and also to regenerate agriculture. Nehru was convinced that the Indian farmers could become the agent of change and modernization of agriculture if he were enabled to do so. Nehru's dream was to introduce cooperative village management but he soon realized that the peasant will not like to part with his land under any circumstances. Nehru's ideas on land reforms were aptly reflected in the *Report of the Congress Agrarian Reforms Committee* submitted in 1949.

This Report is one of the most radical documents on reform of the agrarian relations in India. After laying down the principle of equity and efficiency, the report favoured an agrarian pattern of intermediate-size, village-based cooperative associations as the best safeguard for the legitimate interests of both individual and community. The Report envisaged the abolition of intermediaries, ceilings above the optimum land holding and security of tenure. Two types of farming related to differences in the size of holding were recommended. All holdings below basic size, that is uneconomic farms that could not provide full employment and a reasonable level of living to an average family of five, were to be amalgamated in joint cooperative farms. This would enable the small holdings to increase their output by making use of scientific methods of cultivation. The Committee recommended family farming for holdings between 'base' and 'optimum' size—a limit defined as three times the economic holding. This was only an intermediate stage. The Committee envisaged that ultimately all land would come under joint cooperative management. The Report also underlined the need for fixation of minimum wages for the agricultural labourers. Cooperative village management was to be combined with development of small and cottage industries to provide employment to rural people and relieve the pressure of population on agriculture.[4] This was perhaps one of the most comprehensive, clear-headed and articulate statements of the Congress on agrarian changes under Nehru's influence. By 1949, the rural propertied class therefore, stood warned of the threat to their economic interests by the intended social reforms by the government.[5]

The main objectives of the land reforms legislation enacted by the State governments during the mid-fifties were five-fold, viz., (i) abolition of intermediary tenures; (ii) tenancy reforms comprising regulation of rent, security of tenures and conferment of ownership rights on tenants; (iii) ceiling on land holdings and distribution of surplus land; (iv) consolidation of holdings; and (v) compilation and updating of land records. After the initial burst of enactment of land reform legislation during the mid-fifties, some subsequent legislation on ceilings on land holdings were also passed by the states during the mid-sixties as also during the emergency in 1975.

The implementation of land reforms brings out that while the legislation succeeded in abolition of intermediaries, the other objectives of land reforms were only partially met. The result was that by and large, self cultivation became the dominant mode of production in agriculture and vast sections of peasantry were vested with entitlement to land. However, tenancy could not be abolished and only went underground. Most important, because of the failure of land ceiling acts, land distribution remains extremely skewed in all parts of India with marginal and small farmers constituting an overwhelming proportion of total holdings.

According to the First Five Year Plan:

> "On account of the abolition of feudal tenures, which is in progress in many States, the system of land holding

> over the greater part of the country is beginning to approximate in substance to the ryotwari system. Proposals for land reform raise important questions of policy and finance which call for close co-operation and consultation between the Central and State Governments. Even though the pace of land reform and of economic development cannot be the same all over the country, it is desirable that as between different States there should be a broad, common approach in land reform programmes and, as an essential aspect of the implementation of the Five Year Plan, the stages in which land reforms are to be carried out should be worked out by the Central Government and the States."

In addition to land reforms, other measures taken for regenerating agriculture in India were large investment in irrigation, power, rural roads, markets and communications and scientific research and technology. The Community Development Programme was launched in the mid-1950 with a view to raising their awareness and uplifting the villages. The imparting of extension through village level workers constituted an integral part of the Programme.

III. NEHRU'S IDEAS ABOUT INDUSTRIALIZATION—THE ROLE OF THE STATE

Nehru helped to lay down the development strategy with objectivity, without being too emotional to the fact that the father of the nation, Mahatma Gandhi, had espoused an altogether different development philosophy. Nor did Nehru go full length to accept the Marxian strand of thought or the reasoning of the Fabian socialists with whom he built excellent personal relationships during the years of his study in Great Britain. Nehru, as Morrison-Jones remarked in the 1960s, was a Gandhian without believing in anarchy; he was a Marxian without the logic of Marxism; and he was a Fabian socialist without the required faith in administration. He was politically skilful in deferring discussions on the development strategy that India should adopt during the years immediately following independence. In 1950, the central government took the most important step of setting up the Planning Commission and initiated other active measures for planned economic development.

Nehru launched programmes to build irrigation canals, dams and spread the use of fertilizers to increase agricultural production. He also pioneered a series of community development programs aimed at increasing efficiency in rural India. While encouraging the construction of large dams, irrigation works and the generation of hydroelectricity, Nehru also launched India's programme to harness nuclear energy.

Along with the land reform, the most urgent task was to overcome India's industrial backwardness—the share of modern industries in national income at the end of British rule was only 7.5 per cent. In 1950, the central government took the most important step of setting up the Planning Commission and initiated other active measures for planned economic development. The First Five Year Plan succeeded in most of its objectives. Land reform legislation was implemented by most of the states and in most other sectors, achievements surpassed the targets.

"National income over the five years has increased by some 18 per cent .... On the whole, the results of the Plan have been satisfactory. There is now increasing awareness of the need for development, and it is not without significance that there is demand all over the country for a plan that would secure more rapid advance in all directions." (Second Five Year Plan, 1961).

The successes of the First Plan gave gave immense confidence to the planners. With the launching of the Second Five Year Plan, from 1956 to 1961, emphasis of government economic policy shifted to rapid industrialization based on the development of heavy, capital goods industry, even while encouraging small scale industry, and state ownership and control of the commanding heights of the economy (Bipan Chandra, 1997).

Many economists believe that the Second Five Year Plan which gave high priority to heavy industry was one of major contribution made by Nehru. A great deal of debate has taken place about the heavy industry model propounded by Mahalanobis. It is interesting to note that most of the Indian and contemporary foreign scholars welcomed the emphasis and high priority accorded to heavy industry.

But there were some vehement critics also. Professor B.R. Shenoy wrote a famous Note of Dissent on the Second Five Year Plan which challenged planning and argued that it led to the loss of economic freedom. Until his death in 1978, he tirelessly argued for abolition of planning, denationalization, privatization of public sector enterprises, responsible monetary policy, rejection of foreign aid, open competition, and free trade. A.D. Shroff, a Bombay businessman, started the Forum of Free Enterprise to educate the public about the vices of planning and virtues of private markets. Minoo Masani, one of the founders of the Swatantra Party, launched several freedom organizations. His journal, *Freedom First,* continues to beacon liberal principles and policies.

The other early critic of planning were C.N. Vakill and P.R. Brahmananda who expounded the wage-goods model as a cohesive and serious alternative to the strategy followed in the Second Plan. Their argument was that a heavy industry model which gave high priority to capital goods industry neglected the wage good sector and the existing wage-good gap would act as the main limitation of the heavy industry strategy. In contrast to the strategy of the authorities of raising the investment rate above the voluntary rate and diverting resources to capital goods, Brahmananda argued that unemployment was solely due to the prevalence of the wage-goods gap. The Brahmananda model underscored the important Tinbergen dictum that the investment pattern determines the distribution of income. In other words, if the investment pattern is concentrated on coarse grain and coarse cloth, the income distribution would be tilted in favour of the lower income groups; while if the investment pattern resulted in the production of luxury goods, income distribution would be tilted towards the upper income groups (*The Financial Express,* posted on Feb. 05, 2003).

IV. NEHRU'S CONCEPT ABOUT MIXED ECONOMY

Nehru was not a doctrinaire socialist. He was a realist and pragmatist. He deliberately chose the term mixed economy in which private initiative was to be quite crucial in certain areas. There can be change in the relative roles of private *versus* public sector depending on the level of development of an economy. Although he gave the public sector the core position for the equitable development of the economy, he also did not underrate the initiative and enterprise of the private sector.

In his concept of mixed economy, public sector was to play a central role in the development of rural infrastructure and basic research and extension, social infrastructure like education, health and public services with a view to building an equitable society, but private sector was also expected to play its legitimate role. In particular, public sector was to occupy the dominant heights. The private sector was, however, not to be eliminated. Under government direction, regulation and licensing, it was to play an important role in economic development. India was thus to have a mixed economy, with the public sector gradually dominating it.

There was, however, a major shift in the government's economic policy in 1991 when liberalization of the economy, initiated in 1980, went full speed ahead. The system of controls and licence was mostly disseminated and the public sector started retreating.

V. NEHRU'S ATTITUDE TOWARDS SCIENCE AND TECHNOLOGY

Nehru gave great importance to science and technology and therefore agricultural research and extension were to play an important role in the process of regeneration of agriculture. The Indian Council of Agricultural Research and Agricultural Universities were strengthened on the pattern of Land Grant College in the USA. A large pool of agricultural scientists was created and a network of research stations and laboratories was established to develop appropriate technological packages specifically suited to the agro-climatic conditions in different parts of the country. Since land reforms included cooperativization, the small farms were to be organized into bigger production units for enabling them to make use of modern scientific technology.[6] This, Nehru thought, was essential for increasing productivity and income of a large number of small and marginal cultivators and thereby raising their living standards. Agricultural growth was to proceed simultaneously with rapid industrialization for building a self-reliant prosperous economy. The green revolution became possible because of the establishment of ICAR and agricultural universities.

The Five Year Plans had the objective of guaranteeing free and compulsory primary education to all of India's children. For this purpose, mass village enrollment programmes were created, thousands of schools were constructed. Another important initiative was the establishment of adult education centres, and vocational and technical schools for adults, especially in the rural areas.

Along with primary education, Nehru was also a great advocate of higher education. Many institutions of higher learning, including the UGC, the All India Institute of Medical Sciences, the Indian Institutes of Technology and the Indian Institutes of Management, the ICAR and the agricultural universities were set-up during Nehru's time. Much of the credit for current IT revolution in India and the dividend being reaped through outsourcing should go to the enlightened policy of Nehru on higher education. There is a need to carry on with this heritage. It is a matter of gratification that the present government is also planning to increase the number of central universities, IITs, IIMs and other Institutes of Higher Learning in a big way.

VI. NEHRU'S POLICY OF NON-ALIGNMENT

In a period of intense cold war Nehru along with Nasser and Seokarno and Chou en Lai launched the concept of *non-alignment* and *Panchseel*. From the outset, under Nehru's leadership, India followed an independent foreign policy based on non-alignment and anti-colonialism. Foreign policy has been used to defend and strengthen India's independence and to promote world peace. During the cold war, India firmly refused to get involved in it and opposed the policy of dividing the world into hostile power blocs. It also tried to lessen the mutual antagonism of the big powers. This enabled him to create a wider space of economic and social international cooperation and helped India stay out of the cold war. During the Nehru and Indira Gandhi years, India's foreign policy also contributed to a sense of national pride among the people and thus contributed to national cohesion.

VII. NEO-CLASSICAL CRITICISM OF NEHRU

It has now a days become fashionable to blame Nehru for slow growth of the Indian economy and his planning model which primarily depended on closed economy for having inhibited growth and leading to long term slow growth and stagnation of the Indian economy. A section of economists also believe that export pessimism built into the model was responsible for stunted growth of the economy. They argue that closed economy not only inhibited investment of private multinationals, it also resulted in India not gaining access to modern technology. This criticism has become quite vocal after the initiation of economic reforms in 1991. It is important to critically examine this criticism.

India was able to achieve substantial growth in saving rates and thereby undertake large investment in infrastructural as well as in other capital assets. Huge investments were undertaken during Nehru's period for capital formation in general and in investment in infrastructural projects in irrigation and power (for him Bhakra Dam, etc., were the new temples) as well as in roads, communications, markets, etc. The result was a visible acceleration of the growth rates during the period 1950-51 to 1965-66 as compared with those achieved during the colonial period 1901-04 to 1946-47 before independence.

In terms of growth, Nehru's period 1950-51 to 1964-65 is characterized by high growth of the economy as a whole and in particular unprecedented growth achieved by the manufacturing and the industrial sectors.

During *1950-51 to 1964-65* (the First, Second and Third Plan periods), the overall GDP recorded a growth rate of about 3.94 per cent p.a. compared with a growth rate of only 1.05 per cent during 1901-04 to 1946-47. Similarly, the per capita income growth rate was 1.86 per cent p.a. compared with a paltry growth rate of 0.22 per cent during the earlier period. More important, the *secondary sector* recorded a high

TABLE 1

Growth Rates of GDP and Per Capita Income (at 1993-94 Prices)

Years	*1900-01–1946-47@*	*1950-51–1964-65*	*1967-68–1979-80*	*1981-82–1990-91*	*1992-93–2003-04*	*1950-51–2003-04*
GDP	1.05	3.94	3.44	5.62	6.1	4.33
GDP Agr.	0.46	2.54	2.05	3.08	2.38	2.54
Secondary	1.82	6.88	4.23	7.1	6.29	5.54
Tertiary	1.66	4.76	4.54	6.72	8.22	5.54
Per capita Income	0.22	1.86	1.23	3.5	4.21	2.12

Note: @ Refers to growth rate of National Income at 1938-39 prices.
Source: Sivasubramonian, 2000 and National Accounts Statistics, 2004.

growth rate of 7.0 per cent p.a. in the Nehru period which was more than the growth rate achieved in the post-liberalization period (Table 1).

The critics of Indian pattern of development which attribute India's slow growth and stagnation to Nehruvian policies of autarkic development, emphasis on heavy industry are unable to explain this high growth during the Nehru era. It is true that India's economic growth rate was rather slow during the period 1950-51 to 1979-80. But to deny that nothing happened during the planned period is not borne out by facts. Actually, to some extent the boost in India's economic growth during the 1980s and later on in 1990s owes much to the infrastructural investments undertaken earlier out of rising domestic savings and investment achieved by the economy (Nayyar, 2006).

For example K.N. Raj has the following to say about

that period: "We did not have any foreign aid, but we had only the Sterling balance. How would we raise our savings was bothering us too much because at that time China was talking about leaping forward. We had long discussions with Nehru at the end of which we emphasized that we would fix a rate of savings then itself. Thus we, at the Planning Commission, then worked out a strategy of raising the rate of saving from 5 per cent in 1950-51 to 7 per cent in 1955-56, from 7 to 11 in 1960-61, from 11 to 16 by 1965-66 and from 16 to 20 by 1970-71." (*The economist on ten economic breakthroughs that changed and shaped India since 1947*). It was this higher rate of saving and investment that resulted in higher growth of the Indian economy.

Many neo-classical scholars who are highly critical of Indian path of development are at pains to find explanation for high growth achieved by India during Nehru's period, when India was a closed and planned economy.

How did high growth take place in a closed economy comes as great surprise to these authors since they firmly believe that growth can only take place under an environment of free trade and free enterprise.

Some of them have tried to argue that during the 1950s keeping imports out so that domestic industries could flourish was absent in the thinking of policy-makers. Instead, they were more keen to develop indigenous production structures that could reduce or eliminate the need for imports and free the country from threats of closure of world markets. Against this background it is not surprising that an active policy of raising trade barriers did not accompany the initial launch of industrialization, which principally relied on planning, public investment in heavy industry, and licensing of private sector. According to one of them, this liberalism ows much to the benign neglect of trade policy and active defense of an open foreign investment policy by Prime Minister Nehru (Panagariya, 2008).

This is a rather far-fetched argument. Either Nehru believed in closed economy and thereby did immense harm to the Indian economy or he encouraged foreign investment and believed in open economy model. He cannot be both a planner and a liberaliser at the same time.

The fact of the matter is that Nehru's period (most of the planning period) is characterized by high investment financed out of saving and high capital formation, what is now called perspiration. It is high domestic savings and capital formation that promoted high growth of the economy. But this explanation does not fit in with many of the neo-classical scholars since for them rapid growth can only take place in an open trade environment and trade liberalization can be the only and sole source of growth.

The real stagnation in Indian economy took place after 1964-65, i.e. during 1967-68 to 1980-81, primarily because of crisis in food production, wars with neighbours and the two oil crises that adversely affected the fiscal situation and public and private investment.

SUMMING UP

To sum up, Nehru's economic philosophy evolved gradually over the years alongside the struggle for national freedom and his participation and leadership of the Indian National Congress. Nehru knew first hand the lot of the common people how poor they were and how they made their living. This instilled in him the urgent need to take steps that would eradicate poverty. While understandably blaming the colonial rule for having neglected economic development, he also understood the nature of structural problems like landlordism, illiteracy, superstition, and social backwardness faced by the masses. And, he also realized that mere attainment of independence will not automatically raise the economic, social and educational backwards of masses. This would have to be done through investments for modernizing the economy achieving high growth, industrialization and large investment in education.

Two other influences on Nehru are most important. One is the Gandhian influence. Nehru did not ideologically agree with Gandhi on economic philosophy. But, nevertheless he held him in high esteem and had deep respect and affection for him which Gandhi reciprocated in abundance. The second influence was socialism. Nehru was deeply influenced by Marxism as a philosophy but also the achievements of the Soviet Union when he first visited in 1927. He was specially impressed by the speed at which the Soviet Union was able to transform itself from a backward to a modern economy. But Nehru never agreed with the coercive policies adopted by the Soviet leaders and was critical of that aspect. But he did want India also to industrialize as quickly, if possible. The Second Five Year Plan has to be seen in this context.

But he did not impose his socialist ideas on Congress which was deeply influenced by Gandhi. Historically, with freedom struggle facing resistance, Congress became more and more radical over time. It is interesting to note that even Gandhi gradually shifted his position and became more radical on most of the issues.

Within Congress, it was only during the late thirties that Nehru started exercising his influence. He moved slowly but surely. On land reforms, Gandhi supported him on the issue of abolition of landlordship and on other objectives of land reforms. In fact, the most radical document on land reforms *The Congress Agrarian Reforms Committee Report* was prepared under the authorship of a famous Gandhian J.C. Kumarappa.

Again, although he believed firmly that India could only be modernized and living standards of masses improved qualitatively if she gets quickly industrialized, but in this respect also he moved cautiously. He proposed the radical plan for industrialization and heavy industry only after the successful implementation of the First Five Year Plan, which in fact, succeeded in over-fulfilling its targets in terms of growth of the economy and growth of agricultural and industrial production. On heavy industry strategy also, Nehru soon became aware that it did not generate enough employment and hence he combined the strategy of heavy industry with the need to develop cottage and small scale industries. He wanted rapid industrialization and approached all the countries to get heavy industry. It is also a fact that it was massive aid and transfer of technology and setting up of steel and heavy industries by the Soviet Union that made it possible for India to lay the foundations of heavy industry. The help by the Soviet Union was deeply acknowledged by

Nehru.

One of the problems with the neo-classical economists and those advocating free enterprise and rapid globalization is that while evaluating and criticizing Nehru they try to isolate him from the historical context and want to criticize him from a vantage point of the 21st century.

Despite the a-historical and distortional criticism by the neo-classicals, Nehru's legacy deserves to be remembered with great reverence. Nehru remains the founder of modern India. Much of the high growth in recent years owes much to the policy of modernising the economy, building of huge physical and human infrastructure, revitalizing the educational system, giving very high priority to science and technology and setting up institutions of higher learning. Above all, the achievements during Nehru's period succeeded in instilling a sense of self-reliance, self-confidence and self-respect and pride and dignity among the people of India.

Notes

1. Gopal, *Ibid.*
2. Nehru (1929), *Presidential Address delivered to the 44th Session of the All India Congress* on 26th January, 1929 at Lahore.
3. "Programme of the Independence for India League, UP, 1929", *Selected Works,* Vol. P. 287, Gopal, pp. 113-14.
4. All India Congress Committee, *Report of the Congress Agrarian Reforms Committee.* AICC 1949.
5. Frankell, *Ibid.*, p. 70.
6. For a detailed discussion on Cooperative Agriculture See, Myrdal, Gunnar, *Asian Drama,* Pantheon, Vol. II, pp. 1346-56.

References

All India Congress Committee (AICC) (1949), *Report of the Congress Agrarian Reforms Committee.*

AICC (1972), National Planning Committee of the AICC, *Report of the sub-Committee on Land Policy, Agricultural Labour and Insurance.* Published in *Young India*, August.

Chandra, Bipan (1997), "Evaluaing the achievements and failures during the fifty years of freedom", in Radiff on the net.

Jawaharlal Nehru (1962), *An Autobiography*, 1962, Allied, New Delhi.

Jawaharlal Nehru (1961), *The Discovery of India*, Asia.

Joshi, P.C. (1974), "Land Reforms and Agrarian Change in India and

Pakistan since 1947", *Journal of Peasant Studies*, January and April 1974.

Gopal, S. (1975), *Jawarharlal Nehu—A Biography*, Volume One, Two and Three, Oxford University Press.

Myrdal, Gunnar (1963), *Asian Drama: An Inquiry Into the Poverty of Nations* Volumes 1 and 2, Pantheon, London.

Nayyar, Deepak (2006), "Economic Growth in Independent India" in *Economic and Political Weekly*, April 15.

Nehru, Jawaharlal (1941), *Toward Freedom: The Autobiograplly of Jawaharlal Nehru* (New York: John Day Co., pp. 228-31.

Panagariya, Arvind, 2008, *India: The Emerging Giant*, Oxford University Press, Delhi.

Ranga, N.G. (1937), *Kisan Speaks*, Madras, p. 7.

Shenoy, B.R. (1958), *Problems of Indian Economic Development*, Madras University, Madras.

"The Savant of Society is no More", Story in Web Edition of *The Financial Times*, posted on Feb. 5, 2003.

Vakil, C.N. and P.R. Brahmanand (1956), *Planning for an Expanding Economy: Accumulation, Employment and Technical Progress in Underdeveloped Countries*, Bombay, Vora and Co.

2

Economic Philosophy of Jawaharlal Nehru

Radha Raman Singh and Madhulika

The economic philosophy of Jawaharlal Nehru rests mainly in his efforts to build democratic institutions, forge a united secular socialistic society with a modern scientific outlook and a self-reliant industrial country non-aligned in a world dominated by superpowers. The important components of the philosophy of institutional framework were planned mixed economy, socialistic pattern of society; parliamentary democracy and welfare state. But the ideal economic philosophy of Nehru was accepted and implemented in parts with misinterpretations and distortions. As a result, it has not proved effective in wiping out the emergence of Western type capitalist system and creating an egalitarian society based on the principle of equity and social justice. If Nehru's legacy fell in troubled water, this was partly due to his own prophetic generalizations and more partly irresponsible interpretations and mishandling by whole class of decision-makers who followed him and the inheritors who forgotten them. But its needs to be defended.

I. INTRODUCTION

The economic philosophy of Jawaharlal Nehru rests mainly in his efforts to build democratic institutions, forge a united secular socialistic society with a modern scientific outlook and a self-reliant industrial country non-aligned in a world dominated by superpowers. He was a great pioneer of total struggle for political, social and economic rehabilitation and modernization of free India. In his intellectual make-up, a profound sense of history and a deep commitment to nation building with scientific secular outlook stood with great prominence, which was apparent from his committed efforts to modernize a feudal society, to industrialize a rural-oriented economy, and to mould a fragmented guild of Princely states into a 20th Century nation-state. Jawaharlal Nehru's philosophy of institution building for fulfilling his commitment to a new society provides mainly the basis for his continuing contemporary relevance in India. The important components of his institutional framework of an open and new society were planned mixed economy, socialistic pattern of society, parliamentary democracy and welfare state. These, in fact, were his favoured tools to lead the Indian national revolution towards the accomplishment of the new economic and social order of his dream.

II. MIXED ECONOMY—CONCEPT AND RATIONALE

In the economic philosophy of Jawaharlal Nehru, the concept of mixed economy was accepted and developed to solve the basic problems of planning the economic growth in a democratic set-up. After independence, the country needed multi-class mobilization and setting up of an equitable economic system for achieving socio-economic development of all the classes and sections of the society. The then existing systems of the world like capitalism and communism had inherent nature of inequality and exploitation as well as violence and class conflict respectively, which, in view of Nehru, did not suit the Indian socio-economic fabric. The Indian revolution was not the anti-capitalist revolution like the Soviet Revolution, rather it was a multi-class national revolution supported, helped and fought by all the classes and sections of the society. In this background, Nehru formulated the scope and perspectives of the Indian revolution in a scientific manner and opted for a mixed economy.

The basic purpose of Nehru in adopting of the strategy of mixed economy was to avoid class conflict and mobilize all productive sections of the society against the pervasive economic, social and cultural backwardness inherited from the feudal and colonial periods. From the historical point of view, Nehru saw that the 'shell' of the Indian system was capitalistic while its 'essence' remained feudal and option for capitalistic system would lead to monopolies and concentration of economic power. On the other side, the fully controlled communistic economies leads to authoritarianism and totalitarianism with violent approach, language and thought. He wanted to do away with classes by winning over people, not by aggravating class struggle. He emphasized that the strongest urge today is for social justice and equality and unless state responded to it, "it might well become a police state." Therefore, as writes P.C. Joshi, "Nehru envisaged that a faster growth of public sector in industry, the predominance of the co-operative sector in agriculture, small industry, credit and trade and a channelizing of the forces of capitalist growth to areas of social priority. These and such other factors would prevent the general direction of the total economy and society from becoming predominantly capitalist. This meant that the forces of economic development would have to be consciously channelized in the direction of the predominance of non-capitalist forces. In Marxian terms, Nehru posed the problem of fulfilling the bourgeois-democratic task—which was the main national task after freedom—in a socialist perspective." (Joshi, 1982)

III. PARLIAMENTARY DEMOCRACY AS THE POLITICAL FRAMEWORK FOR ECONOMIC PLANNING AND GROWTH WITH EQUITY

Nehru wanted India to be a parliamentary democracy for various reasons and he conceived it as a favourable political framework for economic growth with equity. He knew that political democracy will justify itself only when it ultimately succeeded in facilitating the vast majority of the underprivileged to become an active political force capable of influencing economic policies and ensuring their effective implementation which will help reduce and finally defuse social tensions including class war. He believed that change is essential but with continuity and therefore future has to be built on the foundations laid in the past and the present. Keeping this in mind, he promoted the concept of mixed economy with economic planning which was to be the main instrument of change without a break with continuity. It was an uncharted path that he took and made it clear that for India, planning was to be a method of trial and error and the suitable model was to be evolved, seeking an alternative to capitalism and communism and striving for economic democracy with equity and social justice. Nehru knew that the economy was in a difficult transitional stage and therefore, he was trying to explore such institutional form which could harmonise the principle of growth with equity. In this background emerged Nehru's concept of open society, planned and mixed economy, parliamentary democracy and the welfare state as the institutional forms of India's transition to a new society.

IV. PUBLIC SECTOR AS A MORTAR OF GROWTH WITH IDEALS OF SOCIALISM

The favourite tool of Nehru to attain the ideas of socialism was the adoption of the concept of public sector as a mortar of growth. This was supposed to play a dominant role in the planned mixed economy in rendering the transition more acceptable to large sections of the society. The concept of socialism was never clarified in specific terms by Nehru, rather he had the picture of the social system in his mind being classless in nature, with equal opportunities for all; founded on planning for the raising of mankind to higher material, cultural and spiritual levels including the spirit of usefulness, service goodwill and love (Singh, 1975) to be achieved without coercion, (Nehru, 1958) that intended to avoid the pitfalls of capitalism of the West and the economic totalitarianism of the East. Nehru sometimes called it the socialistic pattern, at other times socialist pattern and on other occasions simply socialist society, but he made it clear that the three phrases meant the samething—a casteless and classless society.

The approach of Nehru regarding his ideals of socialism was based on his pragmatic considerations and there was a whole theory of transition to more human social orders behind the choice that Nehru made (Chakravarty, 1981). This can be assessed from the speech Nehru delivered at the annual meeting of the FICCI on March 5, 1955 wherein he observed: "Capitalism, Socialism, Marxism, all these are children of the Industrial Revolution. We are on the eve of at least something as great as the Industrial Revolution, perhaps something bigger. It is affecting everything—production, distribution, thinking and everything else. In this context, why was this decision for a socialist pattern of society taken? It was taken to give an indication of the objective and the approach. We have to fit India into the nuclear age and do it quickly." Here we get a clear indication that for Nehru, the process of transition included not merely accumulation of physical assets but also building up of technological capabilities of the highest order for which he emphasized strengthening of the public sector.

V. APPROPRIATE STRATEGY FOR INDUSTRIALIZATION

For Nehru, none of the conventional modes of thinking as well as the existing patterns of social organization were adequate to deal with the technological opportunities that were opening up. He, therefore, wanted the strategy of transition to be worked out in the context of the changed times (Chakravarty, 1981). Along with the emphasis on the so-called heavy industry strategy, simultaneous acceptance of the need to develop the village and cottage industries shows that the aim of Nehru was not, in any way, against the concept of industrialization of Gandhi as criticized by the Gandhians. In fact, it was only an improved interpretation of the underlying spirit and philosophy which is apparent from the statement Nehru made while inaugurating the Perambur (Madras) Integral Coach Factory in 1955 on the eve of Gandhi Jayanti: "Perhaps some people might wonder what is the connection between Gandhiji and this big factory......I feel that this idea is due to a basic misapprehension. I am quite sure, if we had the good fortune to have Gandhiji with us today, he would have been glad at the opening of this factory. Many, I suppose, took the latter of what he said and paid little attention to the spirit, to the underlying philosophy for which he stood. India has to be industrialized as rapidly as possible and industrialization includes, of course, all kinds of industry—major, middling, small, village and cottage... We have to develop the village and cottage industry in a big way, at the same time making sure that in trying to develop industry, big and small; we do not forget the human factor." Thus, the basic idea of Nehru was to make adequate preparations for changing the entire productive base of society with suitable strategy for capital and labour-intensive activities to develop an appropriate sectors of the economy.

VI. OBJECTIVE OBSERVATIONS

From the above analysis, it emerges that Nehru's basic contribution was to present a framework of values and normative principles capable of imparting unity of purpose and direction to divergent social forces in the national movement and these are found to be embodied in his concepts of internationalism, nationalism, democracy, secularism and socialism. To attain these values and principles, Nehru presented an institutional framework consisting of open society, planned mixed economy, parliamentary democracy and welfare state as appropriate tools. Now, it is needed to make an objective assessment whether the institutional framework and the tools thereof, have succeeded in leading independent India towards the accomplishment of the new economic and social order of Nehru's dreams?

The survey of the situation and the emerging scenario shows that the institutional framework of Nehru released two contradictory types of processes simultaneously—one linking the forces of national revolution with those of social and economic revolution and the other delinking national independence from a revolutionary perspective and, in course of time, the latter tendency gained much strength to distort the entire fabric of the ideal institutional framework of Nehru. He himself confessed in his writings and speeches after independence that certain tendencies of the emerging social system did not help in carrying forward the Indian National Revolution in the direction of a socio-economic evolution. The causes of the negative tendencies and the mishappennings are found mainly in the inherent weaknesses in the ideologies and the indifferent implementing authorities.

The tools of the institutional framework of Nehru have not been working in the direction as perceived and dreamt by him and, in spite of development in various economic fields, their effects have not met the tests of desired equity and social justice. The concept of open society has not made India open to the necessary extent and by working in wrong direction, it has created great tension and the liberating potential of national revolution has lagged behind in channelizing it towards a national, cultural, and economic revolution. In both the social and economic spheres, the ideals of Nehru have been so rapidly eroded that the concept of open society has helped in strengthening the acquisitiveness of the new middle class and creating a vast gap between the rich and the poor, village and the town and labour and owner. The concept of mixed economy, on the other side, has not been able to change the property structure in tune with the set objectives of equity and social justice and it has failed in ensuring primacy of growth over consumerism, social purpose over private gain, and mass welfare over elite consumption and has released forces of destabilization by introducing corruption in the political spheres. In ideology, parliamentary democracy was oriented towards the underprivileged, the deprived and the unorganized millions, but in actual working, it has favoured the organized sections as against the unorganized sections, the big propertied class as against the small one and the parasitic non-productive class as against the productive classes. A naked assertion of the philosophy of getting rich quickly accompanied by erosion of moral and social ethics, discipline and the spirit of service and sacrifice, has pushed into prominence the careerist and parasitic tendencies among political workers and the leadership.

The concept of welfare state, another pillar of Nehru's legacy, has been implemented with such distortions that it has resulted in the emergence of high cost and elite-oriented superstructure of education, medical care, housing and recreation; in fact, it has become an instrument of exploitation by the rich and powerful sections of the society than a means of mass welfare. It has been so corrupted by misinterpretation and mishandling that it has remained as a dole and charity in the name of state assistance to the vast majority of the underprivileged population. On the other side, it has been made a perennial source of riches in the hands of politicians, proliferating middle classes, the bureaucracy, the organized white collar workers and rich farmer lobbies. The result is that the entire institutional framework of Nehru and the tools thereof, have taken their worst vulgar shape and in place of equity, liberty, equality and social justice, they have given rise to poverty, bondage, discrimination, corruption, coercion and tension in the society posing threat to integration and sovereignty of the nation.

In spite of good ideals and clear intentions, Nehru's concepts proved to be more prophetic, general and imprecise because he, though, chose policy issues, but never paid enough attention to organizational areas to make them work. He left the interpretation and implementation of his generalized concepts in the hands of the administrative system inherited from the colonial era and with all his foresight, he forged the old and colonial instruments to give substance to his vision without fully understanding the ground realities. The distortions, misinterpretations and the adverse results of the generalized concepts of Nehru without adequate organizational support can be illustrated with the help of the examples present in the socio-economic structure of independent India. For Nehru, socialism was to be a pattern of society, avoiding the pitfalls of the competition of the West and totalitarianism of the East and it inevitably led him to adopt an uncharted middle-of-the-road concept without translating into specifics, which obviously suited the social diversity and cultural heterogeneity to be interpreted and adopted favourably by the vested socio-cultural interests, and thus, bringing the ideologies of Nehru's socialism on crossroads. This is the reason that though as an individual, Nehru continued to be the idol of the masses but Nehruism became the ideology of the rational and elite middle classes. In fact, Nehruism could not draw upon the Gandhian heritage of reinterpreting tradition to suit the needs and compulsions of the modern times and failed to take advantage of the immense reserves of idealism and moral energy which Gandhi had tapped during the period of freedom struggle.

The nature of mix under the concept of mixed economy was never very clearly spelt out. Nehru was free to make his own interpretations as a prophet, but his inheritors fell out. Public sector, for Nehru, was the mortar of growth and private sector, as he once told the Lok Sabha, "has a very important task to fulfil provided always that it works within the confines laid down and provided always that it does not lead to the creation of monopolies and other evils that the accumulation of wealth gives rise to (*India Today*, 1984)." But due to the absence of a concrete code of conduct for the private sector, it expanded vastly on the basis of external economies provided by the public sector and the resources provided by the state agencies. On the other side, private sector never went into priority areas of either capital goods or mass consumption goods but concentrated deeply on the areas of profit-oriented luxury goods production. As a result, concentration of private economic power emerged as a challenge to the very principles of planning and state regulation of the process of economic development. Nehru set-up public sector, but laid down no standard of performance due to the generalized nature of mixture of public and private sectors, and their subsequent handling hampered industrial growth bringing it down from eight per cent from initial period of 14 years (GoI, 1980) of planning to near stagnation in 1966-68 and to -1.4 per cent in 1979-80; it was only 3.7 per cent as against the target of 6.9 per cent growth rate at the end of the Sixth Plan Period (GoI, 1985-90). The reason was inefficient functioning of both the public and private sectors. In fact, due to the dominance of inefficient public sector with unyielding grip on key sectors of infrastructure, basic services and raw materials prevented the revival of the economy. This is primarily due to the fact that no guideline and standard of performance was set either by Nehru or by his successors which Nehru himself realized later. His Community Development Project, land reform measures and other schemes also could not create desired impact and vested interests succeeded in moulding them in their favour.

Thus, the economic philosophy and tools of Nehru's institutional framework, though ideal in ideology, ruined the socio-cultural and economic structure of independent India due to mishandlings and distortions and therefore, it was felt essential to search for suitable measures of remedies and corrections. The reform measures adopted at the end of the 20th century and being continued concurrently manifest the need of the hour based on ground realities and prove that Nehru's philosophy was more prophetic without concrete operational support which was easily distorted by the vested interests hampering the basis of objective results.

VII. CONCLUDING REMARKS

In conclusion, we can say that the ideal institutional framework and economic philosophy of Jawaharlal Nehru was accepted and implemented in parts with distortions. As a result, it has not proved effective in wiping out the emergence of the Western type of capitalist system and creating an egalitarian society based on the principle of equity and social justice in independent India. The concept of free society of Nehru has taken a vulgar shape in which poverty and riches, luxury and starvation are so juxtaposed that tension, corruption, dissatisfaction and discrimination have taken firm root giving rise to violence, class-war, communalism, narrow groupism and other destructive activities poisoning the socio-economic fabric of the country. But Nehru alone cannot be blamed for it. Whatever economic philosophy he presented before independent India was like a tailored suit reconciling together the vision of Gandhiji and his own as well as the tenets of growth with social justice. If his legacy fell in troubled water, it was partly due to his own prophetic generalizations and more due to the irresponble interpretations by the whole class of decision-makers who followed him and the inheritors who forgot them. The need is to defend the legacy of Nehru with renewed promise and dedication, courage and enterprise, spirit of endurance and vision of future to make India develop with equity and social justice as dreamt by Jawaharlal Nehru.

References

Joshi, P.C. (1982), 'Nehru Legacy and Struggle For a New Society' Published in *Development Planning and Policy* (Eds) Gupta, D.B., Y.C. Halan and P.B. Desai, Wiley Estern Limited, New Delhi, p. 4.

Singh, V.B. (1975), *'From Naoroji to Nehru'*, The Macmillan Company of India Limited, pp. 155-56.

Nehru, J.L. (1958), *'A Bunch of Old Letters'*, Bombay, pp. 139-143.

Chakravarty, S. (1981), 'Nehru and the Public Sector', *Yojana,* Annual Number, January 26th, p. 52.

'India Today (1984), June 15, A Troubled Legacy, p. 84.

Government of India, Planning Commission, *Sixth Five Year Plan*, 1980-85, p. 259.

Government of India, Planning Commission, *Seventh Five Year Plan* (1985-90), Vol. I, p. 1.

3

Nehru and the Choice of Mixed Economy: Strategy of Development

SMRITI MUKHERJEE

The paper focuses on Nehruvian choice of mixed economy or the state socialism. Since Nehru was a visionary, his economic ideas were governed by the spirit of the society of his time as well as the economic philosophies that were in currency all over the world at that time, except the communistic economic ideals. He remained a firm believer to his own economic philosophy till his death. An historical account of the concept of mixed economy and various economic policies has been presented in the first two sections. Inefficient functioning of the mixed economy in the third section and resurrection of the market principles in the 1990s that Nehru could not visualize thereby putting the Nehruvian state-led development policies in the backstage in the name of higher growth have been presented in the final section of the paper.

The way to industrialization is confronted with two basic choices namely import substitution and export promotion. Whichever policy alternative is chosen, the next question to decide is the allocation of resources. Under capitalist framework market forces of demand and supply will do this job but if strict socialist framework is chosen government policy becomes the crucial determinant. Besides these two basic forms, the menu consists of still another item which falls midway between socialism and capitalism and is known as the mixed economy principle. Basic characteristics of socialism as defined in the *Communist Manifesto* (1848) consist of social ownership of means of production, distribution and exchange and social welfare as opposed to private profit being the guiding principle of production. In a mixed economy these features apply to public sector while the private sector follows the laws of market.

It is obvious that simultaneous operation of two economic principles in a given economy gives rise to internal conflicts and contradictions. In the present paper we organize Nehru's choice of mixed economy principle under the following heads: (i) Congress Party and socialist thinking; (ii) formulation of the mixed economy idea; (iii) the working of mixed economy and growing pressures; and (iv) the move towards restoration of market forces.

I. CONGRESS PARTY AND SOCIALIST THINKING

The origin of mixed economy idea as a guiding principle for state policy in India cannot be understood without a reference to Congress Party's ideas on socialism during the pre-independence period. Socialism and mixed economy ideas bear close association in the field of India's political thinking. The idea of socialism in Congress was introduced by single handed efforts of Jawaharlal Nehru. In 1929 he happened to visit the erstwhile Soviet Union and was overwhelmed by the new forces released by the revolution, which were then desperately engaged in the economic upliftment of the country. Being a sensitive thinker he was enormously moved by the dignity accorded to human beings in the new Republic. Freedom from poverty and hunger, equal opportunity to all, no fear of unemployment and no exploitation of man by man appealed to him immensely. If a poverty-ridden country with a huge mass of illiterate people is to develop, socialism with a decisive role for the government seemed to be the right answer. At one point he was even prepared to consider the outright nationalization of all means of production. ["Nationalization of the means of production and distribution seems to be inevitable" was stated in a letter to Lord Lothian dated the 17th January 1936].

At the Lahore Conference of the Congress Party held in 1929 Jawaharlal brought forth his ideas on socialism for the first time before the Party. He understood that although a full socialist programme was necessary to put an end to the widespread poverty and inequality, the Party was not yet fully exposed to the idea and hence it might not have been acceptable. At the next two sessions held at Lucknow and Faizpur respectively, he pushed the idea further and a concrete programme of agricultural reforms to ensure fairness in distribution was announced. Afterwards, Nehru could manage a few supporters within the Party and a Congress-Socialist Forum came into existence.

Socialism as it is understood in communist countries looks upon coercive tactics as inevitable. Dictatorship of the proletariat comes through violence, chaos and hatred. Destruction of private property specially in agriculture has been a common feature of collectivization programme in the then Soviet Union. Industrial strikes resulting in loss of coal production affected the farmers badly in winter as a result of which lot of internal strife was there. Nehru as a person was not capable of pursuing anything with ruthless dedication and closeness to Gandhi made his faith in non-violence even stronger. International aspect of socialism promoting world peace and friendship drew him strongly towards it. His dynamic mind also was quick enough to see the way to freedom from aggression for the country. Authoritarian ways of establishing state control was not acceptable to him and supremacy of parliamentary democracy as a way of governance appealed to him most.

Acceptance of socialist ideas by the Congress was at the insistence of Nehru as opposed to a studied appreciation of socialist principles by the rank and file of the Party. Proletariats by no means controlled the Party, the reins lay in the hands of the middle class. This powerful middle class would never lend support to the establishment of a totalitarian state. Progressive ideas appealed to the party supporters who were well informed of international developments but commitment to a principle and upholding it at any cost was largely an impossibility.

Under the given circumstances, dichotomy presented itself on both the fronts, namely, internal and external. Nehru's inner self could never get reconciled to coercion, violence or regimentation of people's lives. Freedom and human dignity were his two basic faiths. Externally, Congress Party, which was a platform of all nationalist forces irrespective of class structure, had a large section of middle class and agriculturists with larger land holdings. Confiscation of land or introduction of collectivization programme would be opposed tooth and nail by this segment of Congress members. Ending of colonial rule was something which acted as a cementing factor and bonded the different groups together. Along with the political agenda of freedom from foreign rule the Party needed an economic agenda as well and socialism was accepted without the dogmatic approach. The way socialism was accepted was not much different from a capitalist welfare state.

There was criticism from those who wanted socialism in the way it has been practised in the communist countries of the world. The confusion regarding terminology symbolized in 'socialism', 'socialistic pattern of society', etc., made Congress brand of socialism unacceptable to the socialists lying outside the Party. They were sure that indecisive nature of economic philosophy adopted by the Party would have repercussions on the functioning of the government.

II. FORMULATION OF MIXED ECONOMY PRINCIPLE

Once the country became independent a policy for economic development attempting to demarcate the spheres of influence for public and private sectors had to be announced. The Industrial Policy Resolution of 1948 largely did this job. Industries were put into three different categories, which were under the management of public sector, private sector and a third sector where both private and public sectors could coexist. "Commanding heights of the economy" were to be owned by the public sector and it had the right to step into the management of industries in the private sector as well. The 1956 Policy Resolution was more cohesive and put industries into three categories. All industries which were of basic and strategic importance or in the nature of public utilities were placed under the public sector. Other industries which were essential in nature and required investment on a scale which the private sector could ill afford were also put under the public sector. The government was expected to assume responsibility of industrialization in a significant way.

The two Industrial Policy Resolutions taken together made it clear that production of capital equipments, essential consumer goods and exportable items were to be the primary concern of the public sector. Cottage and small scale industries being important employment generators could expect assistance in various forms from the government. Cooperatives represented a major organizational change in the case of agriculture and there also government help in the form of special funds was promised at least during the initial stages. Regarding foreign capital something like what we call now national treatment was promised during normal times. In the event of nationalization becoming a necessity, foreign investors were assured of compensation.

Adoption of mixed economy idea was probably a direct offshoot of the emergence of the idea of economic development as a political issue. Increase in the general level of well-being came to be regarded as a responsibility of the government, which required the drawing up of a plan of action on the development front. To implement government ideas a strong public sector and a Planning Commission were found necessary. Planning for economic development was a basic ingredient of socialist thinking and rapid industrialization had to be carried out with the help of the public sector. In a truly socialist economy, the entire economic life of a nation is set into motion by the Planning Commission. Here in India, Planning Commission ideas were to be put into practice through the public sector while private sector followed market economy principles.

About the relationship between public and private sectors it was generally held that both these sectors could coexist to serve the common goal of economic development. But since overall pace of industrialization had to be faster under planning, public sector had to grow at a higher rate and resource allocation to it also had to be made on a priority basis. So not only absolutely, public sector had to grow at a higher rate relatively also. The Mahalanobis model prepared for the Second Plan reflected this idea in a rigorous way. The areas where public sector dominance was not so prominent private sector was to operate under the broad guidelines provided by the Planning Commission. Thus in the case of agriculture land reform, tenancy reforms, and regulation of rent, etc., became directive principles under which agriculture had to progress. Compulsory procurement or compulsory membership of collective farms was never attempted in the case of India as existence of private property and means of production were guaranteed in the Indian Constitution.

The emphasis on socialistic pattern of development introduced by Nehru led many commentators to think that the existence of private sector was a temporary phenomenon. The short duration of the transition phase from capitalism to socialism was compatible with the idea of existence of the private sector. They viewed it more like the period of New Economic Policy as it prevailed in the case of the Soviet Union. Collectivization programme accompanied by compulsory procurement alienated the peasantry who were instrumental in providing the surplus for industrialization. As a compromise solution, collective farm members were permitted to retain some private plot yield which could be sold in the open market. It was a temporary arrangement to win over the peasantry so that their support was available for the development programme. Firm believers in socialism took the view that like NEP mixed economy was there just to fill the gap between capitalism and socialism. Once the change over to socialism is complete, mixed economy idea will automatically fizzle out.

Hard core socialists made a major mistake here. Mixed economy did not represent an idea for an economy in transition, it was going to stay forever. While commanding heights would be owned by the public sector the rest of the economy could safely be entrusted to the care of private sector subject to the broad regulations exercised by the state. A completely state-owned and state-operated system did not seem feasible and as an idea it did not appeal to Nehru also. Concern for welfare of Indian people in general and the need for equality as between different classes motivated him to go for socialism. The ideological or doctrinaire solidarity with socialism was largely absent from Nehru's way of thinking. Dedicated socialists or communists remained outside the framework of socialism put forward by the Congress Party. In the absence of a dedicated and committed group of Party cadres it was very difficult to implement true socialism. What Nehru did was a down to earth approach combining elements of both socialism and capitalism to act as a principle of governance.

The later imbalances that made their appearance in the economy were thought to be mostly caused by the adoption of this hotch-potch idea as a matter of state policy. The attitude that it is neither this nor that failed to give a proper direction to the management of the country. But this criticism does not seem to carry much weight. It is probably unrealistic to assume that planned development would always produce a balance between different sectors. To step up the overall rate of development it may be necessary that one sector grows at a rate higher than those of the others. This is planned imbalance. As an example, one can take up the case of heavy industries during the Second Five Year Plan period in India. Higher allocation of investment in favour of heavy industries at the cost of other sectors was attempted with a view to ensuring uninterrupted supply of capital goods to all the user industries in future. In the Soviet Union, in order to earn foreign exchange exports were pushed to the point where internal starvation became the order of the day. In a similar way one can refer to the Chinese Cultural Revolution where dictatorship of the proletariat was sought to be replaced by military-bureaucratic alliance. In the last two cases, excesses and mistakes were made under the very eyes of socialist approach.

The relationship between public and private sectors in India was one of complementarity and not of conflict. Mixed economy as it was understood in India combined elements of both capitalism and socialism with long-term trend towards pure socialism. Over the short-run, private sector would have a well-defined area of operation and it was entitled to financial assistance from the publicly-owned financial institutions. It was expected to benefit from massive infrastructure development programme undertaken by the government through the five year plans. Without creating any ill-feeling between different segments of the population, the chosen strategy tried to utilise available resources in such a way that there was no wastage. Prohibiting private capital and confiscating it would have brought dangerous consequences for the country. Government take over and payment of compensation without any guarantee for more efficient functioning under government ownership would have meant tremendous wastage for this capital scarce country. To scare away private investors when the economy was still in a premature stage of development would surely have been a short-sighted policy. Had Nehru been able to impose a disciplined form of coercion on the economy the rate of growth could have been higher. He made a compromise whereby the rate of growth came to be slower but the country was spared the agonies associated with the totalitarian alternative. An apt description of mixed economy can probably be state capitalism meaning thereby that the State takes the major initiative for investment without eliminating features of capitalist development as far as private sector functioning is concerned.

III. WORKING OF THE MIXED ECONOMY AND GROWING PRESSURES

Choice of the path of economic development by Nehru was not fault-free as such. The fact was that there were not many leaders with political farsightedness. In the enthusiasm to hold the reins of economic development in its hands the government went on imposing controls after controls. Thus industrial licensing, import licensing and strict control on foreign private investment grew in strength over the years and stifled the economy. It killed legitimate private initiative on the one hand and directed people's energy towards undesirable activities like black marketing in rationed articles or selling import licences at a premium on the other. The normal instruments to control an economy like monetary policy, fiscal policy, etc. were available with the government but to assert the authority of the public sector an elaborate licensing scheme became necessary. And it so happened that established business houses got the lion's share of licenses to be allotted as a result of which monopolistic tendencies grew stronger. Allocation of resources in the most efficient manner was not possible by the issuing of government orders alone. Poor quality of coal was often held responsible for low electricity generation. Selling of substandard food grains through ration shops or diverting rationed commodities to the open market to earn a good margin became common occurrences. Urban inequality in income distribution became more prominent due to growth of monopolies. Monopoly capitalism which the country was experiencing was far removed from the dream of socialist society.

As far as rural poverty is concerned the entire blame cannot be shifted to the mixed economy idea. Even the World Bank followed the percolation thesis in their initial attempt to address the poverty issue. It was believed that faster growth would penetrate the grassroots level and people from the lowest strata would benefit without there being any special effort in this direction. Unfortunately, it did not happen and targeted programme had to be devised to address the issue of inequality. Coming to India also one finds that various schemes like community development program, IRDP, Jawahar Rojgar Yojana and the latest NREGS have been in operation since long. One scheme yields place to the new one without the problem ever getting solved. Accountability was not an integral part of the system and so fixing of responsibility was hardly undertaken. To achieve that a detailed analysis regarding costs and benefits that resulted from the projects had to be undertaken. In a pure socialist system rewards and reprimands are easy to administer as micro level information is meticulously collected. Besides that the continuous pressure exerted by the Party upon the enterprise management to fulfil the targets is another factor for better performance.

The poor performance in foreign trade sector was mostly due to the failure to stage a turnaround in policy. From import substitution the thrust had to be shifted in favour of export promotion which many other countries in East Asia were able to do much earlier. The economy that was built inside tariff walls needed forces of competition badly and globalization brought forth that opportunity. It is quite possible that the remedy was known to the government but the thrust to initiate the change had to come from outside. India's adherence to modified pegged exchanged rate, lack of convertibility, and almost zero capital mobility made the system quite outmoded. Reforms that were necessary to correct these rigidities had no conflict with the mixed economy principles but it was simply not done. The initiative to undertake extensive reforms waited till the international agencies came forward to do so. Reforms at the behest of outside institutions had a couple of advantages which no one can deny. Firstly, probability of incurring unpopularity due to harsh measures is avoided, the whole blame can be shifted to international power games. Secondly, synchronization of policies as between different countries made the implementation of reform package more efficient. There are certain policies where international policy coordination is necessary to render them more effective. It was precisely this necessity that prompted countries to go in for pegged exchange rate during the Bretton Woods days. And lastly, reforms initiated by outside agencies save the government much embarrassment in a country whose economic policies proved to be ineffective.

The delay in lifting the tariff walls really made the economy stagnant. When foreign producers can enter, range of alternatives available to the consumer increases and this can give a spurt to consumer expenditure. Inequality in income distribution is a fact and this has to be openly recognized. Purchasing power of urban middle class has gone up considerably over the years and more important, size of middle class itself is growing at a fast rate. In the absence of open access to international branded things well known centres came into existence where imported things were freely available. Once buying and selling in foreign made goods are regularized both consumers and government are likely to derive benefits from the process. Side by side if a thrust on production and export with a view to capturing the foreign markets can be built up, all round stagnation that was visible in economic life can largely be done away with.

One interesting question relating to the economic crisis that was slowly building up in the economy is the fact that the crisis was not something unique to India. Many other countries had to undertake structural adjustment programmes to remove the mess that engulfed them. Oil crisis, debt crisis, and last of all the financial crisis that frequented the world economy during seventies, eighties and the nineties was caused by imbalances in the domestic as well as international fields. East Asian economies that went for reforms much earlier than India experienced enviable rates of growth for sometime and then were led into a financial crash. Government policy played an active role in shaping these tigers from Asia but still the crisis could not be averted. The policies that they adopted intended to usher in a faster rate of growth but imbalances developed in certain areas of the economy which ultimately developed into a crisis. Sometimes preconditions for success were not there, sometimes proper safeguards were not applied so that ultimately the International Monetary Fund had to come to the rescue and formulate a recovery programme.

Those who argue that the adoption of the mixed economy principle by India compromised with the rate of growth probably do not tell the whole truth. There was no proper monitoring and internal checks and balances were not timely applied. Public sector was not functioning in an efficient manner but disregarding that it went on to expand its area of operation. It should have really stayed away from the sphere of consumer goods production. When tackling inflation demand management was given due importance by manipulating monetary and fiscal policies. The other side of the story dealing with aggregate supply behaviour and per capita availability position were not always given due attention. Distributional equality is a good policy criterion but it has its limits. Unless the size of the resources to be distributed increased growth cannot take place. Investment and technological progress in agriculture which can augment supply and successfully tackle excess demand situation was viewed with complacency.

It is pointless to multiply such instances. Pressure points developed from time to time and stop-gap measures were applied to solve them. A thorough overhauling of the system was postponed probably due to the fear of loss of popular support base. The fact is that such sectoral imbalances could arise in the case of socialist economies also. The economies in transition which encountered considerable difficulties under socialism will lend credence to this view. Efficient functioning of an economy requires the detection of crisis at an early stage and then apply corrective remedies. If the crisis can be predicted before hand it is all the more desirable but for that one requires extensive research and policy coordination between government and research institutions. Models on market failure or crisis forecasting can achieve a lot in this regard.

IV. THE MOVE TOWARDS RESTORATION OF MARKET FORCES

The move towards liberalization sweeping through the Indian economy since the 1990s is a part of global experience. To put the disequilibrium economies back to the path of equilibrium a move towards privatization and greater role for market forces was envisaged. Actually two alternatives were available to restore equilibrium: one was to go for exhaustive controls by the government and the other was for relaxation of controls and give more importance to market forces. The world in general voted for the later course of action.

The reasons behind the reversal of the earlier approach are not difficult to seek. Since the end of the Second World War providing aid to facilitate the survival of the other half was looked upon as a sacred duty on the part of developed nations. All the Presidents of the United Nations have time and again reminded the developed nations about this obligation to the world community. Bilateral and multilateral aid were directed towards less developed countries with a view to stepping up their rate of growth. The recipient countries in their turn mostly chose import substituting type of industrialization as a matter of growth policy. High tariff walls restricted the entry of outside producers and the economies that resulted were invariably high cost economies. Export competitiveness of products turned out by import substituting industries was not up to the mark and exports were handicapped due to the lack of currency convertibility. Although pegged exchanged rate system came to be largely discarded since the seventies there were a few countries which hang on to pegged rate till the nineties and they needed a substantial depreciation to give stimulus to exports. Withdrawal of tariff restriction coupled with a general regime of depreciation could lead to a broadening of export markets. Such a strategy was expected to benefit both the developed and the developing countries since general accessibility to markets would increase and at the same time need for official development assistance would decrease.

The second aspect related to this new strategy of development was the tapping of private funds for development purposes. Many investors in developed countries were quite willing to have a change in portfolio composition in the sense that emerging market financial assets started becoming attractive in their portfolio. This new group of investors did not consider it risky to send their savings to far away countries. The newly gained economic strength on the part of several developing countries enabled them to compete freely in the international capital market to attract foreign private funds. Excessive dependence on official assistance on the part of developing countries was explained by the fact that their economic prospects did not evoke response from the investing community. Now as private investors were showing interest there had to be an international move to regularize the mobility of capital involving all countries irrespective of economic performance.

The qualitative change in development pattern that has

been discussed above brings us face to face with Nehru's choice of mixed economy idea as a policy of governance. When Nehru as well as the Congress Party accepted socialism as the goal and the mixed economy was supposed to be the vehicle to reach that goal the world environment was different. The East European socialist bloc was considered to be the new centre of power and for many years to come this belief proved to be true. The erstwhile Soviet Union, the leader of the bloc, inspired many countries in Asia and Africa to follow the path of public sector-led development. Since that experiment could not produce faster growth and divergence between rich and poor countries was not showing any sign of coming down, something new had to be thought of and there emerged the new ideas regarding globalization, liberalization and privatization, etc. The poorer countries disenchanted by now with the results of public sector-led development strategy just gave in and started preparing their own reform programs within the broad guidelines provided by the initiators of reform agenda.

Nehru, of course, could not foresee it. It was impossible for him to judge that socialist countries would disintegrate some day and the other bloc led by the U.S.A. would have more weightage in deciding the strategy of world economic development. The tilt towards the market economy and hence the private sector is the accepted philosophy not only in the U.S.A., but in European Union also. All these countries, however, have faith in economic welfare which Nehru fondly cherished in his heart. He did not believe in any dogmatic approach and had he been alive he most probably would have given his consent to the suggested revision. If a policy cannot produce the desired results he might not have any hesitation in joining the group advocating globalization. Being an international citizen at heart, he would have gone willingly with the rest of the world in its attempt to maximize the rate of growth.

References

Boffa, G. (1972), No Models for Socialism, *Indian Left Review*, Vol. 1, No. 10, March-April.

Dandavate, M. (1973), Approach Without Policy Frame, *Indian Left Review*, Vol. II, No. 2, April 1973.

Ganguli, B.N. (1964), Nehru and Socialism, *The Economic Weekly*, Sp. No. July, 1964, pp. 1213-18.

Ganguli, B.N., Institutional Implications of a Bolder Planning, Planning Commission, Papers Relating to the Second Plan.

Government of India, Planning Commission, Papers Relating to the Formulation of the Second Five Year Plan

Government of India (1956), Planning Commission, *Second Five Year Plan: A Draft Outline*, February.

Namboodiripad, E.M.S. (1964), Modernism, *Seminar*, November, pp. 34-37.

Nove, A. *The Economics of Feasible Socialism*, chapter 4.

Raj, K.N. (1964), The Congress and the Class Conflict, *The Economic Weekly*, Sp. No. July, pp. 1231-34.

Raj, K.N. (1973), The Politics and Economics of Intermediate Regimes, *Indian Left Review*, Vol II, No. 9, November, pp 35-51.

Rangnekar, D.K. (1964), Nehruism and the Second Plan, *The Economic Weekly*, Sp. No. July, pp. 1235-42.

Rao, V.K.R.V. (1983), *Indian Socialism: Retrospect and Prospect*, Concept Publishing Company.

Rao, V.K.R.V. (1974), Fundamental Aspects of Socialist Transformation, *Indian Left Review*, Vol XII, No. 11, pp. 8-19.

Savyasachi, (1964), Nehru's Concept of Socialism, *The Economic Weekly*, Sp. No. July, pp. 1227-30.

Shah, K.T., *India's National Plan*, Vora and Company Publishing.

Sen, M. (1964), The Socialist Democracy, *Seminar*, November, pp. 15-18.

Shankar, K. (1973), Needed: Institutional Changes, *Indian Left Review*, Vol. II, No. 1, March, pp. 55-58.

Singh, V.B. (1976), *Capitalism, Socialism and India*, Sterling Publishers Private Limited.

Singh, V.B. (1972), Indian Socialist Democracy, *Indian Left Review*, Vol. I, No. 9, Jan.-Feb.

Singh, V.B. (1964), *Indian Economy: Yesterday and Today*, People's Publishing House, September.

Singh, J. (1964), Nehru and the ISM; A New Legitimacy, *Seminar*, November, pp. 27-33.

Wiatr, J.J. (1972), Conflicts in Socialist Societies, *Indian Left Review*, Vol. I, No. 10, Mar-April.

The Socialist Legacy, *The Economic Weekly*, Sp. No. July 1964, contributed article, pp. 1219-25.

A Selection from the Writings and Speeches of Jawaharlal Nehru, *Seminar*, July 1964, Jawaharlal Issue.

4

Nehru: A Synthesizer of Two Extreme Economic Doctrines

Mrinal Kumar Dasgupta

Nehru's economic philosophy is based on multi-dimensional aspects of economic behaviour of mankind in relation to the economic institutions. He wrote on various economic topics viz., on planning, land reform, mixed economic system, industrial growth, and further on related economic topics viz., socialism, education, science and technology and so on. He was very much anxious to maintain justice and equity for the vast Indian masses. But his entire economic philosophy should be understood from his historical aspect. His book, "The Discovery of India" provides the key to his development philosophy. Time and space are the two very important aspects of Nehru's economic philosophy. His economic thought is not only concentrated on domestic politics but also on global perspective. In the global context, Nehru tried to understand the two extreme forms of economic institutions, one based on the Marxist philosophy and the other capitalism led by neo-classical group of economists. Domestically, he did not contradict Gandhian idea of Sarvodaya and Gram Swaraj, but he had other intentions. He laid the foundation for economic modernization, which had a kind of relative autonomy both at the domestic level as well as at the global level. In the process of modernization, he included centralized planning and public sector as two basic instruments. In this paper, however, we concentrated on Nehruvian approach to two basic doctrines of economic institutions viz., capitalism and socialism of Indian variety.

I. INTRODUCTION

Economic ideas of Jawaharlal Nehru were a product of two basic doctrines of economic institutions viz. (a) uncontrolled capitalism, and (b) socialism in the line of former Soviet Union's command economy. However, his views stemmed from a long process of interactions, compromises and accommodation of diverse ideas and ideologies. On the one hand, he visioned openness and global innovations to be incorporated in the Indian economy, on the other hand, he tried to introduce government interventions to protect the rights of Indian masses. To fulfil the second aspect he advocated for strong state-controlled sectors to reduce income inequality and to bring justice for the large part of the population living below the poverty line. His approach was always to maintain balance between free enterprise economy along with the policy of liberalization and the strict control on several sectors even at the cost of growth. He envisaged that until distributive justice is not attained through government protection, the vast masses with the lack of basic amenities like food, shelter, education, sanitation and health will plunge into darkness of poverty for a long time. Again, he tried to compromise between domestic and global compulsions in his economic policy approach.

In his development strategy, he tried to blend the neo-classical free economic system with the planned development process where plan called for the establishment of centralized planning, the imposition of rigorous economic controls, the introduction of public sector large scale industry and that of radical land reform in the agricultural sector For his economic policies, he argued for an interventionist state which sought to take an active role in the development process. The success of planned economy in the former Soviet Union influenced him to adopt centralized planning technique in India after independence. For the purpose, he took the initiative for implementing a plan model which would be commensurate with the Indian conditions and the Feldman-Mahalanobis model served the purpose. As for co-existence of private sector along with the dream public sector projects, Nehru took the Industrial Policy Resolutions of 1948 and 1956, which emphasized a progressively active role for the state in the development of industries coupled with a valuable role for private enterprise, properly directed and regulated.

Nehru's views on equity and justice, however, are different from Gandhian Sarvodaya system, though he tried to incorporate the neo-classical version of equity and justice without shunning the Gandhian doctrine. But he emphasized the role of state in this matter very emphatically. Thus, Nehru tried to synthesize the Gandhian view, the neo-classical idea of justice and equity under free market economy and modern welfare economics and finally, the role of state particularly in case of heavy and large scale industries such that a mixed economy can bring the optimum solution.

II. NEO-CLASSICISM AND NEHRU

Nehru, basically, being a liberal had many reservations about neo-classical economic ideas. He never automatically adopted the overall perspectives of a free enterprise economic society as there are unquestionable limits of the aspirations of a free society. His views were exceptionally liberal and he distanced himself from the sycophants of inequality, alienation, destruction of the environment, imperialism, racism and the subjugation of women. Thus in his opinion the basic terms of neo-classical economics viz., 'utility', 'consumer sovereignty', 'marginal products', etc., cannot bring optimal allocation of resources at various sectors and thus cannot solve automatically the primary problems of hunger, basic health and sanitation, primary education and many others. Further, the neo-classical jargons like 'free choice', 'competition', 'market', 'private ownership', etc., cannot be removed from Nehruvian concept of welfare state. But Nehru did not believe the neo-classical argument that everything outside the efficient productive engine, every aspect of human relations is taken as outside economics. In his study of neo-classicism he observed that this subject encompassed vast arena viz., pure theory including value and distribution, monetary economics, international economics, welfare economics, growth economics and many others. Basic objective of the subject was to study the economic variables for the determination of value and allocation of available resources in an optimum manner. In doing so they had set common assumptions such as:

1. Uncontrolled capitalism as the institutional structure.
2. The premises of social harmony which indicates that except a few frictions there is no conflict among social groups.
3. Individual freedom is accepted religiously.
4. The state is absolutely impartial.

According to Nehru, the problem arises from there. Accepting the above assumptions and to arrive at the optimality there are tremendous distortions which have been experienced by a large group of population. Thus growth and economic justice in his opinion (horizontal, vertical and distributive justice) have become incompatible with the prevailing feature of economic studies.

Nehru very inquisitively examined the Great Depression during the initial part of 1930s and felt that the neo-classical economics, to be built on the basis of 'perfect competition', and *'laissez-faire'* could not be applied in the Indian context. Rather, he closely observed the Keynesian approach, emerging out of the devastations of the Great Depression, which intensified the state control in the free market economy. Keynesian view induced him to think for the mixed economic system in India.

III. NEHRU ON COMMAND ECONOMY

Nehru had great appreciation for the Soviet experiment of centralized planning and for the emergence of 'developmentalism' as a new philosophy of economic policy. But Nehru did not approve the complete state control over both the production sector and consumer sector under a totalitarian framework. Nehru observed that a socialistic pattern of society would be the most desirable one and that the dominant role of the state in the economic development should continue for the developing countries. Nehru was very much concerned about the controversy regarding the two extreme economic systems, one complete free enterprise economy and the other perfect command economy. He witnessed a temporary and relative stabilization of capitalism during the 1920s. He further heard the main arguments against Marxist-Leninist economic theory and its conclusions concerning the general crisis of capitalism which took the form of boasts about the economic prosperity and claims that the mass production and availability to some working people of relatively cheap consumer durables showed that the capitalist system was viable, sound and enduring. But Nehru was never convinced of the superiority of the market competition system over the Soviet ideas of economic planning. But the disastrous economic crisis of 1929-33, which hit all the capitalist countries, induced Nehru to revisit the situation of Soviet-led command economic structure which successfully restrained the great depression of the capitalist world. Nehru was very much encouraged to observe the successful fulfilment of the USSR's First Five Year Economic Development Plan. He felt that the advocacy of the ungovernable market economy would be quite non-sensical and marked the demise of the bourgeoisie neo-classical school in view of successful implementation of anti-cyclical measures to stop such global depression under the command economic framework.

IV. NEHRU, A SYNTHESIZER

After independence, Nehru as the Prime Minister of

India faced a challenge towards development either through complete free enterprise economy or adopting a socialist state. The world at that time was economically divided into two extreme forms:

1. complete free enterprise economic structure,
2. totally controlled economy.

But the experience of the Great Depression raised certain uncomfortable questions for the advocates of free enterprise economy and they were searching for some adjustment to get-rid-off the maladies of unbridled capitalism. In that process the American economy took the help of some social measures and a liberal mixed economic system was adopted to counter the depression like crisis of the unbridled capitalism. Nehru also advocated for a mixed economic system which he called a socialistic pattern of society. Thus, his mixed economic system was tilted towards the socialist system. Actually, not only India under Nehru's stewardship but the World economy as a whole faced two alternative extreme market situations to fulfil the maximum number of the desired objectives which may often be non-commensurate and conflicting. As we have already seen that the first one is the perfect market mechanism or unbridled capitalism and the second is the complete state controlled or command economy. Nehru tried to synthesize the basic benevolent qualities of both to reach an optimum point in a feasible region. This situation can be seen in the following diagram.

X and Y axes represent the complete controlled economy (C) and uncontrolled capitalism or free market (F), respectively. The countries on the X-axis adopt centralized planning technique to follow an alternative growth strategy where role of decisions of individual entrepreneurs are completely ignored. The Central Planning Board, which is assumed to have the total information of economic situation, takes the decision regarding the choice of technology and adopts the requisite growth path. After the Second World War besides Soviet Russia, China, Cuba and several other East European countries on the X-axis followed the state dominated growth path. But in reality absolute free enterprise

DIAGRAM I

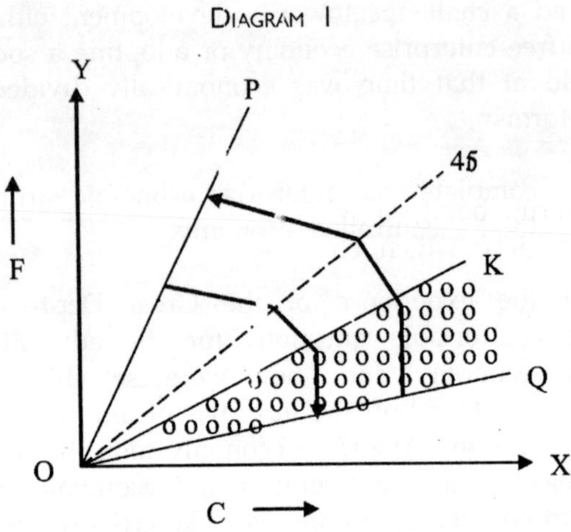

economy is non-existent. Thus most of the countries which like to follow free market mechanism fall from Y-axis to region YOX. The new developing countries also who want to adopt some sort of market mechanism, are free to choose any point on the region YOX. Suppose for some sort of adjustment they remain below OP, as after 1954 (the year of Stalin's death) the countries adopting fully controlled economy had to adopt some sort of liberal attitudes and could not remain on X axis and had to shift to the region YOX and could choose any point on YOX. Again, suppose for some sort of adjustment they cannot remain below OQ, then, OP and OQ are the two demarcating lines, like ridge lines, and POQ is the actual feasible region. Nehru in his effort to synthesize both the systems prefered to adopt conceptualized planning as a first step towards the goal of a socialist society. But as he was a confirmed democrat, the objectives like efficiency in production and distribution, consumer sovereignty, etc., were most important democratic values for him which need to be followed and achieved. Thus he endeavoured to reconcile the beneficial aspects of both societies to reach to a dream society that would be based on democratic socialism. Still his inclination was slightly towards socialism. Thus in the feasible region he tried to remain in KOQ space (all the lines OP OQ and OK are taken arbitrarily). Thus as per the actual need, customs and resource-base countries will move arbitrarily towards any of the two lines OP and OQ as indicated by arrow marks in the diagram.

V. COMMENTS AND CONCLUSION

Nehru, being a visionary, sometimes dreamt of a utopian society which could reject all the evils of various institutional framework. In his effort to synthesize the two extreme forms of institutional framework—(a) market economy, and (b) controlled economy—he could not foresee the difficulties of social decisions in such synthesized form of the institution; the distortions of both the systems could cripple the mixed economic system. In the first system, to fulfil the objectives, private owners with least interference through market mechanism arrive at their decisions. But in that system as they cannot shun the goal of maximizing self improvement, profit maximization objective become their major instrument. Allowing free entry and free exit in such a market may lead to worst form of private monopoly. In such cases in the production market only those private goods are produced which can hardly serve the social ends. On the other side, in the second system, distrust of politicians and fear of the government power again bring distortions. Bureaucratic pressure often leads to serious exploitation by producing goods that serve the private interest instead of fulfiling social needs. Thus in both the systems difficulty arises in arriving at a social decision.

Nehru, while trying to remove such anomalies from both the systems, brought certain new dimensions in the mixed economic system. In his approach to synthesize the beneficial aspects of both systems he searched for maximization of efficiency in economic activity so that social welfare is maximized. To achieve this target, Nehru stressed on distributional efficiency. Nehru at the AICC's Economic Programme Committee in January 1946 proposed radical measures to bring about equitable distribution of the existing income and wealth and prevent the growth of disparities with the process of industrialization.

Thus, in the liberal democratic process social justice

and equity in the Nehruvian economic thought could be attained in the structure of centralized planning system. The 1956 Industrial Policy Resolution and the adoption of Second Five Year Plan founded the development strategy of India which ensured that equity and justice could be obtained in India. Nehruvian justice and equity unlike that of Gandhi who studied these more philosophically than economically, was interpreted in economic term where the state had a great role to play. Thus, according to Nehru, the benevolent role of the state is very important even in the framework of liberal democracy. As a synthesizer, Nehru's effort will ever be remembered in the history of Indian economic thought.

References

Bardhan, Pranab (1986), *The Political Economy of Development in India*, Oxford University Press (Delhi).

Betaille, Andre (1983), *The Idea of Natural Inequality and other Essays*, Oxford University Press.

Datta, B (1982), *Social Justice in a Mixed Economy*, University of Calcutta.

Desai, A.R. (1984), *India's Path of Development: A Marxist Approach*, Popular Prakashan (Bombay).

Gopal, S (1975), *Jawaharlal Nehru: A Biography*, Oxford.

Kothari, Rajni (1989), *Politics and the People: In Search of a Humane India*, Vol. I, Ajanta Publication (New Delhi).

Nehru, Jawaharlal (1961), *The Discovery of India*, Asia Publishing House.

Sarkar, Sumit (1983), *Modern India 1885-1947*, Macmillan (Delhi).

Shenoy, B.R. (1958), *Problems of Indian Economic Development*, Madras University.

5

Jawaharlal Nehru—Rationale of His Socio-Economic Vision and Ideas

Kapil Sharma, Neeraj Sharma and Hemant Kumar Sharma

How did Nehru transform pure socialist thought with which he had an acquaintance in his early years of life to democratic socialism in a mixed economy setting has been elucidated in the initial pages of the paper. The paper aims at linking Nehru's foreign policy with the then state of India's economic development. Being a progressive and pragmatist national leader, Nehru yearned for integration of the Indian economy with the rest of the world. Nehruvian ideas of socialism can be fitted into the shibboleth of globalization. Nehru's hunger for industrialization through the means of economic planning is not subject for scrutiny. All these facets of Nehruvian economic philosophy have been knocked in the last section of the paper.

I. INTRODUCTION

Nehru, born in Allahabad on November 14, 1889, in a

respectable and rich family, made his home in the hearts of the poor and down-trodden. He is a legend in the annals of socio-economic and political history of India. His thinking was affected by the evil consequences of the First World War, the Home Rule League movement inspired by Lokmanya Tilak and Mrs. Annie Besant, the Jalianwala Bagh massacre, the policy of Ahinsa and the peaceful coexistence of Mahatma Gandhi and the widespread public movements. These incidents induced him to give up a life of leisure and jump into the national movement to liberate India from the evil clad clutches of the British. It was in 1912 that he started his political life and attended as a delegate in the Bankipore session of the Indian National Congress. He was influenced by his father, from whom he inherited integrity, courage, capacity for hard work, and freedom from pettiness. It was from his father that he acquired the gift of persuasive advocacy, freedom from doctrinaire rigidity and capacity for maintaining friendliness with political opponents. No leader was as free from the bonds of orthodoxy and sectarianism as Moti Lal in his time and it was, therefore, but natural for Jawaharlal Nehru to imbibe the tradition of liberal secularism.

Nehru was deeply touched by the circumstances also what India was facing at that time—like general mass poverty, unemployment, political instability, economic crunch and precarious global scenario. He became very much concerned on all fronts—national and international.

II. DEMOCRATIC SOCIALIST

Nehru was essentially a democratic socialist, but his views on democracy and socialism were not shaped by particular theory. His views were shaped by his practical bent of mind and an acute sense of justice. He regarded socialism as a panacea for all social and economic evils. To him democracy was more than a mere form of government. It was a way of life which tolerates differences of views and prefers reasoning, persuasion and consent to force in the conduct of public affairs. He thought that democracy demands discipline, tolerance and mutual respect.

Nehru had a kind of attraction towards Marxist

philosophy of historical interpretation and justice for general mass. This inclination got vitality and articulation when he was out of India during Brussels Conference and four days visit of Europe including Moscow in 1927. This Moscow visit gave a sharp turn to Nehru's economic ideas and stirred his interest in practical Marxism leading to planned economy.[1]

Nehru had deep admiration for massive intellectual construction of Marxism but drawn towards its constantly underlying passion for social justice. When Nehru realized the menace of Fascism and Nazism which was overshadowing every other thing, he preferred socialist direction. He expressed in his autobiography—"The world today is between some form of communism and some form of fascism—I am all for the former that in communism but would be far from being a staunch communist."

In post-independence period Nehru gave a slight shift to his socialism towards pragmatism. He denounced any economic dogmatism and in 1956 addressing All India Manufacturers' Organization he was glad that his evidence of capitalists agreed with the *Avadi* declaration of socialistic pattern of society and added in his usual ambivalent strain. "Some people seem to make fine distinction among socialistic pattern of society and socialism. They are all exactly the same thing without a slightest difference. But they are—is not such a very easy thing to define.... doctrinaire thinking leads to rigidity.... leave us high and dry."

Categorically, Nehru found in Marxism, a scientific approach to the solution of socio-economic problems, and a deep moral concern for the down-trodden masses. But Nehru was convinced that the details of Marxism could not be applied everywhere unthinkingly and without necessary modifications. Therefore, Nehru's socialist thought between 1935 and 1955 underwent a great change. Nehru thought in the late thirties that there was no middle path between capitalism and socialism and that the world had to choose one or the other. But in 1955, realizing a change in the nature of old-style capitalism, he abandoned his extreme position and held that it was possible to adopt a middle path between the two rival economic systems.

Nehru was a firm believer in socialism but he had his

love for democracy also. Socialism demanded the centralization of all the means of production and distribution and vesting the ownership only in the hand of State to wage the marathon war against poverty and the people have to sacrifice all non-economic values for waging the war successfully. Nehru certainly did not want this type of war against poverty. He chose the socialistic pattern which will have the economic ideals of socialism and democratic values of capitalism. The combination of the ideals of socialistic and capitalistic economy resulted in the mixed economy. Nehru, the great visionary, gave this economic system to India which is being followed even today.

Nehru also asserted that the democratic method is the only method for the attainment of a socialistic state as also for building it up on a firm foundation. Nehru believed that both the public and the private sector were indispensable in India's economy. The public sector is essential because Indian private capital is not sufficient to carry out huge projects such as the manufacture of arms and ammunition, the production and control of atomic energy, and the ownership and management of railways. The less vital industries would remain in the private sector and this would be advantageous for the economic development of the country. Nehru asserts that in a mixed economy there is also a place for the development of cottage industries which, by remaining in the private sector, can solve the problem of unemployment to a considerable extent.

Jawaharlal Nehru accepted the idea of decentralized village industries, but only to a limited extent and as a "subsidiary part of nation's economy." "Industrialization" was the only panacea to build up the infrastructure of the economy. He believed that, if industrilization is socialized, it would be free from the evils of capitalism, because the state ownership will eradicate them, and trusteeship will be built. Every type of human association has some philosophy of its own and they change with the order of the time to benefit humanity. And a reformer has to have a revolutionary outlook for the benefit of the society. Their views can be termed as different schools of thoughts. Jawaharlal had a "modern view" based on industrialization and a rational scientific way of life, as Ranade and Raja Ram Mohan Roy had viewed earlier. Jawaharlal's approach appeared as a bridge between Marxism and Gandhism and quite reconcilable as a "Specialism."

Nehru's economic connotation was instinctive; something natural. His new economic order, in the form of 'mixed economy', was based on his experience of his life and this was his firm belief that dexterity needed moral ethos to prove Economics as science and art both, because life is a composition of facts and norms both. He did not attach importance to theories or dogmas and advocated a policy implementation with a sense of pride, as a way of democrat's life, which, at no cost, should enthuse juvenile delinquency and a rejection of spiritualism or basic national culture. This is why, he advocated a policy for Indian Economic System, which should grant and guard freedom of the citizens and guide them for just course of economic path. He was cautious to avoid extremes of all kinds, so the policy could spell the responsibility of all the conscious citizens to apply the learning inputs in the most lucrative ways.

His idea of socialism therefore, was ultimately converted into practical form of mixed economy and encouragement of public and private sectors, and the mechanism what he prescribed to exercise his mixed economy was economic planning. Nehru's conception of socialism was inevitably tied to democracy and his mixed economy system was possible only in a democratic set-up. He did not want socialism without freedom or freedom without socialism. Nehru's idea served as a bridge between democratic socialism and Gandhian Idea of Swaraj and Welfare. His socialism was not a dogmatic ideal but an ever growing and changing philosophy, which moulded society and has the capacity of change according to the demand of time. Nationalization of the key industries was to be undertaken but a wide field was to be left for private entreprises.

Broadly speaking, Nehru did not confine himself in the limits of any particular political philosophy. He developed a working philosophy of his own by choosing pieces from Marxism, Gandhian and western liberalism. He judged people more by their conducts and character rather than their 'isms'.

III. FOREIGN POLICY

Since Nehru's socialism flourished in a democratic set-up, he took keen interest in framing India's constitution and formulating India's foreign policy in that light. After independence, Nehru declared, "Ultimately foreign policy is the outcome of economic policy." Since the freedom from want was of fundamental need, naturally a significant foreign policy could be developed on the basis of a vital internal policy. It is evident that when Nehru expressed his views he must also have had in his mind the compulsions of economic development as an input in policy-making. Nehruvian idea of Socialistic Pattern of Society was also reflected in his foreign policy of non-alignment. Nehru encouraged an amalgamation of Soviet and Western pattern, keeping non-attached policy with either of the blocs and maintained non-alignment as the basic character of his foreign policy. Nehru's contribution to international affairs has been an important one as his contribution in the domestic field.

Jawaharlal Nehru was in vanguard of the great world struggle against colonialism. The non-aligned movement which emerged as a counter-balance to the two big power blocs owed its origin to the initiative taken by Jawaharlal Nehru along with a few world leaders. Nehru's approach to foreign relationship did not evolve in a vacuum. Nor did it originate at that point in his life when he assumed political power for guiding the destinies of India. He was conscious of India's having to interact with other countries and with other societies when she became independent, however, remote the prospect of this independence might have been. He had given deep thought to the state of the world and to international relations for nearly 25 years before he became the Prime Minister of India. In fact, foreign policy was one field in which Nehru's democratic outlook and his world perspective had a chance to build a conceptual framework and concrete policies which have endured and survived unshaken even after his death.

During the years of power, Nehru made constant efforts to seek peaceful solutions for international conflicts. To these peaceful courses Nehru is disposed partly by nature and partly by Gandhi's impact. Pursuit of peace is Nehru's ideal which came to him as a legacy of Gandhi. But he believed in the pursuit of peace in the framework of possibilities. Nehru, broadly speaking, applied the teaching of Gandhi in foreign affairs, self-reliance, respect for the enemy, constant search for areas of co-operation, persistent refusal to surrender the essentials in negotiations, and refraining from causing hurt to others.

For economic development of the country, Nehru realized that peace was very essential and his clear understanding of international forces convinced him that India could progress only if she kept away from 'Cold War' and 'bloc' politics. Hence, the policy of non-alignment, peace, and emphasis on negotiations for the settlement of international disputes were the essential conditions for India's economic development. Nehru strove hard to achieve this objective.

IV. NEHRU'S IDEOLOGY AND GLOBALIZATION

Nehru was never against the policy of globalization. He was of the opinion that the development of a nation is not possible and cannot be sustained as well in isolation. It was because of this reason that he invited the co-operation of the people not only from India but from other countries of the world also in developmental activities. He wanted the emotional integration of his country with the rest of the world. He invited foreign capital and technology in order to achieve a faster economic growth.

With globalization trends all round, Indian economy has presently witnessed significant trends towards privatization, marketization and liberalization—all taking place since 1991 with the introduction of the new economic policy. Over more than the last one and a half decade, public sector has been yielding place to the private sector. At the macroeconomic level, there has been a marked shift towards indicative planning, industry, capital markets, banking, telecommunication and foreign investment. It would not be an exaggeration to state that the Government is withdrawing, though slowly, from the economic field and relegating itself to regulatory and monitoring roles.

Presently, the economy is in the process of recession. Sharp rise in the consumer price index and mounting unemployment have been the characteristic feature of post-reform developments, which have marginalized an increasing proportion of population. Various measures of decontrol in the economic sphere without alternative regulatory legislation or commensurate legislative changes have caused a series of national level scams and frauds disrupting smooth flow of economic activity. In such conditions, Nehru's idea of Socialistic Pattern of Society is of vital importance in the present context of globalization.

Nehru, being progressive and pragmatic in his outlook, broadly speaking, had picked up the practical side and accepted the concept of globalization and internationalism. Globalization is generally defended as the expansion of economic and political activities across the boundaries of the nation. That is way it means different things to different people. More importantly, perhaps, it refers to a process of deepening economic integration, increasing economic openness and growing interdependence between the countries of the world economy.

But for Nehru, Globalization meant something different from what is understood and practiced today. Nehru, of course, wanted the integration of his country with other countries of the world and always looked for co-operation of the other countries in socio-economic development of India, but he did not want the progress of his country at the cost of exploitation of its people by foreign countries.

Nehru was of the opinion that no nation can progress in isolation. He suggested for the globalization and internationalism of today and for acting globally. The main purposes of globalization and Jawaharlal Nehru's socio-economic ideas have been to make India economically strong, stable, self-reliant and economic and political freedom more relevant and meaningful.

His economic freedom is the central point of economic reform and globalization whose main aim is to reduce the gap between the favoured few and unfavoured millions also support the same concept. After the completion of about two decades of globalization and liberalization, a critical comparative analysis has compelled everybody to give top priority to Nehruvian models along with economic reforms and globalization for sustainable, balanced economic growth and stronger economy to achieve socio-economic and welfare in the new millennium. Nehruvian ideas are still quite relevant and useful.

V. PLANNING AND INDUSTRIALIZATION

To Nehru, planning was an inevitable process of a socialist economy in a democratic structure. Talking of the elements of the new economic system visualized by him, Nehru said : 'Political change there must be, but economic change is equally necessary. That changes will have to be in the direction of a democratically planned collectivism... A democratic collectivism need not mean an abolition of private property, but it will mean the public ownership of the basic and major industries. It will mean the co-operative or collective control of the land. In India especially it will be necessary to have, in addition to the big industries, co-operatively controlled small and village industries. Such a system of democratic collectivism will need careful and continuous planning and adaptation to the changing needs of the people. The aim should be the expansion of the productive capacity of the nation in every possible way, at the same time absorbing all the labour power of the nation in some activity or the other are preventing unemployment... An equalization of income will not result from all this, but there will be far more equitable sharing and progressive tendency towards equalization'.

This system, in short, emphasized democratically planned development within the framework of a mixed economy with private, public and co-operative sectors to achieve the objectives of modernization, growth and social justice. The objective of achieving growth with social justice is as relevant today as it was ever before.

Jawaharlal Nehru was initially responsible for creating an awareness and laying the foundation for social planning in India. He was so much eager that as soon as he became the

Vice-President of the Interim Government, he set-up a Planning Advisory Board in September 1946. Nehru wanted to have concrete plans and for that purpose an economic as well as statistical unit was set-up in the Cabinet Secretariat. He also invited an American expert, Dr. Solomon Trone, to study and report on some of the aspects of Indian economy. The expert recommended *inter-alia* the setting up of a permanent Planning Commission. The Congress Working Committee recommended the setting up of a Planning Commission in January 1950.

Nehru wanted the objectives of the plan to be well-defined. He, however, was not dogmatic about the objectives. He wanted the Commission to be dynamic in its outlook. Countering the mischievous propaganda that planning meant regimentation and the rise of totalitarianism, he declared that planning meant the most rational use of available resources to achieve certain nationally accepted goals which could bring about an improvement in the standards of living of the people and strengthen political independence of the country. It did not mean the negation of freedom of the people. Planning means an all round development of national economy and national life.

Nehru reiterated: "Let us have as great a measure of self-sufficiency as possible. If we are not self-sufficient, we are dependent on other countries, may be for food, may be for other thing. If we are dependent we may get into conflicts while we may avoid them if we have a large measure of self-sufficiency." "Planning means having some conception of the goal we are striving for, of the kind of society we are aiming at, trying to work up towards that end harmoniously and peacefully with as few upsets as possible, laying down targets so that on all sectors we may advance simultaneously. It we advance on one sector and do not advance on others, even that one sector will come to a stop, and we will face bottlenecks and difficulties."

Internally, Nehru was of the view that there was no hope for the transformation of the Indian economy into a modern one without planning and without active state intervention. The role of the state in the economy was perfectly justified "because, after all, state is the expression of society." In India, planning and the active intervention by the state in economy were indispensable. The key industries must inevitably be controlled very closely by the State. "Talking of industry as it is in India today sometimes to be a misnomer. Most of our so-called industrialists are hardly industrialists. They are in reality financers; that is not industrialization. They are buying up industries here and there but there is hardly an industry as much. The prime need in India is industrial power. Without power we can achieve little. It is power that we want and there are big schemes to be operated: unless we have planning, we cannot achieve anything."

The policy of the Government was oriented towards encouraging industrialization of the country so that India's manpower was most rationally and fully utilized, no one who wanted and was capable of adding to the national output was denied the opportunity to do so and in this industrialization there was no essential conflict between the cottage industries and large-scale industries. As the large-scale industries will not be in a position to absorb the vast manpower of India for a long period of time, the development of both types of industries could be adjusted which also necessitated planning.

For Nehru, the main problem of India was to increase its national output, which was increasing at a minimal rate. But, this did not mean that the problem of distribution would be neglected and it was wrong to say that "distribution would look after itself; in future, if there is no proper distribution and no proper social justice, there are going to be conflicts on an enormous scale. Therefore, distribution must be taken in hand and considered as a highly important factor."

Nehru had a solid reason for giving primacy to production over distribution and it had much to do with his conception of building a self-reliant economy for India. The resources for such an operation had to be largely raised from internal sources and the tasks of capital accumulation would become easier if the production increased at a faster rate to yield a higher rate of savings and capital accumulation.

Nehru regarded planning as an ever-flowing stream,

because only then there was a rhythm of expansion in the development of the people. Indeed, perspective planning is the essence of the planning process. As this process develops, there is a certain rhythm of expansion in the development of the people, and a sense of enterprise and achievement comes to them..." Nehru was never deterred by the problems, however, severe they may be, which came in the implementation of the plans. At the time of the massive Chinese attack on India, when there was confusion even in the high circles about the continuation of the plan, Nehru was strongly against any pruning of the Plan. Just two days after the attack he said, "We are at the cross-roads of history and are facing great historical problems on which depends our future. The Plan was the warp and woof of our national life and it was the war-effort itself that requires the Plan. The basis of the Plan is to strengthen the nation, to increase production...The basic objective of the plan was to strengthen the nation and, therefore, the plan should be looked upon as an essential part of the national effort." It was, alone, his determination and support which was responsible for the continuation of the plan.

VI. INDUSTRIALIZATION

On April 1948, India adopted what Nehru called a mixed economic system based on both public and private enterprise. Industries were divided into three categories; those which were to be exclusively owned and managed by the state, those which could be run by both state and private enterprise, and those which could be left in the hands of the private industrialists but subjected to some official controls.

Nehru said that "We have in our Industrial Policy Resolution laid down a broad approach of what is called a "mixed economy" which combines public enterprises and private enterprises." The doctrine of mixed economy was a combination of the merits of two economic systems—socialism and capitalism. The public sector is given the main responsibility of developing the economy while the private sector is also given an important role to play in the economic development of the country. The reliance and faith in this economic system was given shape through the Industrial Policy Resolution of 1948.

Nehru was of the opinion that without industrialization, the basic economic problems of poverty would remain unsolved and even the political foundations of independent nationhood would be threatened. It was not, therefore, a matter of moral or aesthetic choice. It was a simple fact of modern life, determined globally by the condition of modern day economic production. Nehru argued that an economy based on cottage and small scale industries was 'doomed to failure' because it could only 'fit in with the world framework' as a 'colonial appendage.'

Nehru was fully conscious that industrialization—setting up of basic industries and big industries in addition to the cottage and small-scale industries—was fundamental to the rapid economic progress of the country. As early as December 21, 1938 in his first note to the National Planning Committee, Nehru said. "There can be no planning if such planning does not include big industries, but in making our plans we have to remember the basic Congress policy of encouraging cottage industries." However, Nehru laid great emphasis on basic and heavy machine-making industries, as they were the very basic of industrial growth.

Nehru put emphasis on rapid progress of heavy machine building, heavy electricals and other basic industries. As a result of Nehru's initiative and strong support, the production of capital goods would increase to facilitate the country's march towards the achievement of a self-accelerating and self-reliant economy. Furthermore, the increased production of food and agricultural raw materials is necessary to keep pace with rapid industrialization. To this end, the increased production on agricultural implements, machinery for irrigation and fertilizers will be of immense help.

He said: We shall find what this industrial progress cannot be made without agricultural advance and progress. The fact is that two cannot be separated. Nehru argued that unless India is self-sufficient in agriculture, she cannot be able to advance in the industrial sector. Nehru said : "It seems to me that the only way to solve outstanding Indian seems to me that the only way to solve outstanding Indian problems is to have an all-embracing planned system of Indian economy, dealing with the land, industry—big scale and village—social service, etc. Nehru's rationale was that without industrialization and technology it would not be possible to create employment opportunities.

Jawaharlal Nehru wanted to make a harmonious balance between industry and agriculture to put India on the road of economic developmen and prosperity. Nehru said in 1957, 'Planning essentially consists in balancing between heavy industry and light industry, the balancing between cottage industry, and other industry. If one of them goes wrong then the whole economy is upset'. Nehru was a great visionary and he provided the fundamental idea in the realm of economic policy for developing a strong and self-reliant India with a just social order. These ideas continue to be of great relevance and will remain so in future also.

References

B.N. Ganguli (1977), *Indian Economic Thought*, Tata McGraw Hill Publishing Co., Ltd., New Delhi, p. 239.

Bagchi, Shantanu; *Ideas on Socialism and Social Justice: A Study of Jawaharlal Nehru*, Kanishka Publishers, New Delhi, 2002, p. 31.

Ghosh, Shankar (1992), *Jawaharlal Nehru: A Biography*, Allied Publication, New Delhi, p. 240.

Grover, Verinder, Jawaharlal Nehru, *"A Biography of his Vision and Ideas"*, Page XV, Deep and Deep Publications, New Delhi, pp. 128, 423-24.

Jawaharlal Nehru (1956), *An Autobiography*, Bodley Head, London, p. 529.

Jha, Nalini Kant (2002), Domestic Foundation of Nehruvian Foreign Policy in Nehru's World View in Nizami, T.A. (ed.): *Nationalism* Vs. *Internationalism*, Threeways Publishers, Aligarh, p. 42.

Michael Brecher (1969), *A Political Biography*, Abridged Edition, Oxford University Press, London, p. 72.

Mukherjee, Hirendranath (1964), *The Gentle Colossus*, Manish Granthalya, Calcutta, pp. 162-63.

Nanda, B.R. (1955), *Jawaharlal Nehru: Rebel and Statesman*, Oxford Unversity Press, New Delhi, p. 185.

Nanda, B.R., *op. cit*, p. 190.

Nayyar, Deepak, 'Globalization: What does it mean for development', in Debray, Bibek (ed.); *Challenges of Globalization*, Konark Publishers Private Ltd., New Delhi.

Nehru Jawaharlal (1964), *The Discovery of India*, Asia Publishing House, p. 559.

Nehru, Jawaharlal, *India's Foreign Policy*, pp. 592-93.

P.D. Kaushik (1964), *'Congress Ideology and Programme'*, Allied Publishers Pvt. Ltd., Bombay, pp. 120-22.

Raj Kumar, N.V. (1952), *The Background of India's Foreign Policy*, A Collection of Resolutions of I.N.C, New Delhi, AICC.

Rao V.K.R.V. (1960), *"Planning without Dogma"*, A Times of India Publication, Bombay, p. 306.

S. Gopal (ed.) (1984), *Selected Works of Jawaharlal Nehru* (Second Series), Vol. 1, New Delhi, p. 320.

Singh, R.S. and Shrivastava, M.P. (2004), *Socio-economic Ideas of Nehru and Globalization*, Anmol Publication, New Delhi, p. 68.

Smith Donald Eugene (1959), "Nehru and Democracy", London, pp. 124, 129.

Supra Note, pp. 239-40.

6

J.L. Nehru—A Model-maker of India's Democracy and Development

DEBES MUKHOPADHAYAY

"But for him, India would have left much less the winds of change that had been blowing over the world; he made us aware of them and also more receptive. Yet he failed his people insofar as he could not adequately execute the great mandate he had from them because he just was not relentless enough. He was our beautiful but ineffectual angel, beating his beautiful wings largely in vain." Hirendranath Mukherjee (1964), The Gentle Colossus: A Study of Jawaharlal Nehru

There was Jawaharlal Nehru in India who designed the country's destiny after attaining independence through his two commitments of nationalism and socialism in a democratic polity. He is called a model-maker of democracy and development. The multi-faceted Nehru raises some issues and penetrating questions on economic planning and the state-dominated industrialization of the country. Section I of the paper presents Nehru as a builder of modern India—'a modernizer par excellence'. He was a visionary "who experimented with socialist planning or Indian version of state planning. Section II describes Nehru's ideas on planning since 1930s. But he faced some opposition from Sardar Patel and Gandhiji. After their death, he became an unchallenged man in government and policy-making. Nehru's vision on industrialization/planning has been presented in Section III. This section speaks about contradictions in planning policies and programmes experienced during his lifetime and afterwards. This section also touches upon Nehru's vision of self-reliance/import substitution. Section IV deals with the errors of commissions and omissions made by Nehru and the legacies that the country experienced thereof.

I. INTRODUCTION

Jawaharlal Nehru—a dedicated democrat, a veritable renaissance man, an aristocrat and an idealistic intellectual, founding father of institutional democracy, the architect of modern India, both political leader and a chief planner, "the gentle colossus"—has thus had "a peculiar mixture of liberal socialism of the West and the experiments in planning in Soviet Union that often prevailed over the philosophy of decentralized rural-oriented production (Subramanian, 1978)." Impressed by the economic gains of the socialist Soviet Union consequent upon economic planning, Nehru applied the concept of socialism on the Indian soil on Gandhian lines (that is, "an Englishman in Indian clothing", as said by Acharya Kripalani), paraphrased by Nehru as the 'socialistic pattern of society' where the principal means of production would be under social ownership or control. Being a true nationalist, his only concern was 'India first and India last'. Thus he had two commitments interlinked to each other that he maintained all through his life—Nationalism and Socialism.

Nehru—The Builder of Modern India

Behind these perceptions based on the understanding of the problems faced by the countrymen before and after independence and understanding of the country based on socialist passion as well as Gandhian influence and message of emphasising the need for self-reliance and self-development, this political giant stepped in formulating economic policies for building a Modern India. It is because of differences in perception, policy-making of different leaders is expected to be non-homogeneous. In fact, he met strong opposition from the 'iron man' of his cabinet, Sardar Patel and Gandhi, in his initial years of Prime Ministership. The legacy of pre-independent debate—the Gandhian approach and the Nehruvian modernising approach—carried on till December 1950 when these two almost unyielding stalwarts passed away. Following their demise, Nehru became the unchallenged leader of the independent India and rose to an iconic status during his life time.

Nevertheless, his economic convictions and beliefs came in for sharp criticisms from many quarters both during and after his lifetime. There are some people who believe that this or that policy of Nehru was wrong and the crises that the Indian economy experiences today owe greatly to his cult figure. Debunking such criticisms, Meghnad Desai articulated that many of the problems faced by us 'began with the daughter, and not the man himself'. Nehru's admirers argue that he is the apt symbol of India's sixty years of independence as his legacy continues even today. Contemporary economic thinking of the 1940s, 1950s and 1960s 'influenced the logic of India's plans, and correspondingly, development theory was for a while greatly influenced by the Indian case', said Sukhamoy Chakravarty (1987). "Most Indians—even those who during his life-time were his harsh critics—hark back to the Nehru era, identify with him, and draw inspiration from his life and work, his social vision, ... The legacy he left behind is in many respects a sheet-anchor for the Indian people who are today buffeted about in a sea of despair. What more could a people ask from a leader? Has any society, any people, the right to ask a leader, however great, to solve all its problems once for all? (Chandra *et. al.*, 2000)." Sukhamay Chakravarty held him in high esteem and resolutely mentioned Nehru 'as a modernizer *par excellence*'. Throughout his life, he relentlessly engaged himself in what he called 'nation-building' through a combination of economic growth and development with modern agriculture and industry and the parliamentary form and process of democracy.

Nehru's Vision

The Nehruvian view—derived predominantly from Fabian Socialism endorsed the need for rapid development bolstered by planning and state economic activity with greater emphasis on the expansion of public sector industrial enterprises. "Economic policy-making is basically derived from the politics of policy-making and the politics of policy-making is derived from the political leaders' view of the kind of policies that will serve their ends (Sengupta, 2002)." Nehru's experiment with democratic pattern of socialist planning or Indian version of state planning, not available in bookshelf as a reference, was considered to be a new model for Asian and African development. Planning Commission set-up under the aegis of Nehru attracted many stalwarts such as Ragnar Frisch, Jan Tinbergen, N. Kaldor, Rosenstein-Rodan, Ian Little, Richard Goodwin, Oskar Lange, Brian Reddway, etc., who gave advice and learnt a great deal from the Indian experiment of planning. "Nehru's vision of a mixed economy moving towards a socialist pattern of society appeared to the theorists of reformed capitalism as an answer to the challenge posed by the model of growth presented by Mao's China", says Sukahamay Chakrabarty (Sengupta, 2002). However, Nehru was a hard core pragmatist and not a doctrinaire one. Once Nehru told Dr. V.K.R.V. Rao: "It is not a question of theory of communism or socialism or capitalism. It is a question of hard fact. In India, if we do not ultimately solve the basic problems of our country ... it will not matter we call ourselves capitalists, socialists, communists or anything else." All these are evidence of Nehru's economic maturity, though he was not a professional economist. No other individual has left an indelible imprint on independent India's economy as Nehru did.

II. NEHRU'S PLANNING FOR PLANNING

To start with, the three pillars of development strategy as designed by Nehru were planning for: (i) rapid agricultural and especially industrial growth, (ii) a public sector to develop strategic industries, and (iii) a mixed economy. Nehru has to be credited for implanting and popularizing the concept of economic planning on the Indian soil. From the point of understanding the past regarding economic planning as a tool of development, we must note that the Congress Working Committee constituted a National Planning Committee in 1938, though one could notice tensions within the Congress in the form of a battle between 'left' and 'right'. It may not be irrelevant here to mention that the word 'socialism' did not get moorings in the concept of economic planning in 1938. It was only later that the Congress Party and Nehru in particular candidly pleaded that 'planning' was a step toward socialism in India. Although the arguments and counter-arguments that continued between the 'left' and 'right' forces within the Party relating to the shape of planning and the powers and influence to be divested inside the government gathered strength after independence, Gandhi stood as a reconciliatory force, albeit temporarily, between Nehru and Patel—the 'Duumvirate'. After Gandhi's assassination in January 1948, Nehru's position and influence came to be almost unassailable, even though he had to contend with Sardar Patel, the Deputy Prime Minister. Meanwhile, he renewed the idea of establishing the Planning Commission in 1949, but again met tough opposition from Patel. However, as economic crises became critical in the post-independent period, private entrepreneurs rallied behind Nehru. Anyway, after prolonged debates, the Planning Commission came into existence on March 15, 1950.

After the demise of Sardar Patel on December 15, 1950, Nehru became the unquestioned authority as the arbiter of the Congress Party, government and national policy-making. The final version of the First Plan saw the light of the day in December 1952 in which one could see 'a discernible change in tone and emphasis on the approach to industrial development (Frank, 2005)'

III. NEHRU'S VISION ON INDUSTRIALIZATION/ PLANNING

Although Nehru had the distaste for capitalism and affection for socialism, he was never a dogmatic and inflexible person. He viewed planning as necessary for a national consensus on matters affecting the welfare of the entire people of India. It is said that India's plans of the early years were drawn within the ambit of the then politico-economic development and social change having three closely related objectives viz., (i) pursuit of people's welfare, (ii) the search for equality, and (iii) the desire for more even distribution of economic power (Singh, 1974). The purpose of planning, as proposed by Nehru in the meeting of the National Development Council in 1954 and in the *Avadi* session of the Congress Party in January 1955, was 'the establishment of a socialistic pattern of society where the principal means of production are under social ownership and control', and there was to be a 'plenty of room for private enterprise provided the main aim is kept clear' (Tomlinson, 1998).

From M. Visvesvaraiya, an engineer-administrator but the first Indian planner, to Nehru, all the 'pioneers' dealt with planning as a mere economic exercise. Whenever they talked of 'planning', they thought that planning was an effective method of industrializing the Indian economy. As a result, the issue of agriculture was dealt with in a perfunctory manner—sometimes as an addendum, sometimes only as a matter of technology (Chattopadhyay). Nehru's speech in the Parliament in 1952 to vent his justification for policies to be followed in the First Plan goes like this: "If our agricultural foundation is not strong then the industries we seek to build will not have a strong basis either." Underlining the interconnection between agriculture and industry in the early period of development of the Indian economy, Second Five Year Plan document reads: "In India, agriculture and manufacturing industries are completely interlocked. Economic progress depends on the advance of both." In his scheme of things, Nehru reiterated substantial increases in agricultural production and productivity as the "keystone of our planning" through the routes of institutional measures of land reform (instead of a technological one) and efficient use of available resources of land and labour. However, as events turned out, agriculture represented a 'bargain sector' (Rao, 1971). Nehru himself, in 1964, six months before his death, admitted that, "Though we all know that agriculture is essential and basic, it has been rather neglected." Possibly because of this kind of ambivalence and the urgency of repairing the post-partition problems, the First Plan was prepared on a 'rush order' and put emphasise on infrastructure—power, transport and communication. The First Plan being a rudimentary one did not assign industry as the 'leading sector of growth'.

Economic development, as was argued by Nehru, strongly demanded industrialization of India by building up 'temples of modern India'—iron and steel and fertilizer industries—the essence of the so-called Nehru-Mahalanobis Strategy of the Second Plan. The Second Plan being a more sophisticated one put emphasis on comprehensive industrialization. Not only in terms of industrialization, but also in respect of economic independence or self-reliance as well as import substitution and left-wing economic ideas of socialism, Nehru had his own views and observations. As Nehru by his sheer personal domination in the system, charisma, power and influence relegated the Planning Commission as an advisory body, a decisive role in the drafting of the Second Plan was played by him.

Public sector dominated 'industry-first' policy was believed to be the 'engine' of India's economic growth as the public sector was destined to occupy the 'commanding heights' of the economy and that import substitution (IS) policy would be used to stimulate growth. It was a settled fact that along with Mahalanobis, Nehru wanted to push heavily to "make machines to make machines", while simultaneously encouraging, influenced by Gandhian philosophy, small and cottage industries to provide adequate employment such that economic and social disparities get reduced. Nehruvian idea of a mixed economy got translated in the building up of three steel plants in the Second Plan in collaboration with both the socialist USSR and capitalist

Britain and West Germany. This 'indicates the emergence of a global outlook in the industrial programme of the country'.

The central premise of the Second Plan was industrialization. And Nehru categorically stated that this plan document 'stands as the most elaborate statement of his economic policy'. However, he had been nurturing such a dream for comprehensive industrialization since the 1930s. Nehru's address to Congress in 1936 goes: "I believe in the rapid industrialization of the country; and only thus, I think, will the standards of the people rise substantially and poverty to be combated (Nehru, 1958)." By industrialization, he meant heavy and basic industries—the sinews of getting India modernized so as to create foundations of a self-reliant industrial economy. Nehru's industrialization programme has had the four objectives: welfare and employment, import substitution to save scarce foreign exchange reserves, export promotion to earn foreign exchange and lastly, self-reliance.

Thus the Nehruvian vision laid emphasise on 'growth with equity'. Commenting on this Nehru-Mahalanobis strategy, Bipan Chandra and others said that "... the strategy did not posit equity against growth but assumed that higher growth enabled higher levels of equity and was critical for meeting the challenge of poverty; utmost attention was therefore given to rapid growth (Nehru, 1958)." This is what may be called the "trickle down hypothesis" (Galbraith, 1992).

Contradictions in Planning Policies and Programmes

By the end of 1950s it became obvious that Indian planning contained serious contradictions of aim and flaws in implementation and such contradictions between plan policies and programmes grew worse at the beginning of the Third Plan. Commenting on the policy implications of the Nehru-Mahalanobis import substituting industrialization strategy, Arjun Sengupta says that although this strategy talked about producing machines to make machines which needed to be sold in the market to meet the demand, the mechanism to match demand and supply is quite different in a partially controlled economy from that of a Soviet-type centrally planned economy. He articulates: "In the very partially planned economy like India, where the overwhelming part of the economy is privately managed or market-oriented, planning has to play a different role where prices and markets will have to be given major importance. From the very beginning this important role of the price system was neglected because of the influence on our planning model of the central plan model of the Soviet Union. This was a major mistake made by us at that time. No fault of Nehru. No fault of Mahalanobis either. This was a genuine misunderstanding of the viability of the central planning model" (Arjun Sengupta, 2002).

After assuming office, the third in a row, in August 1963, Nehru's idiosyncratic brand of economic policies came in for sharp attack. His concept of socialism came into disrepute as it failed to achieve either the goals of rapid progress toward a self-reliant economy or the aims of reducing social inequalities of vast Indian masses. Nehru's model of bourgeoisie democracy with a centralized tendency thus conferred benefits to the ruling classes and elites. In spite of best intentions of its framers, benefits of it did not percolate to the poor Indian people—a kind of 'distorted model of both democracy and development' (Kothari, 2002). The entire rationale of development planning then raised a big question mark. Rammanohar Lohia forcefully stated in the Parliament that two-thirds of Indian population was earning an average of 3-*annas* a day, while Nehru as a Prime Minister claimed it was five times higher than Lohia's estimate. "The Planning Commission, drawn into the Lok Sabha debate with the request to issue an authoritative estimate, disputes Lohia's figures as too low, but had to concede it was closer to reality than the one used by Nehru." This is a clear reflection of 'fundamental class structure of the Indian economy'. It was roughly 7.5 *annas* a day.

The political compulsions of accommodating both large farmers and traders, as revealed in the final version of the Third Plan, were the main source of contradiction. Some higher-up authorities believe that concessions awarded to the propertied classes that emerged out of accommodating politics were so expensive that it hindered the 'possibility of carrying out institutional change on any meaningful scale.' The cult of patronage and power that came to the surface with a headlong speed by the early 1960s were nothing but the 'sign of political decay', leading to a crisis of governance: "Officers of the police, the judiciary, the state and local revenue and development services, and even the vaunted Indian Administrative Service, were all engaged in selling influence (often at fixed prices and graded fees) to individuals ranging from industrialists, contractors and suppliers, traders and large agriculturalists, to the chief ministers and ministers of state and central governments. As corruption became institutionalized into a distributive device, those who could not afford to pay found themselves at the bottom of the list in the allocation of access to the "public" goods and services (Frankel's, 2005)." It is because of bureaucratic control that Nehru's brand of socialism brought in was a kind of 'licence raj', a term coined by C.R. Rajagopalachari.

The ultimate result of such accommodating politics, instead of being an integrative device, was the absence of consensus, stability and integration thereby putting the rationale of national development planning into question. Simultaneously, as institutions of the democratic polity were going to be increasingly dependent on key individuals, often called 'extra constitutional' individuals and groups for which Nehru himself was to be blamed, there developed some sort of perverted model of both democracy and development. In fact, 'de-institutional process' or the so-called 'institutional failure' started gathering its get-up-and-go mood during Nehru's regime causing low level of development. Nehru's iconic status both as a planner and a national leader of high calibre was then not a smooth sailing one. Step-wise de-institutionalization coupled with the rise of individual opportunism and the resultant corruption led to 'growth-through exclusion', the emergence of a 'soft state', in the words of Gunnar Myrdal, and the growing discredit of parliamentary democracy. It may be convincingly argued that our failures are mostly to be attributed less on ideology and more and more on poor management.

As a national leader, he failed to stop leadership contest among Congressmen in the General Election of 1962. The Chinese aggression in 1962 further ridiculed Nehru's

Panchsheel. Coming out of the shell of sycophancy and all-please mind-set toward Nehru family, V.K. Krishna Menon, Defence Minister in Nehru's Cabinet and a staunch leftist in the Congress Party questioned Nehru as an arbiter of national policy. The result was the dismissal of first Krishna Menon and then K.D. Malaviya (allegation for misusing election funds) from the Cabinet.

Search for Economic Independence and Self-reliance/ Import Substitution

It may be mentioned again that the prevailing economic philosophy of 1950s and 1960s 'influenced the logic of India's plans'. In her search for economic independence after getting political independence, the policy prescription for India's industrialization was bolstered by the promotion of domestic production through import substitution—the substitution of domestic production for imports of manufactured articles. However, the roots of self-reliance can be traced to the Swadeshi movement and the Gandhian idea of village-level self-sufficiency. Like all, since Nehru was the product of a certain society and age, the spirit of the then society and age demanded the employment of IS (Import Substitution) policy.

On IS policy, Nehru asserted: "I believe as a practical proposition that it is better to have a second-rate thing made in one's own country than a first-rate one has to import." Interestingly, one may, without any iota of doubt, submit that such inward-looking policy prevailed till 1991. The IS-oriented policy of industrialization was adopted in India on the grounds of: (i) 'export pessimism', and (ii) the protection of infant industries. The exploitative British rule shaped Nehru's future economic policies. He strongly suggested that India should not be dependent on external forces in designing her economic and political policies. And as far as economic policies of the country were concerned, Nehru was convinced that India must be independent of foreign capital or foreign aid. By building domestic industry base, Nehru suggested that the country should build up her own defence potential. The economic implication of such independent policy-making is that the scarce foreign exchange reserves need to be conserved with great care. If leakage of foreign saving is not plugged, India's economic policies might become subservient to foreign countries. Hence the IS was a valid approach toward the country's the then industrial development.

It may not be irrelevant here to say that Nehru's vision of self-reliance need not to be associated with IS. It did not imply zero aid, but basically putting a restraint on the flow of foreign capital, given the arm-twisting nature of the benefactors. Thus, India's industrial structure could be carried forward 'on the basis of the country's own domestic and foreign exchange reserves'. Building of such industrial structure necessitated, dominated by the then economic thinking, IS policy.

One may, however, contest the reasoning for using IS strategy of industrialization, but export stagnation in the 1950s was the ground reality, constituting the rationale of the then economic policy. Very rightly, says Arjun Sengupta: "But what is relevant here is that the export pessimism of that period and the import substitution policy was not Nehru's contribution. That was a contribution of the policy-makers or the economists on the basis of their judgment and study of the foreign trade situation (Sengupta, 2002)."

IV. NEHRU'S ERRORS OF COMMISSION—BUREAUCRACY AND REGULATION

For creating 'commanding heights of the economy' by building public sector enterprises in the years to come, Nehru was then contemplating control and regulations of the private sector. To this end in view, the Industries (Development and Regulation) Act, 1951 came into force. But because of his softness toward the propertied classes and the concept of diluted version of socialist planning applied on the Indian soil, he did not wage any attack on the institution of private property.

Nehru as an Institution-builder

Nehru being a mass leader adopted "mass approach" for propagating his dual perception of 'development' and 'democracy' of the parliamentary variety. Participatory democracy is expected to educate vast Indian masses so that they can fruitfully integrate themselves into the system. To this end, the first few years attached a great deal of attention for establishing various institutions. That is why, under Nehru's initiative not only institution of the Planning Commission was set-up but also institutions like Community Development Projects, Panchayati Raj Institutions (PRIs) had been planted to blossom in the newly independent India. In fact, a whole gamut of paraphernalia of institutions was conceived in the early years of planning. But conflicts and tensions often ruled over these institutions. As the Congress Party failed to come closer to the masses for not being a cadre-based. party, most of these institutions came to be administered by the government officials and bureaucrats. As a result, the autonomous character of these institutions was robbed of. Above all, it created enough room for loyalties and manipulations and sycophancy. Its consequences were disastrous, as was argued by Rajani Kothari, "... there took place a gradual decline in the effectiveness of even government bodies and the civil services, at any rate at the state and lower levels, with the rise of 'extra constitutional' individuals and groups. Nehru could be blamed for all these developments as he destined to enjoy the unique position till he is alive. ...Patronage and sycophancy became important and even elements in civil society—the literati, the artists, the intelligentsia and the scientists—became hangers-on on the Nehru Household (Kathori, 2002)." It is alleged that he embodied paradox and autocratic tendencies with a profound belief in democracy.

Nehru's Errors of Omission—Neglect of Primary Education

Advanced countries of the world are supposed to invest more in education or in a broader sense in the knowledge industry. It is an irony that a man like Nehru brought up both in the British and Indian traditions failed to attach any importance to the primary education where the number of illiterates at the time of independence stood at 82 per cent. In fact, for the success and efficient functioning of the parliamentary democracy, such oversight of primary education to educate the mass of the population especially in the rural India could be envisaged as a 'cruel neglect'. In comparison, other Asian countries that attained independence around late 1940s and early 1950s leapt past India in later decades. Unbelievably, a very insignificant amount of fund was allocated to education and other social services in the Second Plan! Pulapre Balakrishnan's comment captures this error of omission with much clarity: "One cannot overlook the likelihood that the very face of India, not to mention the rate of growth of output via human capital accretion, may have been vastly different had much more attention been paid to primary education at the very outset." He adds further "...that the man whose birthday is celebrated as Children's Day in India had actually managed to do very little for her very young (Balkrishnan, 2007)." However, the Nehru's legacy continues even in the 21st century and we did not learn any lessons from our recent past. This may be attributed to a 'lock-in' effect of the Nehruvian strategy.

But we have another Nehru, a dreamer, a visionary who at the same time with great enthusiasm attempted to build up the 'temples of science and technology' to liberate the country from dependence. A large number of luminaries of Indian science—Meghnad Saha, C.V. Raman, S.N. Bose, Homi Bhaba, and Vikram Sarabhai—were placed at the helm of affairs by Nehru. His government oversaw the establishment of many institutions of higher learning, including the UGC, the All India Institute of Medical Sciences, the Indian Institutes of Technology and the Indian Institutes of Management in different parts of the country.

CONCLUSION

"Whatever the weaknesses that emerged later, Nehru's economic policy did prove to be the right one for India and as a result her economic achievement was substantial (Chandra *et. al.* 2000)."

As far as nation building role was concerned, Nehru without organizing and mobilizing and educating Indian people believed that the exercise of adult franchise would ultimately educate people to vote in their own interests. That is, this kind of participation in elections would propel 'parliamentary democracy to serve as an instrument of nation-building, social change and equity.' This is the area where we faulted because very little importance had been given to primary education. Electoral politics only strengthened the hold of the elites and privileged groups of people. People in power could not come closer to the people.

India had to inherit many economic problems from the past and had to confront many built-in disadvantages but succeeded in developing and modernizing independent economic base bolstered by industrial growth via mainly the public sector. Although Nehru, till date, is the longest serving Prime Minister (1947-64), Nehruvian legacies continued until 1991, when the new *mantra* of 'liberalization, privatization and globalization' (LPG) replaced the old economic policies. It would be a great mistake to assess Nehru in the light of the so-called LPG model and the consequent 8-9 per cent growth rate achieved so far. No one should doubt that today's growth is a function of yester years, though the pre-conditions for take-off were in a state of pitiable condition during the regime under consideration. Thus measured by any historical standards, Nehru's achievements and greatness can never be run down. I close my discussion with a quote from P.C. Mahalanobis: "Through his leadership, he has brought about profound changes in social and productive forces which will continue to influence the course of events in India in the most decisive way."

In his life time, Nehru had the experience of seeing the tentacles of corruption, bureaucratization, careerism and many other evils and ills that he denounced in an unwavering manner: "We may point to some of the large areas of neglect which have today assumed monstrous proportions: the entire educational system was left untouched and unreformed, and failed to reach the majority of the population; no worthwhile political and ideological mass struggle was waged against communalism as an ideology; the tardy and inadequate implementation of land reforms left a legacy of economic inequality, social oppression and political violence in rural India; the inadequate steps taken to curb corruption in its initial stages, led later to its assuming shocking dimensions and pervading almost every area of life, administration and politics (Chandra *et. al.*, 2000)."

References

Mukherjee, Hirendranath (1964), *The Gentle Colossus: A Study of Jawaharlal Nehru,* Manisha Granthalaya, Kolkata.

Subramaniam, C. (1978), 'Indian Experience in Economic Development', *Yojana* 16, June.

"Terms of Trade Thesis" popularized by Sir Hans Singer and Raul Prebisch calling for "Import substitution Policy", "Dependency Theory" of neo-Marxist authors, etc., of 1940s, 1950s and 1960s had influenced Indian policy-making after getting political independence.

Chakravarty, Sukhamoy (1987), *Development Planning: The Indian Experience;* OUP.

Chandra, Bipan, Mridula and Aditya Mukherjee (2000): *India after Independence: 1947-2000,* Penguin Books.

Sengupta, Arjun (2002), *"The Planning Regime since 1951"* in N.N. Vohra and Sabyasachi Bhattacharya (eds.), *Looking Back in the Twentieth Century,* National Book Trust, India in Association with India International Centre.

Frankel, Francine R. (2005), *India's Political Economy: 1947-2004;* OUP.

Singh, Tarlok (1974), *India's Development Experience,* Macmillan, India.

Tomlinson, B.R. (1998), *The Economy of Modern India, 1860-1970;* Cambridge University Press.

Chattopadhyay, Raghabendra 'Indian Business and Economic Planning: 1930-56' in D. Tripathi (eds.) *Business and Politics in India.*

Rao, V.K.R.V. (1971), In his book *"The Nehru Legacy",* Popular Prakashan, Bombay, Rao stated: "In fact, of the total investment undertaken during the first three five year plans ...agriculture, including irrigation, accounted for Rs. 3,446 crore, or 22.7 per cent, while economic infrastructure, like transport and communications, and power, accounted for Rs. 5,737 crore or 37.7 per cent and social services for Rs. 2,760 crore or 18.1 per cent. Industry accounted for only Rs. 2,651 crore or 17.2 per cent of investment in the public sector during the 15 years covered by the three Plans." However, Raj Krishna articulated that agriculture had not been neglected during Nehru's regime. For the debate between the importance/ neglect of agriculture and industry, see Raj Krishna's "Assessing India's Economic Development ", *Mainstream,* October 25, 1982; and Pulapre Balakrishnan's The Recovery of India: Economic Growth in the Nehru Era; *Economic and Political Weekly,* Nov. 10-16/17-23, 2007.

As far as the design of the Second Plan was concerned, Mahalanobis version came to be known as 'Plan frame', while Economic Divisions of the Planning Commission and Finance Ministry's outline of the Second Plan came to be known as "Tentative Framework for the Second Five Year Plan."

Nehru, J.L. (1958), *Toward Freedom,* Boston: Beacon Press.

Galbraith, J.K. (1992), "Trickle-down theory—the less than elegant metaphor that if one feeds the horse enough oats, some will pass through to the road for the sparrows." *The Culture of Contentment.*

Kothari, Rajani (2002), *The Nehruvian Political System and Its Aftermath* in N.N. Vohra and Sabyasachi Bhattacharya (eds.) *Looking Back in the Twentieth Century,* National Book Trust, India, in Association with India International Centre.

Balkrishnan, Pulapre (2007), The Recovery of India: Economic Growth in the Nehru Era, *EPW,* Nov. 10-16/17-23.

7

The Economic Ideas of Pandit Jawaharlal Nehru and their Relevance in the Changing Scenario

Swami Prakash Srivastava

Nehru had the privilege to develop and pursue his thought not only on socio-political issues but also on a host of economic topics, which are relevant not only to the contemporary Indian economic situation but to the situation in most of the developing countries of the world. Nehru was not an economic theoretician but an ideologist and a great politician. As such he did not hesitate to compromise with the orthodox leadership of the nationalist movement in the expression of his socialist ideas. Still it cannot be denied that because of Nehru's influence socialism has become a vital issue in Indian politics and economics. It may not be possible to forecast if socialism of Nehru's perception will be the long-term destiny of the Indian people but there can be no doubt that it shall remain the dominant issue in times to come. His economic ideas bear an unmistakable mark of a synthesis of Gandhi and Marx besides other democratic socialists of the nineteenth Century. Nehru wanted to work for certain objectives like self-sufficiency in food, clothing, housing, education, sanitation, etc. He was very much in favour of modern means of transport and many other developments.

I. INTRODUCTION

The plan of the paper is as follows. The paper has been divided into ten sections. The first section gives a brief introduction. The second section deals with the Nehru's Economic ideas of Planning. The third section reveals the facts on Nehru's views on Cottage and Small Scale Industry. The fourth section depicts the Co-existence of Gandhi and Nehru. The fifth section focuses on Nehru-Mahalanobis model. The sixth section gives The Peculiar Growth Model. The seventh section outlines Nehru's views on Industrialization. The eighth section focuses on Nehru's views on capitalism. The ninth section deals with the Nehru's views on socialism. In section tenth, we shall present the broad conclusions of this study.

Nehru had the privilege to develop and pursue his thought not only on socio-political issues but also on a host of economic topics, which are relevant not only to the contemporary Indian economic situation but to the situation in most of the developing countries of the world. Nehru was not an economic theoretician but an ideologist and a great politician. As such he did not hesitate to compromise with the orthodox leadership of the nationalist movement in the expression of his socialist ideas. Still it cannot be denied that because of Nehru's influence socialism has become a vital issue in Indian politics and economics. It may not be possible to forecast if socialism of Nehru's perception will be the long term destiny of the Indian people but there can be no doubt that it shall remain the dominant issue in times to come. His economic ideas bear an unmistakable mark of a synthesis of Gandhi and Marx besides other democratic socialists of the nineteenth Century. Nehru wanted to work for certain objectives like self-sufficiency in food, clothing, housing, education, sanitation, etc. He was very much in favour of modern means of transport and many other developments.

This paper is prompted by two developments. In the public sphere there is today an unusual degree of interest in India's recent past, especially the Nehru Era. Much of this is negative in its judgment. Perhaps buoyed by the extraordinary current rates of growth of the Indian economy, there is a certain despondency induced by a sense of an allegedly "wasted past" [Das, 2000; Srinivasan, 2004]. Indeed, some have gone on to lay the blame squarely on Jawaharlal Nehru and the policies adopted under his leadership. These are serious allegations and need to be addressed.

II. NEHRU'S ECONOMIC IDEAS OF PLANNING

Before independence whatever development took place in India it was only to serve the interests and needs of the British economy. Immediately after independence the country bore the scars of the Second World War and the partition of the country, shortage of food and manufactured articles, transport dislocation, relief and rehabilitation problems, and severe inflation. The achievement of economic freedom was the necessary follow-up of political freedom. Under the given circumstances, Nehru visualized rapid economic growth through the instruments of economic planning, for which he had drawn inspiration from the achievements of Soviet Russia. Nehru's faith in economic planning speaks of the impact of Marxism and socialism on his economic ideas. Even before independence Nehru advocated planned economic development of India.

Nehru can rightly be called the father of the concept of economic planning in the Indian perspective. Nehru wanted to make India industrialized through economic planning. The original idea behind planning had been to further industrialization, without which the problem of poverty, unemployment, national defence and economic regeneration could not be solved. A national industrialization plan was therefore necessary to cover heavy key industries, medium scale industries and cottage industries. At the same time planning could not ignore agriculture. The scope of planning thus become wider, as the social services were also brought within its net. Nehru believed in state planning. He also perceived how national independence depended upon a strong base of industry and power resources and how a free India had to join the race of technological development for its survival as an economically independent nations.

Nehru was convinced that, without an activist kind of planned industrial development, with a socialistic regulatory control mechanism, the objectives he had in view, would be frustrated. It was not enough, as in the last century, to plead only for state assistance and initiative in order to build a private enterprise economy dominated by foreign economic enterprise. The nineteenth century thinkers were caught in this dilemma, the nature of which they correctly understood. In the world of Gandhi and Nehru, this lesson of the past had already been carefully absorbed, and the necessity for some kind of regulatory mechanism to obviate the difficulties created by uncontrolled private enterprise, whether foreign or domestic was considered almost axiomatic.

III. NEHRU'S VIEWS ON COTTAGE AND SMALL SCALE INDUSTRIES

In spite of the fact that Nehru believed in large scale industrialization, he did not fail to see the important role which the cottage and village industries could play in India. During the national movement Gandhi encouraged Swadeshi, and Khadi become a symbol of India's socio-economic and political revolution. Nehru realized that "for keeping balance in the economy, self-sufficiency was to be promoted and for that as well as for the provision of work and employment, village and cottage industries are of paramount importance."

Nehru was not opposed to the development of agriculture or cottage and small scale industries; rather he laid great stress on the development of agriculture and small scale industries in the true Gandhian spirit. He simply contended that the development of other sectors of the Indian economy are directly correlated to the development of modern heavy industries and application of modern science and technology. He was also not unaware of the constraints faced by underdeveloped countries before they cross the critical threshold of self-sustaining growth. In the initial stages, i.e., the teething period, there was no escape from the difficulties of foreign exchange and 'tied' foreign aid. The internal social and political forces could tend to sustain sharp inequalities of income distribution, socio-economic stagnation and regional imbalances. However, Nehru believed that in the long-run these difficulties would resolve themselves.

Nehru did not think that small scale industries could be rival to large scale industries for these were indispensable for country's progress, but village industries could certainly help accelerate production and provide employment to the people. Government was to give all the required help to cottage industries but they were not to depend solely on state help. If these industries do not have inherent strength and vitality of their own, they cannot survive for long. Moreover, as democracy should have decentralization at certain levels Nehru believed in 'more village industries in cottage industries to balance the heavy ones'. The small scale sector mainly flourished in urban areas. The rural and urban India were to be brought together and a bridge could be provided by village industries . Therefore, in a mixed economy, these small scale, village and cottage industries were to have a real important role to play in contributing to the welfare of the common masses. What Nehru deemed essential for the successful realization of a democratic socialist society in India was "to activize and dynamize the base of the Indian social structure.... Which means millions and millions of villagers, millions of workers and small earners, unemployed people and people on land."

IV. CO-EXISTENCE OF GANDHI AND NEHRU

Many phrases used by Gandhi confused Nehru, but his theory of 'co-existence' provided a backbone to the Indian people and Nehru accepted that wholly. His stress through "character and pity", was disliked by Nehru although he had accepted the policy of 'sacrifice' for the millions. Nehru's scientific temper was disliked by Gandhi and Sardar Patel. Jawaharlal disliked Gandhi's ideas of favouring a system which was decaying, so he stressed on "industrialization" for modernization, which was inevitable. But Gandhi stressed that "true socialism lies in the development of village industries. We do not want to reproduce in our country the chaotic conditions prevalent in the western countries consequent on mass production." Weighing the situation in India, Jawaharlal commented that "events are undoubtedly the most powerful education," which have to be understood properly. For Gandhi even 'Taj Mahal' was an embodiment of "forced labour", although his dependence on Gandhi was "almost filial", he disagreed with him on many strategies.

V. NEHRU-MAHALANOBIS STRATEGY

Though narrowly identified as the model for the Second Five Year Plan, nothing is more iconic of the economics of the Nehru era and representative of the means adopted to pursue its goals than the "Mahalanobis model." The model was intended to provide the analytical foundation for the project of raising the level of income via industrialization already deliberated upon in the National Planning Commission of the Congress, which was chaired by Nehru at the request of Subhash Chandra Bose in his capacity as the short-lived Party President. For this reason, it is often referred to as the Nehru-Mahalanobis strategy. This was a model to serve the end of rapidly raising the level of income through accelerating growth, as raising the level of income was considered the means to eliminating poverty.

VI. THE PECULIAR GROWTH MODEL

Keynesian approach appealed to Jawaharlal for its applicability to practical problems and policy matters. This had dual implications: (i) He believed that economic activity was to be stimulated and regulated by "non-market agencies", particularly the State; and (ii) he held that Keynesian approach implied the understanding of the structure and functional relationship of the Indian Economy. The first was "overtly recognized", and the second was "implicitly accepted". With its imperfections, Keynesian approach, in a way suited the "underdeveloped economies." Two alternatives were presented in 1969 that either the Indian economy should be "converted" into a socialist system by a radical alteration of its structure, especially the "ownership of resources" or "accept the system to work through its own growth mechanism." Jawaharlal had already viewed these and had opted for the latter for India's peculiarities and synthetic nature.

Another view highlights remarkable truth in favour of Jawaharlal's policy that "there existed a functional justification for inequality of incomes if it raised production for all and not consumption for a few." He is of the view that "the road to eventual equalities may inevitably be through initial inequalities" and he shared the same experience that "most of the population had remained virtually untouched by the forces of economic change since economic development had become warped in favour of a privileged minority", and it revealed that "a rising growth rate is no guarantee against worsening poverty", and production and distribution policies must be coordinated. This analysis identified "seven sins of development planners": "preoccupation with econometric models at the cost of economic policy formulation, excessive economic controls, investment illusion implying the concern with the level of investment overriding productivity, focus on the immediate problems and short-run solutions involving relative neglect of longer-run considerations of structural changes; divorce between formulation of plans and implementation; neglect of human resources; and fascination for high growth of GNP at the cost of equity and social justice."

VII. NEHRU'S VIEWS ON INDUSTRIALIZATION

Nehru was fully conscious of the possible consequences of his own line of thought and action in the matter of heavy industrialization. It was argued that heavy investment in basic industries might be counter-productive to the creation of demand for consumer goods on the one hand and absorption of large quantity of unemployed labour force caused by the rapid population growth, at least in the short-run, on the other. Naturally, any attempt in the direction of balanced industrial development calls for a well-organised effort for adoption of labour-intensive production techniques so as to generate employment opportunities on the one hand, and ensure adequate supply of much needed consumer goods on the other so as to prevent consequent inflationary pressures, which might be associated with the process of economic development based on heavy industries. As a safeguard against these problems, Nehru did not lay emphasis on the development of employment-oriented small scale sector besides the large scale industries in the private as well as public sector. This fact is very well evident in the Industrial Policy Resolution initiated by Nehru in 1948 and gave it a socialistic bias in 1956. Nehru wanted to work for certain objectives like self-sufficiency in food, clothing, housing, education, sanitation, etc. He was very much in favour of modern means of transport and many other developments.

Nehru's view on heavy industries has been a centre of controversy, especially in the post-independence period. Nehru believed that a strong industrial base is vital for the rapid economic growth of the Indian economy. The British rulers did not bother to build a sound and strong industrial base for India and whatever industrial development took place in the pre-independence period was solely motivated by the imperialist designs of the colonial rulers. Obviously, independent India had to choose one of the two possible alternative, i.e., either the main thrust was to be given to the development of consumer goods industries to meet the basic needs of the poverty-stricken masses or lay a sound foundation for long-term economic growth through the development of heavy industries like steel, cement, heavy machine tools, heavy electrical, heavy chemicals and industries connected with the development of the infrastructure like power generation, transport, communication and irrigation, etc. Nehru preferred later on the basis of his firm belief that India possessed vast natural resources and substantial manpower potential.

He believed that India's economic development could

be achieved only through modern industrialization, which alone could ensure the self-sustaining growth and real economic independence—other economic objectives like poverty, employment and better living standards can be achieved as a consequence of such a development strategy, which required huge capital investment, imported technology, and low profitability ratio in the initial stages of industrialization. Being highly capital-intensive it did not ensure adequate employment potentials in the labour-intensive and agriculture-based economy of India. Under the given circumstances the Gandhian approach of self-sufficient rural economy with employment-oriented development of Khadi and Village Industries appeared to be a better and more realistic strategy.

VIII. NEHRU'S VIEWS ON CAPITALISM

Tracing the growth of imperialism to the rise of capitalism in the West, Nehru observed, "Capitalism has led to imperialism and to the conflicts of imperialist powers in search for colonial areas for exploitation, for areas of raw produce and for markets for manufactured goods." In this connection he further states, "The whole basis of capitalism is cut throat competition and exploitation, and imperialism is an advanced stage of this." About the capitalist society Nehru said, "The rich people today are those who have plenty of surplus, the poor have none at all. It is not so much because one person works more than another, now-a-days a person who does not work at all gets the surplus, while the hard worker often gets no part of it." Nehru believed that the crisis of capitalism, essentially lies in the ill distribution of world's wealth, to its concentration in a few hands. He states, "Capitalism have solved the problem of production, helplessly faces the allied problem of distribution and is unable to solve it. It is not in the nature of the capitalist system to deal satisfactorily with distribution and production alone makes the world to heavy and unbalanced."

As regards the industrial development under capitalism and its consequent impact on the socio-economic order Nehru remarked, "Capitalistic industry was dynamic by its very nature, it grew bigger and bigger and its hunger was never satisfied. Its distinguishing mark was acquisitiveness; it was always out to acquire and hold, and then acquire again. Individuals tried to do so, and so did nations." Further elucidating his argument he states, "Capitalism stimulated acquisitiveness and these deeper instincts which we want to get rid of now. It did much good also in its earlier stages and by rising production greatly increased the standard of living. In other ways too it served a useful purpose and it was certainly an improvement on the stage that proceeded it. But it seems to have outlived its utility and today it not only bars all progress in a socialist direction but encourages many undesirable habits and instincts in us. I do not see how we can move along socialist lines in a society which is based on acquisitiveness and in which the profit motive is dominant urge." These comments made in 1936 hold good even today when India stands committed to socialism within the framework of an economic order largely based on capitalism.

IX. NEHRU'S VIEWS ON SOCIALISM

Nehru had his disagreement with those Indian socialists of the contemporary era who borrowed the socialist ideas from Marx and Lenin but did not realize its implications in the context of the Indian situation. In his *'Autobiography'* (1936) he writes: "I was by no means a pioneer in the socialist field in India. Indeed I was rather backward and I had only advanced painfully, step by step, where many others had gone ahead blazing trail. The workers' trade union movement was ideologically definitely socialist, and so were the majority of the youth leagues. A vague confused socialism was already part of the atmosphere of India when I returned from Europe in 1927, and even earlier than that there were many individual socialists. Mostly they thought along utopian lines, but Marxian theory was influencing them increasingly, and a few considered themselves as hundred per cent Marxist. This tendency was strength ended in India, as in Europe and America, by developments in the Soviet Union and particularly the Five Year Plan."

In the Indian context Nehru was convinced that vast

changes that socialism envisages cannot be brought about by the sudden passing of a few laws. Basic law and power are necessary to give direction of advance to lay the foundation of the structure in which the edifice of a socialist society can be built through the active involvement of the people whose emancipation it seeks to bring about. In his presidential address to the Indian National Congress (1936) Nehru remarked, "I am convinced that the only key to the solution of the world's problems and of India's problems lies in socialism. I see no way of ending the poverty, the vast unemployment, the degradation, and the subjugation of the Indian people except through socialism. That involve vast and revolutionary changes in our political and social structure, the ending of vested interest in land and industry, as well as the feudal and autocratic Indian state system that means the ending of private property, except in restricted sense, and replacement of the present profit system by a higher ideal of co-operative services."

Nehru had a firm conviction that socialist objectives need not necessarily be achieved through violent revolution and at the cost of individual freedom and liberty. He saw great merit in individual liberty and freedom and to some extent in the institution of private property.

X. CONCLUSION

Any evaluation of the success or failure of Jawaharlal's Economic Thought has to be made with an eye both on the 'philosophy' permeating the Indian planning process as well as "the specific targets it set for itself." Jawaharlal Nehru never suffered from any status fobia or 'fascination for grandiose', even notions like 'death knell of Khadi' or 'no logic in the apparatus of planning' and 'imitative model' were many unpleasant criticism, which generally falsified his pure economic policy. The 'strategy' incorporated in the plans was sound and well spelt out, and he conceived of a Balanced Economic Development in the country. He tried "to solve each problem as it arose", and his approach was "inclusive."

Finally, it may be pointed out that Nehru's systematic approach was relevant in the context of the terrific strains of the legacies of feudalism, autocracy, rampant communalism, social disorganization, compulsions of casteism and religious heterogeneity. The view expressed by some of his pronounced critics that Nehru's synthetic approach in the form of vacillating decision and his efforts to placate the various sections of the society, i.e., the capitalist as well as the working class or the neo-feudalists and the poor rural masses, was an attempt to keep himself in power is not a fair assessment of his personality. His economic ideas bear an unmistakable. mark of a synthesis of Gandhi and Marx besides other democratic socialists of the nineteenth century.

Jawaharlal Nehru stood for a "mixed economy" which was 'Socialistic' to a great extent, but he was not a Marxist; his socialistic ideals implied "planned production and its equitable distribution", which was to be inculcated "legitimately and peacefully." His action programme included land reforms, equitable distribution of income, development of cottage industries and amiable relations between capital and labour. The masses depended on agriculture for their living and 'emphasis' was shifting to "proletariat". The programme was as socialistic and progressive as it could be under the circumstances which aimed at ameliorating the lot of downtrodden masses. Jawaharlal's economic policy became progressive and it "concerned Socialism." In a wider sense of the term he aroused an "Asian Sentiment" and conscience of planning for shaping India's destiny. Any evaluation of the success or failure of Jawaharlal's Economic Thought has to be made with an eye both on the 'philosophy' permeating the Indian planning process as well as "the specific targets it set for itself."

Jawaharlal's economic ideas took a definite pattern in the wake of independence. In a true democratic fashion he designed his policy. He was clear about his basic objectives and means to achieve them. He made his position clear about the pattern of ownership and succeeded in unifying the conflicting interest groups. In achieving his objective, he accorded primary position to planning. Indeed to him, the role of planning in ushering in a socialist pattern was crucial. While emphasizing the need to develop heavy industries, he was fully conscious of the need for all-round development—

especially in the sphere of agriculture and rural industries and added special emphasis on land reforms. Production, according to him, was essential both in agriculture and industry to fight poverty and raise standard of living. He aimed to modernize the tradition-bound society with the help of science and technology and he pinned much hope on the technique of planning to entail happiness to his people. The process of policy formulation, the choice of middle path and the creation of social institutions, evealed his true democratic character and deep love for his people. His foreign policy was a counterpart of his economic policy and aimed to achieve a trusteeship of nations in the process of country's development. He became the true Trustee of the nation.

A 'viewer' accuses the "foundation of "Nehru's policies" for the present day "sufferings." It is easy to give precept than example. The change in the Janata Government policies and the strong government during the Emergency could not achieve what Jawaharlal achieved for India. Some people only like to criticize for their pleasures. Why don't they direct even some sections of the society according to their wishes to see the benefits of their ideals or even their own families to stand the judgment? Whatever the shortcomings of the public sector, it has survived the onslaughts of the critics and it is commendable on the part of the private sector that they responded promptly to the stimulus provided by the public sector. India's development experience during 1951 to 1964 can be summed up in the words of an eminent administrator who was closely associated with the work of the Planning Commission from the beginning as a secretary. The Nehru era witnessed a "(i) sustained economic growth, (ii) expansion of economic capacity, (iii) utilization of manpower and provision of work opportunities, (iv) economic stability, (v) balanced social development, and (vi) progress towards a more unified and integrated economy."

He dedicated himself to create a "just state by just means" and "a secular state in a religious country" even being surrounded by a Saturn's Ring of 'holistic politicians." The basic principles of his philosophy "have sunk (deep) into the minds of people. Yet "raucous voices" cannot be neglected which need sensitive attention to "his general direction and broad strategy", which shall remain valid in the context of economic problems of today.

REFERENCES

Dantawala, M.L. (1969), *The Economic Ideology of Nehru*, Popular Prakashan, Bombay, p. 74.

Desai, SSM (1981), *Development of Indian Economic Thought*, p. 229.

Ganguli, B.N. (1978), *Indian Economic Thought, 19th Century Persepectives*, Tata McGraw Hill Publishing Co. Ltd, First Reprint, pp. 253-54.

Gopal, S. (1975, 1979, 1984), *Jawaharlal Nehru: A Biography in 3 Volumes*, Oxford University Press, Delhi.

Kaushik, P.D. (1964), *Congress Ideology and Programme*, Allied Publishers Pvt. Ltd., Bombay, p. 325.

Nehru, J.L. (1965), *Glimpses of World History*, Lindsey Doummond Limited; First published in India in two Vols., Gulford Place, London W.L.I, pp. 562-63.

Nehru, J.L. (1936), Presidential Address, Indian National Congress, Lucknow, edited by Jagat S. Bright, Lahore, The Indian Printing Works, 1945, p. 37.

Singhania, Hari Shankar (1980), *Today and Tomorrow*, Nehru House, New Delhi, p. 38.

Soviet Russia-Jawaharlal Nehru (1965), p. 5.

Surinder, P.S. Pruthi (1967), Management of Plans, Ahmedabad Management Association, Implementation of National Plans, p. 4.

8

Nehru's Economic Policy and Current Global Crisis

Raghubansh Singh

Nehru translated the mixed economy philosophy into action and as a result public sector assumed the 'commanding heights' of the economy supported by private industrial magnates of the country to achieve the goal of 'growth with justice'. Making a detailed discussion on the Nehruvian concept of mixed economy, the paper intends to explain how the economic policies, that is, Nehruvian socialism, went into oblivion into the hands of the members of the same Congress Party in 1991. Against the backdrop of current global crisis, policy-makers are advised to go to the days of 'the government-financed infrastructure model' adopted during the Nehru era.

I. NEHRU'S MIXED ECONOMY

In our recent history, one mass leader who understood the vital relationship between republican aspirations and the economic independence was Jawaharlal Nehru. The basic contribution of Nehru consisted in presenting a framework of an economic foundation that endows people a meaning to freedom. He observed that India after independence was confronted with two basic challenges. The first challenge lay in utilizing political independence as a means of economic independence of the country and social regeneration of the Indian people. To this was added the equally important task of creating a social system within which justice would be achieved for the vast masses.

Nehru indicated that the classical path of unbridled capitalism was not likely to achieve either the task of national development or of social emancipation. This was because of the massive character of the problem of arrested development and incapacity of capitalism to cope with it within a few decades and also because of inequity being inherent in the very operation of the capitalist system. Nehru was the first outstanding national leader who formulated in a scientific manner the thesis that the continuation of national revolution in India did not lead to the perception of capitalist development but to the socialist perception. Nehru observed, "In Europe, an economic revolution preceded a real political revolution and so when the latter came, certain resources have been built up by economic change. In Asia, political revolution came first, followed immediately by demand for social betterment."

Nehru concluded from this premise that the path of economic revolution must confirm to the demands of political revolution. The economic revolution must become an instrument of realizing equity for the vast masses and not as means of widening the already existing inequity. Thus arose the need for working out such institutional forces as helped to harmonise the principles of growth with principles of equity.

In the post-independence era, the policy which Nehru nurtured sought to create the structure of his future economic policy on the basis of a so-called 'middle path', so as to maintain some continuity with the past. He spoke in the words of Karl Mannheim in pointing out that "it was not easy or desirable to upset old ways of living too suddenly, change is essential but continuity is also necessary. The future has to be built on the foundation laid in the past and the present."

The so-called middle path of which the mixed economy was the strategic functional expression was regarded by him to pave ways for a higher and superior forms of social institutions. The future Indian society must not be dominated by the urge for private profit and individual greed. There ought to be a fair distribution of political and economic power. Nehru pronounced the concept of a mixed economy which would be based on a regulated private sector in industry and trade. Private sector should reconcile the element of self-interest with the element of social interest and in certain cases, the survival of private enterprise may be made conditional to its serving the community at large. The concept of mixed economy was expected to accelerate growth through multi-class mobilization and to promote equity through protection of weaker sections of the society.

In a mixed economy, the government has a positive role to play in the field of economic activity. Nehru observed, "If you want to achieve something we cannot live it to chance. In any country which has to cover a great deal of growth quickly, there is no possible way except planning." Nehru did not want society to be subjected to the chaos of uncontrolled economic forces. He said, "There are many other forces at play which come in the way of balanced growth and we are forced more or less to plan our economic development." By opting for a planned economy Nehru wanted to obviate the anarchy and anomalies of an uncontrolled market. The 'invisible hand' praised by Adam Smith did not always allocate resources and commodities in a manner conducive to the welfare of the majority. The market had a tendency to bring resources to those who already had them in plenty. It would thus increase the wealth of the affluent without diminishing the miseries of the masses. In the planned economy, the state is to direct its policy to secure a better distribution of ownership and control of the material resources of its community and to prevent concentration of wealth in the hands of a few and the exploitation of labour. Nehru conceived that it would be impossible for the state to attain the ideals of the Indian Constitution that the state would serve to promote the welfare of the people by securing and protecting a social order in which justice, social, economic and political shall inforce all the institutions of nation's life, unless the state itself enters the field of production and distribution. This explains the rationale behind the deliberate policy of expansion of the public sector to promote rapid industrialization and self-reliance. To protect the weaker section, the state is also expected to control the distribution of essential commodities.

A pragmatic planning leading to the process of growth with social justice and the basic industries in the state sector was the decided objective of Nehru's economic policy. The Industrial Policy approved by Nehru opted for a mixed economy in which both the public and private sector would exist as a part of a planned economy but in which the public sector would have control over the commanding height of the economy, undoubtedly Nehru's efforts bore a positive fruit in acquiring primacy of public sector over the private enterprise. In the three successive five year plans, the ratio of the total investment in pubic sector to that in the private sector had increased at a significant rate. This ratio which was 46:54 in the First Plan rose to 55:45 and 61:39 in the Second and Third Plans respectively.

Nehru's thesis of providing public sector a dominant role in the nation's economic growth was supported by the contemporary Indian business magnets. In fact, the major Indian capitalist groups led by Tata and Birla formulated a plan of economic development, the Bombay plan, and urged the state that the economic reconstruction of the country be undertaken by the creation of a large public sector. This was so because the private sector itself does not have the means to undertake building of the costly non-profitable but vital infrastructures for economic development on capitalist lines. In fact, late G.D. Birla reassured his fellow capitalists that public sector was not trading on the toes of the private sector. Rather, the public sector was going to act as a generator of the private enterprise.

The advance attained during the Nehru era in the heavy industry, chemicals, power and transport sectors has provided India with the broad foundation of modern economy. The country has today, thanks to Nehru's policy, the basic facilities required for almost all branches of modern manufacture, a large community of scientists, engineers and technocrats. Between 1951 and 1965, the index of industrial production registered an average growth rate of 7 per cent per annum. The index (1950=100) rose from 74 in 1951 to 182 in 1966. The public sector was also conceived as an instrument and agent for resource mobilization. This is evident from the following excerpt from a speech by Nehru on the occasion of the inauguration of the second Hindustan Machine Tools factory in Bangalore in 1961: "There is certain uniqueness about this function and the factory. The uniqueness lies in the fact that this factory has been made out of the profit or surplus of the older Hindustan Machine Tools Factory." It is a little known fact that during Nehru era the savings of the public enterprise grew faster than those of the private corporate sector.

Critics have propagated the view that the very economic policy pursued by Nehru was flawed and hence it was destined to fail. But in answer to such criticism, it must be noted that when we scrutinise the trajectory of growth in the twentieth century we find that the dominant break occurs around 1950, the year planning was launched for industrialization of the country. The development strategy took India in the position of the tenth most industrialized country of the world. The Nehru's era was an irreversible break with a declining economy and achieved a growth rate faster even the then contemporary China. Not only the Nehru era gave birth to a genuine republic but nourished it with a huge economic expansion.

II. THE NEW ECONOMIC POLICY

However, the direction of economic policy has changed significantly in the past few decades especially from launching of New Economic Policy and the Seventh Five Year Plan. The mood of NEP was in the direction of a large scale integration of the Indian economy with the international capitalist system. In determent of Nehru's objective of developing the public sector, NEP proposed to reduce outlays in public sector for its alleged inefficiency. With the New Economy Policy gaining currency there appeared to have been a sharp deviation from the original position of Nehru's thrust on public sector to a generalized dilution of basic tenets of socialist pattern relegating the public enterprise system into background while giving primacy to private enterprise and competitive market forces.

Nehru's economic policy is being gradually discarded and abondoned. It is being widely publicised that the government is an incapable owner, controller and manager of the economy. Nehru's economic legacy is now being considered as an impediment to country's progress and growth. It is being widely propagated all over the economic sphere that future must emphasize individual initiative, private enterprise and must de-emphasize the government's role in economic affairs.

Accordingly, a new development path known as Liberalization and Globalization has been adopted in India since 1991 following an unprecedented forex crisis. Prior to 1991, India was pursuing an inward-looking policy measures but the post-reform phase has been a turnaround. There has been a shift in policy stance from inward looking to outward oriented, i.e. opening up of almost all sectors for the demoestic and foreign private sectors. Import and multilateral commerce have now been accepted by almost every one in India. It is being advocated that government monopolizing from making bread to running airlines denies scope to individual talent and initiative, saddles the public exchequer with huge public enterprise and vests the bureaucracy with inordinate power.

III. CURRENT GLOBAL CRISIS

But it must be recognized that it is a fact of history that the repudiation of any economic policy at a given time does not mean its death or irrelevance. The recent global financial crisis has proved beyond doubt that even when we remove governmental control on economy and use market machanism for growth, some sort of state intervention is considered indispensable to sustain the economic growth.

It has been the philosophy of the United States of America and its cohorts of free market economists, that the best government is the least governments and markets are supposed to be self-correcting and their own best guardians. But following the worst financial crisis in the U.S.A.'s history after 1930, this ideology of free markets is now out of window. Capitalism is now in reverse gear meaning more governmental control over the economy. In the capitalist countries, such as the USA., Iceland, etc., the stage is now set for partial government ownership of banks.

The threat of a systematic meltdown exposes the weaknesses of the unbriddled market system. And people are now beginning to realize in Britain's Prime Minister, Gordon Brown's words that "man does not live by market alone." The British premier falling in with his assertion that in extra-ordinary times with financial market ceasing to work "the government cannot just leave people to be buffeted about. The government's response is classic—Keynes throwing money at it and in such programmes as building capital infrastructure, housing and energy." What is central to Brown's recipe is the warning that man being a predatory animal, the private sector needs firm but understanding guidance and control if it is to benefit all and not just a few operatores.

Similarly, Nicolas Sarkozy, the current French President was forced to comment that the idea that "markets are always right was a mad idea-that America's *laissez faire* ideology was as simplistic as it was dangerous." It would be a great ironies of history if the authoritarian Chinese regime which highly controls the exchange rate and does not allow free capital movement, rescue the U.S. economy.

India is also facing danger since we too trade with the West, seek Western investment and hold our reserves in dollars. Today in India the scenario is marked with falling growth rate, falling rupee, falling corporate margins and shelving of investment plans. It must be recognized that India cannot remain unaffected when the global economy and financial system are in deep trouble. Our stock market and the exchange rate of rupee are under pressure due to capital outflow of foreign institutional investors. It is indeed unfortunate that India's rapid growth is now being disrupted due to the financial crisis in the U.S., Europe and Japan.

Policy-makers in India have been busy in assuring the country that the fundamentals of the Indian economy are strong. It is being asserted that India's banking system is sound and well capitalized. It is not exposed to the types of assets which have given rise to the current crisis. But our policy-makers particularly the reformers in our government would do well to recognize the reasons our banks were not hit was not because they are better regulated, managed and capitalized but because they are government-owned and therefore confidence was never an issue. The assurance does not go far as gowth rates in various sectors of the economy are declining. The Planning Commision, the RBI and even the Prime Minister have predicted a slowdown in India's growth.

Thus to avoid slowdown, the Reserve Bank of India has taken important steps with the twin objectives of increasing liquidity in the system and reversing the outflow of funds on account of selling by the Foreign Institutional Investors. For the former, the RBI cut the cash reserve ratio from 9 per cent to 5.5 per cent. It has also reduced the repo rate to 7.5 per cent. To achieve the latter objective the RBI has given more freedom to FIIs, raised the limit for investment in bonds, has increased interest rate on foreign deposits.

Increased liquidity in the system coupled with interest rate cuts may save financial institutions and banks but they are bound to lead to increased inflationary pressures. Thus policy-makers are in a dilemma. They want to stablize the price of the rupee, they want FIIs to come back and invest in stock, they want banks and financial institutions to start lending to increase investment and simultaneously they want to control inflation. The policy-makers should realize that it would be difficult to achieve all those objectives with these instruments.

Thus in addition to the well thought out monetary and foreign exchange policies, we need to do more to restore confidence so that the businesses feel emboldened to scale up operations with reviving demand and overtime begin to re-look at shelved investment plan. We could think of a return to the predominently government-financed infrastructure model that we have adopted during the Nehru era. It is true, that given the issues of project implementation, service quality and maintenance standard, this may not appeal to many. But sustaining growth demands that these investment be made and public investment even with the drawbacks is better than no investment at all. In such situation, the Prime Minister Manmohan Singh's suggestion that the government should go in for the radical option of sharply raising the spending on infrastructure has a considerable merit. Such focussed pump priming rather than generalized pay-outs involving substanitial leakages of money is actually required during a downturn. The need today is for infrastructural spending as India has a massive infrastructure gap which tells on growth even in the best of times.

But unfortunately even this option is constrained by the state of public finance. In the past few months the public exchequer is burdened with subsidies, loan waiver and salary hikes. The option for counter-cyclical fiscal measures may be limited, but there is scope for releasing investment already planned and budgeted in the country. Apart from pumping demand in the economy, the infrasctructure deficiency which reduces the competitiveness of the Indian economy in the global environment and adds to transaction costs and delays, would get addressed.

The Commission on Infrastructure had envisaged expenses of approximately rupees twenty lakh crore over the Eleventh Plan, 70 per cent of it from government funds and the remaining from private and foreign sources. Such a large fund infusion into the economy would help higher growth. If speedy release of funds for infrastructure could be carried out, it would provide a major boost to the infrastructure sector and to the economy as a whole. Thus the government's role as a financier of infrastructure may be significant in the current economic meltdown.

To conclude, the world over the role of government in economic performance is being reconsidered. We in India too need to do the same but not lose sight of the bitter lessons from the past.

REFERENCES

Gopal, S. (ed.) (1976), *Selected Works of Jawaharlal Nehru*, Vol. VIII, OUP.

Joshi, P.C. (1972), *Nehru Model of Economic Development*.

Singh, Manmohan (H.K.) (1975), *Jawararlal Nehru and Economic Change, EPW Spl. No.*, August.

Narsima Rao, K.T. (1975), *Profile of Jawaharlal Nehru*, Bombay Book Centre.

Nehru, J.L., *An Autobiography*.

Nehru. J.L., *India Today and Tomorrow*.

Rao, V.K.R.V. (1972), *Nehru's Legacy*, Bombay Book Prakashak.

Secular Democracy, Nehru Annual Member, 1976.

Current Global Crisis, Recent Economic Newspapers.

9

The Nehruvian Legacy: Its Impact on the Indian Economy

ASIM K. KARMAKAR

Nineteen forty-seven was a fateful year in the life of Jawaharal Nehru and in the turbulent history of India. For both, it was a year of mixed fortunes. For Nehru, the joy of Independence was tempered by the sadness of Partition. And then there occurred the death of Gandhi, his beloved mentor. The Gandhi era in Indian politics had come to an end. The Nehru era began. To his people, Nehru, at the Indian Independence Day, addressed among other things, "production was the first priority. But equitable distribution was also essential." He also emphasized the necessity for a rapid and radical reform of the archaic land tenure system. India was fortunate to have a broad societal consensus on the nature and path of economic development to be followed after Independence. For example, the Gandhians, the socialists, the capitalists, as well as the communists were more or less agreed on the following agenda: a multi-pronged strategy of economic development based on self-reliance; rapid industrialization based on import-substitution including of capital goods industries; prevention of imperialist or foreign capital domination; land reforms involving abolition of zamindari, tenancy reforms, introduction of cooperatives, especially service cooperatives, for marketing, credit, etc., growth to be attempted along with equity in favour of the oppressed in Indian society, the Scheduled Castes and Tribes; the state to play a central role in promoting economic development through the public sector, and so on. However, Nehru's role in the planning process was crucial, despite the fact that he lacked knowledge of economics and finance. In fact, his influence spans the entire process, from the drafting stage to implementation, because he stood at the centre of the decision-making structure by virtue of his position as the Prime Minister, the Chairman of the Planning Commission (established on 15 March, 1950), and the Chairman of the National Development Council—and because he was Jawaharlal Nehru. He was the link between the planning agencies and the Government. Secondly, he was the pivot around which discussion and decision revolved. Nay, he was the most effective salesman of planning in the country as a whole. Constant reference to the plan in his speeches had helped to make the Indian people plan-conscious, indeed, had inculcated the belief that in planning lay the realization of their hopes for higher standards of living, education for their children, better health services and employment. This might well be his most important contribution, spreading the gospel that planning was the key to welfare. For with general acceptance of this view comes greater co-operation and a spirit of sacrifice, and with that the likelihood of a more rapid pace of development.

This paper in the above context, however, endeavours to show whether his vision of transforming the archaic India into a New India has become a reality? Section I analyzes the presumption that by industrialization of the Indian economy, what Nehru essentially meant. Section II discusses Nehru's idea of self-reliance and the distinctive features of his economic policy. Section III is the concluding observations.

I. NEHRUVIAN MODERNIZATION

By modernization of the Indian economy, Nehru essentially meant 'industrialization.' Nehru believed that a great break-through could be achieved by massive investment in the industrial sector; he saw India close to the famous 'take-off into self-sustained growth'. For Nehru and his associates industrialization was a conduit of technology and scientific sprit, and thus played the same role as industrialization had played in the Western economies. Agriculture was associated with the traditional mode of production, and thus was seen as providing little scope for the application of new technology, which demanded sharp changes in the organization of production. HYV seeds and related methods of cultivation were introduced in India only towards the end of the 1960s. Till then, land reforms and irrigation were seen as sources of growth. Minor irrigation or water management proved to be a major source of growth in agriculture, but these concerns did not receive much attention.

Industrialization was also seen as a method of providing employment to new entrants to the labour force, as well as to the huge masses of underemployed agricultural labourers. At that time, more than 70 per cent of the population depended on agriculture and related activities. Withdrawal of labour from agriculture to other productive occupation was viewed as almost equivalent to economic development. Industrialization, on the other side, would act and trigger the process of virtuous circle of growth, because industry was imbibed with the larger scope for absorbing physical capital, thereby raising productivity at a much faster rate. The disquieting fact is that the supply and the demand side interdependence between industry and agriculture was not fully recognized in the Nehruvian-Mahalanobis model of India's Second Five Year Plan process, in the sense that there was a mismatch of the programmes for industrialization and employment generation with the supply of wage goods, consisting of foodgrain and other agriculture-based products. This resulted in the *ad hoc* and piecemeal agricultural policies, until the period of green revolution came as a rescue for the Indian economy.

II. NEHRU'S IDEA OF SELF-RELIANCE AND HIS DISTINCTIVE FEATURES OF ECONOMIC POLICY

One element of Nehru's approach to development policy relating to self-reliance had an enduring impact on India's economic development. The fact is that, more or less, in some form or other, successive governments in India have subscribed to this principle, though not always fully agreeing with all its implications. For Nehru, self-reliance for the Indian economy meant independence from foreign capital. The structure of the economy should develop in such a manner that no relationship of dependence would emerge so that the political dominance of the aid-giving countries would be avoided and the withdrawal of foreign capital, or a reduction in its flows, would not seriously disrupt the functioning of the economy. Policies for self-reliance should be so designed that there should be a deliberate attempt to reduce these requirements to zero within a short period of time. For Nehru, India's freedom to choose its own path of development; it will not accept any finanancial assistance from international agencies with their conditionalities and advocacy of the private sector and to downgrade public sector and withdrawal of public sector, was non-negotiable. We must remember that even after Nehru, the appeal of this assertion of national independence in development grew such deep roots that the policy of self-reliance remained central to our development planning. Moreover, the case for a policy of self-reliance was also strengthened by the experience of Latin American countries whose receipt of foreign private capital constrained their freedom to pursue independent monetary and fiscal policies. Even during Nehru's time, there was alleged pressure from the United States against the expansion of the steel industry under the public sector.

Although India's economic policy during the Nehruvian era was dominated by inward-looking import-substitution strategies, it should be noted that the concept of self-reliance did not mean autarky. What it meant rather, minimizing the current account deficits of the balance of payments. But this, however, did not mean that it was necessary to minimize either exports or imports. The bias toward import substitution in India's economic policy was derived from an empirical presumption that India's exports could not be raised significantly in the near future or even in the medium-term. In the 1950s and the 1960s, export pessimism was belief of the day in almost all developing countries. India was of no exception. The argument in case of India was that she should expand the supply of industrial products more than the domestic demand. In other words, increasing export was invariably linked to increasing industrialization. As long as exports expanded not at a sufficient rate, a policy of self-reliance implied an overall control over imports. That is why the Nehruvian-Mahalanobis model was essentially a closed economy model; there were no exports. A country's prospects for growth was viewed in this way at that time.

The most distinctive feature of 'Nehruvian' economic policy was central planning and government-directed development. In the early 1950s, good weather, the cultivation of new land, more intensive use of labour, and improved irrigation increased agricultural production, following the First Plan, which ran from 1951 to 1956. The result was that although economic growth during the First Plan was not spectacular, it was adequate. This gave the Planning Commission the heart to move on to industrialization, the real objective, in the Second and Third Plans (1956-1966). These gave a central role to government-owned factories. In 1956, an Industrial Policy Resolution divided Indian industries into three parts. The Second and Third Plans set-up state-owned factories that produced everything from cars to chemicals. By the late 1950s, the Nehruvian economy was well-established, with its tight regulation of industry, import controls, planning, and mixed government and private ownership. The tariff barriers and quantitative restrictions protected domestic manufacturing. Many businessmen found all this to their liking, and the output of heavy industry grew rapidly. Between 1951 and 1966, industrial output more than doubled, and the share of manufacturing in the national product grew from 10 per cent to 16 per cent. India could now produce many goods that had to be imported in 1947; there is thus little doubt that none of this would have happened without government direction and state-owned factories.

But the Second and Third Plans were less successful than anticipated. Agriculture remained stagnant, so total economic growth was modest. All the while, population was growing more rapidly than ever before. We may succinctly describe this period as 'India's dilemma: dynamic industrialization and static agriculture,' though rural India was crucial to the Nehruvian economy. The First Plan attacked the problems of rural poverty by calling for peasants with under five acres of land to merge their plots into cooperative farms. This was not effective, as most peasants had no desire to pool their resources with neighbours whom they knew only as rivals in the competition for scant resources. The Second Plan did little for agriculture beyond urging the states to limit the amount of land one person could own; the excess to be confiscated and given to labourers and smallholders. This was a direct attack on the wealth of the rich peasants who were Congress stalwarts in the countryside. In the early 1970s, 39 per cent of India's land was controlled by 6 per cent of its households. The Third Plan all but gave up on state-driven agricultural development. It advocated private investment in fertilizers and irrigation, but beyond that, it left it for the wealth that would be generated by industrialization to trickle down to the peasantry. Rural India, however, remained poor and was unable to play the part assigned to it in the Nehruvian economy.

Meanwhile, the government was unable to invest the sums called for by the plans. Much of the reasons was the need for imported machinery, which could only be bought with foreign currency. At first, India drew on the Sterling Balances, the debt that Britain had run up during the World War II, which it put toward imports from countries that accepted the British Pound. But the Sterling Balances were spent up in 1956. Indian exports was rapidly declining due to rising prices and poor promotion (for example, in 1955 India supplied 46% of the world's peanut oil exports. The figure shrunk to just 1 per cent only five years after). This also led to a severe balance of payments crisis in the winter of 1956-

57. By the mid-1957 the foreign exchange position was pretty alarming, as T.T. Krishnamachari, the then Finance Minister, told his Prime Minister, Nehru and the Cabinet that if immediate steps were not taken the economy could grind to a halt and India would lose her international creditworthiness. Nehru confirmed the crisis in discussion with the Cabinet. This left plan expenditure dependent on budgetary deficits, higher taxation, and—increasingly—foreign aid for both food and for plan financing.

The above results pinpoint to the fact that there were some basic flaws in Nehru's policy. He believed that the state would occupy 'the commanding heights of the economy' so as to prevent the rise of monopoly capitalism. Since India has had a vast home market he felt that an industry producing goods which had so far been imported had an enormous scope and should have high priority. During his lifetime he witnessed remarkable progress along those lines as outlined above. But in the long-run his policies proved to be self-defeating. The lack of competition in particular bred inefficiency and corruption, the public sector enterprises operated at a loss, the emphasis on protectionism and import substitution and the neglect of export-led growth deprived Indian industry of stimulating challenges. Nehru did a great deal for starting national research institutes devoted to industrial development, but in the absence of such challenges, they did not perform the task assigned to them. The representatives of Western nations who aided India's industrial development after 1957 did not admonish Nehru to change his policies. They were glad to sell their machinery to India and involved their taxpayers in providing 'development aid'.

Another flaw of Nehru's policy was his neglect of Indian agriculture. Since agricultural production was in the hands of millions of peasants, there was hardly any scope for state intervention. Nehru was mainly interested in keeping food prices low so as not to encumber industrial growth with wage prices. There was, nevertheless, a substantial increase of agricultural production in Nehru's time, but it was due to the extension of the cultivated area. This meant that marginal soils were ploughed which would not yield any harvest if rains failed. Nehru died before the great drought hit India in the mid-1960s and was thus saved from witnessing the collapse of his policy in this field. (*Hermann and Rothermund, 1986*). The year 1967 was a bad year for India : it was the second year of a devastating drought, which not only meant a great setback for agriculture but also brought about an industrial recession

III. CONCLUSION

Nehru was faced towards the end of his life and even before the Chinese invasion of 1962 and its disastrous implications for planning with evidence that the pace of change was inadequate to transform India's economy and society in the way he had wished. He confided this to T.T. Krishnamachari, and latter warned him that available statistics were already showing that the targets for the Third Plan (1961-66) were again not being met and the plan was going awry. In retrospect, it seems clear that Nehru's model of planned economic transformation was flawed in the context of India's democratic polity. Nehru could see where there was a problem, but he often could not see how to resolve it, and in particular how to achieve serious implementation of policy. As he aged, he could perfectly see how did his vision of creating New India get frustrated. After he was dead it become dramatically obvious that his policy of planned economic transformation, however idealistic,—particularly in the context of his time—had only worked in India to constrain economic growth and burden the economy with the weight of government control. The seeds of the Kafkaesque web of licence-quota rules and control were so much laid that in later years it was found that it was not easy to dismantle a system that had acquired a vicious stranglehold over the Indian economy.

References

Brecher, Michael (1998), *Nehru: A Political Biography*, Oxford University Press.

Brown, Judith M. (2003), *Nehru : A Political Life*, Oxford University Press.

Krishnamurti, Y.G. (1942), *Jawaharlal Nehru: The Man and his Ideas*, Bombay.

Kulke, Hermann and Dietmar Rothermund (1986), *A History of India.*

Routledge Mahalanobis, P.C. (1958), Science and National Planning, Anniversary Address to the National Institute of Sciences of India.

Majid Khan, Abdul (1951), *Jawaharlal Nehru and His Ideas*, New Delhi.

10

Pt. Nehru on Industrialization

T.G. Gite

This paper addressees Nehru's approach to the industrial economy—the mixed economy in which both private and public sectors march hand in hand. Although rapid economic development necessitated industrialization based on basic and heavy industries, the importance of small scale and cottage industries had not been underrated in Nehru's scheme of things. However, industrial growth during this regime had not been outstanding but not an unimpressive one. For further development of the country, public sector must get its pre-eminence and small scale units need to be developed along co-operative lines.

I. INTRODUCTION

Pandit Jawaharlal Nehru laid the foundation of modern India. His vision and determination have left a lasting impression on every facet of national endeavour since independence. It is due to his initiative that India now has a strong and diversified industrial base and is a major industrial nation of the world.

The first Prime Minister, Jawaharlal Nehru, who introduced the five year plans—agreed that strong economic growth and measures to increase incomes and consumption among the poorest groups were necessary goals for the new nation.

Effective from January 26, 1950, India became a republic. Nehru, the best-known leader of the independence movement next to Gandhi, served as Prime Minister until his death in 1964. During that time he succeeded in putting his imprint on the new nation. His guiding principles in domestic affairs were democracy, socialism, unity, and secularism. In foreign policy, he attempted to steer a non-aligned course between the Communist and the non-Communist powers, hoping to maintain peaceful relations with all nations. Indian industrialization was impressive relative to both other developed and developing countries in the mid-20th century. The Indian Government played an important role in industry since independence.

India embarked on planning process in 1951. The first Five Year Plan ended in March 1956. It laid the foundation for achieving the socialist pattern of society—a social and economic order based upon the values of freedom and democracy, without caste, class and privilege, in which there would be a substantial rise in employment and production and the largest measure of social justice attainable.

The Second Five year Plan focused on rebuilding rural India to lay foundations of industrial progress, and to secure to the greatest extent feasible opportunities for weaker and under-privileged sections of our people and balanced development of all parts of the country.

Unlike Gandhi, Nehru favored industrialization, and under his leadership India made substantial progress. Under the first two five year plans (1951 to 1956 and 1956 to 1961) national income rose 42 percent. Great strides were made in the steel, electric power, cement, and fertilizer industries.

II. NEHRU'S APPROACH TO INDUSTRIAL ECONOMY

Nehru's pragmatic and cautious approach led him to apply a novel variation of socialist economic planning to

India's industrial economy. It was a combination of free enterprise and state-controlled economy avoiding either of the two extremes. Nehru termed it as a 'middle way' or a 'mixed economy' which in his opinion was particularly suited to India's conditions. He firmly believed that we cannot think of this country in terms of what is happening in the United States. India with her very limited resources and under-developed economy could not embrace either of the extreme ideologies but had to find her own way.

The concept of mixed economy envisages the division of country's economy in two main sectors—the state-owned public sector and the private sector. A public sector and a private sector are essentially combined in such a mixed economy. It is a capitalistic economy with a great deal of state control or a capitalistic economy plus a public sector under the State. He further clarified that such an economy was deliberately accepted not because of giving some protection to vested interests but because 'under the existing conditions, we thought that this is the best way to attain our objectives—the immediate objectives being to stir up the machinery of production, to build it up which may lead to more and more wealth, in production in every way. Pt. Nehru believed that we should have two basic objectives to be achieved: one to have as much production as possible through all the means at our disposal and the second is prevention of accumulation of wealth and economic power in individual hands.

Role of the Private Sector

Nehru firmly believed that private enterprise on a big scale inevitably leads to private monopolies and the dominance of the few over many obstructing the progress of many others and opposing the ideals India stands for. Nehru wanted to limit more and more the scope of private sector. Nehru was firm that India's aim of 'developing into a welfare state and toward a large measure of equal opportunity... does not fit in with the growth of private enterprise in a big way'.

Role of the Public Sector

Nehru's stress was on bringing more and more vital enterprises under State control. In an underdeveloped country like India, Nehru was of the firm view that India cannot progress except by state initiative, except by enlarging the public sector and except by controlling the private sector at important points. As far as the basic and heavy industries were concerned, they would be kept under the public sector so that concentration of power, political or economic, might be avoided and equalization of wealth might flow. The public sector would necessarily be dominant, with a complementary private sector organized on cooperative lines. For achieving rapid economic growth, industrialization, particularly the development of heavy and machine-making industries would have to be speeded up

Heavy and Basic Industries

Pt. Jawaharlal Nehru was of the view that the barrier of underdevelopment could not be crossed without industrialization and industrial growth. Basic industries were at the heart of industrialization, and India should build these heavy basic industries. The renowned statistician Prof. Mahalanobis also contributed this view on industrialization especially of heavy and basic industries and the need for technological and ultimately economic self-reliance.

Small and Cottage Industries

While Nehru was a believer in the need of large-scale industrialization, he did not undermine the need for a healthy growth of small and cottage industries. These industrial sub-sectors play a vital role in a developing India. Small scale industries could not be a rival to large scale industries. Small scale industries are vital to help in accelerating production and providing employment to rural, semi-urban masses. He was a staunch advocate of development of small and cottage industries as he firmly believed that in a mixed economy, these smalls scale village and cottage industries were to have a real important role to play in contributing to the welfare of the common masses. Nehru's whole emphasis was on industrialization, planning and utilization of the latest scientific techniques and to make India materially advanced and prosperous nation.

Industrial Policy Resolutions of 1948 and 1956, coinciding with the launch of the Second Five Year Plan 1956-61, was called by some as the Economic Constitution of India. India witnessed a massive expansion of public sector through new units and nationalization of existing units during 1950-60. The Government of India reserved 17 industries for exclusive development in the public sector. The most important features of the 1956 Industrial Policy were the classification of all industries into the following three categories, Schedule A, Schedule B and Schedule C. The schedule A listed 17 industries reserved for exclusive development in the public sector. The schedule B listed 12 industries to be progressively owned by the Government and in which the Government would generally set-up new enterprises. The Schedule C industries contained the rest of the industries, which were left to the care of private sector but under general control of the government.

The Industrial Policy Resolution of 1948 was followed by the Industrial Policy Resolution of 1956 which had as its objective the acceleration of the rate of economic growth and the speeding up of industrialization as a means of achieving a socialist pattern of society. In 1956, capital was scarce and the base of entrepreneurship not strong enough. Hence, the 1956 Industrial Policy Resolution gave primacy to the role of the State to assume a predominant and direct responsibility for industrial development

Jawaharlal Nehru had an alternative idea of development over *Swadeshi.* Instead of becoming locally sustainable India went through a period of rapid westernization and industrialization. This happened because the three main interest groups with political power backed Nehru. The capitalist merchants and industrialists, technical and administrative bureaucracy, and rich farmers all wanted rapid industrialization because they stood to personally benefit from it.

Nehru felt that villages were backward with no culture or intellect, and so progress could not come from them. India also eventually opened up its borders to 'free trade' with other nations. The result of Nehru's plan was increased consumption and wealth for a few people and poverty for many. There has been increased urban congestion and increased air, water, and noise pollution.

It is true that the transition from an agrarian society to an industrial economy has always been a difficult one. But industrialization offers new opportunities and hope, especially for people in rural areas displaced by agrarian change. It is the responsibility of government to ensure that displacement does not lead to impoverishment; that those who lose land do not lose livelihoods; and, that those who have lost employment get better opportunities.

Industrialization and urbanization will generate demand for first rate infrastructure. The expansion and modernization of our highways, roads, railways and airports is visible proof of our efforts to meet this demand. Much more is needed and will be done. At India's independence, industrialization in India was viewed as the engine of growth for the rest of the economy and the supplier of jobs to reduce poverty. By the early 1990s, substantial progress had been made, but industrial growth had failed to live up to expectations. Industrial production increased at an average of 6.1 per cent in the 1950s, 5.3 per cent in the 1960s, and 4.2 per cent in the 1970s. The emphasis on large scale, capital-intensive industries created far fewer jobs than the estimated 10 million annual entrants into the labor force required.

Industrialization is a process that starts with the establishing and developing the industry for production of means of production and completes when the whole economy is transferred to the industrial methods of production. The most pressing problems of economic development of India could be solved only on the basis of industrialization. In the long-run, the aim should have been (and in fact, it was, at least on ideological level) to eliminate heterogeneous structure, integrate the economic system, ensure extended production on a national basis, eradicate unemployment and raise the nation-wide labor productivity.

Instead, the old methods of production had to be replaced with the modern industrial methods. This required, among other things, two major transformations: one, changing the old feudal property relations in the rural landscape and two, introduction of modern means of production and technology into the lower socio-economic structure so that they too would be brought within the commodity-money and market circulation.

Nehru's industrial policies were intended to encourage the growth of diverse manufacturing and heavy industries, yet because of state planning, controls and regulations the result was impairment of productivity, quality and profitability. The Indian economy lumbered along with an anemic rate of growth, and chronic unemployment amidst entrenched poverty continued to plague the population.

From 1951 to 1979, the economy grew at an average rate of about 3.1 percent a year at constant prices, or at an annual rate of 1.0 percent per capita. During this period, industry grew at an average rate of 4.5 percent a year, compared with an annual average of 3.0 percent for agriculture. Many factors contributed to the slowdown of the economy after the mid-1960s, the main one was the socialist policies pursued by Nehru and his cabinet.

CONCLUSION

Development depends on industrialization and industrialization depends on industrial policy. The first industrial policy of the Government of India was announced in 1 April 1948. Subsequently Industrial Policy Resolutions of 1956, 1980, 1990 and 1991 were announced. The Government believed that "It is necessary that proper amenities and incentives should be provided for all those engaged in industry. The living and working conditions of workers should be improved and their standards of efficiency raised. The maintenance of industrial peace is one of the prime requisites of industrial progress. In socialist democracy, labour is a partner in the common task of development and should participate in it with enthusiasm. Some laws governing industrial relations have been enacted and a broad common approach has developed with the growing recognition of the obligation of both management and labour. There should be joint consultation and workers and technicians should, wherever possible, be associated progressively in management. Enterprises in the public sector have to be set an example in this respect.

Nehru felt that India needed an infusion of modern science and adaptation of large scale industrialization. Prosperity was to come through rapid industrialization and urbanization. As a result of this strange ideology, the Indian Government put the majority of its resources into developing industry and neglected agriculture.

Nehru's firm conviction was that rapid industrialization particularly the development of heavy basic industries is very much needed to attain faster economic growth. Both the public sector and the private sector must function and grow, and the former should grow much faster. Along with the public and the private sector the cooperative sector should be helped to grow. This was the only way in which small units could gain advantages similar to those enjoyed by large units.

References

Jawaharlal Nehru, A Biography by Sarvepalli Gopal, 1979.

Jawaharlal Nehru, Centenary Volume: Edited by Sheela Dikshit and others, 1989.

Selected Works on Jawaharlal Nehru, 1st May-20th June, 1956, Second Session-33.

International Round, Round Table, Vijay Bhavan, Ministry of Education, Govt. of India, Sept. 26-29, 1966.

http://www.indianchild.com/india_industry.htm

11

Relevance of Nehruvian Economics under Globalization Regime

UGRA MOHAN JHA AND NARESH JHA

Nehru wanted to have a rapid development of the country as soon as India got her independence. He charted out a roadmap for India's state-led industrialization by developing the steel industry—one of the 'temples of modern India'. However, the rise of the public sector till 1991 and the policy-induced shrinking of the same thereafter have been addressed in this paper. The process of globalization challenged Nehru's economic identity for which Nehru could not be held responsible as globalization is deemed to be the current milieu from which one cannot remain insulated. Economic crises (e.g., severe foreign exchange shortage) that blew up before the completion of the Second Five Year Plan forced India to seek more foreign aid. This flustered policy-makers and forced them to permit MNCs to operate in this country. There are as many as three contradictions in Nehruvian strategy of development. The onslaught on the Nehruvian economic identity through the process of globalization needs to be reversed for evolving a genuine economic identity of India.

I. BACKGROUND

Nehru was the harbinger of change. He had been the architect of the focal point of Indian polity and policy for forty years. He was a great advocate of an economy which should be self-reliant. He did not make his debut in a spectacular manner but it was surely a slow and gradual growth. In the final stage of his life, he become a whirlwind and exercised tremendous influence on Indian economic substratum. His focus, his thrust and his momentum are still potent and powerful. R. Venkatraman, Former President of India has pointed out that Nehru set-up the Planning Commission for bringing about economic democracy in the country, encouraged balanced regional development and developed scientific temper by setting up a large number of national laboratories

Abid Hussain has pointed out that both Gandhi and Nehru wanted India to be self-reliant and self-sufficient. None of them wanted Indian economy to be dependent on the world economy. At the same time both wanted that the common man should be the focus of economic progress. Gandhiji wanted to wipe away every tear from the eyes of the poor and Nehru wanted economic development with a 'human face'. It is true that both of them differed from each other as regards the methods and means of achieving there two ideals.

Nehru's perception and concern for the amelioration of the socio-economic condition of the Indian rural people may be observed from his speech in the Lok Sabha on 11 April 1955: "We talk about socialistic pattern of society, industrialization for removing unemployment, of higher education and so on. What is really necessary is somehow to activise and dynamise the base of Indian social structure.

I want this House to approve and appropriate this phrase. No doubt there must be approaches from the top but there has been too much activising from the top layers of society all the time. We do not solve our problems unless we activise the base of Indian society which means millions and millions of villagers, millions and millions of workers, small earners and unemployed people of the land." Nehru wanted that public sector should occupy and utilize strategic position or commanding heights or positions of advantages and control.

Nehru was a great fighter for India's independence and he was in the company of other dignitaries and more dedicated persons. He was working under the inspiration and guidance of Mahatma Gandhi. Nehru was associated with all the Congress resolutions dealing with the condition of Indian economy and miserable plight of the Indian people under foreign domination. The *Karachi* Session of the 1930s, the *Avadi* Session of the 1950s and the *Bhubneshwar* Session of the 1960s are landmarks and Nehru played a great role in the formulation of the policies of the Indian National Congress.

There was the question of development path to be taken by India after independence. India had not become independent but all possibilities pointed out that independence was on the cards and not far way in the future. Debate was raising in business circles regarding the path to be taken. The industrialists in 1944 came out with a detailed plan for the economic development of the country and their refrain was that it is the Government which has to take the first step to achieve this end. Private sector was of the opinion that it cannot do anything because of the shortage of capital and funds. The businessmen and business houses expressed their inability to make massive investments. At that time India could not produce even a knife or a match box. These things were used to come from England and Germany. Even cement used to come from foreign countries. This was the situation and condition of the Indian economy.

Under these circumstances, Jawaharlal Nehru, as the (first) Prime Minister of India had no option but to establish and forge public sector. Public sector was not only necessary for the economic development of the country but it was still more essential and needed to strengthen the Indian economy. Hence public sector in his days discharged two functions—function of economic development and function of retention and strengthening of the freedom which has been attained. Steel plants were urgently needed because they could be the only foundation of development. The private sector was neither willing nor able to invest in it. The Government of

India had no money. The private sector had already declined. The only option was to have a steel plant from a foreign country. Nehru approached the USA for a steel plant but the USA declared that India did not need a steel plant. India could be supplied steel goods if needed. Nehru approached Britain and all other countries and no country was prepared to give a steel plant. It was the Soviet Union which accepted the proposal and gave one (Bhilai Steel Plant). Seeing this, UK and Germany also came forward to set-up steel plants in India (at Durgapur and at Rourkela). Soviet Union gave plants in all spheres and finally gave a plant to produce plants and this took place in Ranchi and this was known as Heavy Engineering Corporation (HEC). Hence the greatest contribution of Nehru to the Indian economy was the establishment of public sector in all spheres of economy.

After the death of Nehru the very name 'Public Sector' fell into disrepute and the word Nehru also become a term of derision and of sarcastic remark. Public sector became a term of disapprobation. People came to regard public sector as a cesspool of inefficiency and corruption and a white elephant which gobbled the resources of the country and gave no return. It was declared to be flabby and overcrowded and overstaffed. It was a burden on the exchequer. Hence Nehru's achievements in the shape of the public sector were converted into a stumbling block in the development of the country. The result is that India's development required elimination of public sector as a pre-condition. The Cabinet created a Department of Disinvestment. This is the sorry pass to which Nehru and his achievements have descended. The private sector regards the public sector as a 'miltching cow' and flourishes at its expense. If the public sector is overstaffed then the workers who have been appointed are not responsible because they have not appointed themselves. The appointment has been made by some authority, which should be identified and punished.

II. NEHRU'S ECONOMIC IDENTITY *VIS-A-VIS* GLOBALIZATION

By imposing colonialism and imperialism, the British

deprived India of its 'economic identity'. During the freedom struggle, great leaders like Dadabhai Naoroji, Mahatma Gandhi, Jawaharlal Nehru and many others thought about an 'economic identity' for India. However, the privilege of constituting and implementing it mainly went to Pandit Nehru. The 'economic architecture' of post-independent India was largely Nehruvian. Nevertheless, in the (new) globalization era, Nehruvian ideas were dismantled by the neo-liberal globalized economic forces.

As India was nearing freedom, there arose multiple views on the 'economic identity' for the emerging Indian nation among the members of the Indian National Congress. While leaders like Sardar Vallabhbhai Patel and C. Rajagopalachari stood for a Western type liberal economic order for India, the Marxist-oriented members, including M.N. Roy, Netaji Subhash Chandra Bose, Jayaprakash Narain and others advocated for 'socialism'. Gandhian economists like J.C. Kumarappa wanted the emerging Indian economy freed from any type of foreign influence. Pandit Jawaharlal Nehru assimilated all these suggestions and put forward an integrated economic identity for India.

Pandit Nehru as the grand architect of the Indian economic identity; instead of following the Western type 'capitalism' or the Russian type 'socialism', he wanted India to follow a 'mixed economy'. So he perceived that the good elements of capitalism and socialism be combined in the 'mixed economy'. Instead of socialism, he proposed the formulation of a 'socialistic pattern of society' with public sector achieving the 'commanding heights'. He was also hopeful of blending a democratic polity with a planned economy.

In the above perspective, Nehru started steering the Indian economy. The remarkable achievements of the First Five Year Plan imparted great optimism to him and he, with the intellectual collaboration of the great statistician, P.C. Mahalanobis, prepared an ambitious model for the Second Five Year Plan.

The 'model' set economic growth and social justice as the twin broad objectives of the Plan. It prescribed a 'two-pronged industrialization' strategy to achieve these goals. For rapid economic growth, the perspective was to build up heavy and key industries, particularly in the public sector. It was hoped that the 'forward' and 'backward' linkages of it would generate a revolution in industrial and agricultural growth and thereby in economic growth. In order to realize 'social justice', the model suggested the development of light industries. It was hoped that this segment of industries would provide jobs as well as 'wage goods' to ordinary people. For the just advancement of rural agricultural economies, the model recommended land reforms, community development programmes, and cooperative institutions including cooperative farming.

As India inherited a tradition of cottage and small scale industries, the model did not anticipate any constraint in their promotion. But as India was lacking in modern technology and capital, the country had to depend on the Western sources for building up heavy and strategic industries. Since India then possessed a huge foreign exchange reserve, the model-builders thought that Western machinery and expertise could be bought by using the foreign exchange reserves.

Though the Nehru-Mahalanobis model was a magnificent one, the country failed to make a headway in the actual implementation of it in the Second Five Year Plan. This was largely due to the 'neo-colonial' intervention in the political economy of India in those times. The Western capitalist forces did not welcome the development of the country through an indigenous pattern of economic identity. As the Second Plan had to buy foreign technology and capital from abroad for building up the heavy industrial sector, the available foreign exchange was quite insufficient to meet the then requirement. So by 1958-59 there arose a severe foreign exchange crisis in India compelling the government to seek foreign assistance. The Western forces, particularly the multinational corporations, found it a congenial situation to make India to oblige to their conditions. These capitalist forces, through multilateral institutions like the World Bank and IMF, required India to undo 'the socialistic pattern of society', with 'public sector achieving the commanding heights'. So during the Second Five Year Plan the government was forced to succumb to the diktats of the global capitalist forces in allowing the private market forces sufficient role in the functioning of the economy.

This intervention of multinational corporations and their patrons wreaked two havocs on the Second Five Year Plan. One, though India required foreign capital to build heavy and key industries, the MNCs took keen interest in the consumer goods sector only. Two, to a large extent it resulted in the displacement of indigenous industries and a big blow to the Indian economic identity.

Though Nehru initially compromised with neo-colonialism, subsequently he initiated a new international strategy in the formulation of Non-aligned Movement (NAM) to break the onslaughts of global capitalism on the Third World. In international relations, India leaned more to the side of the Soviet Union. It enabled India not only to obtain Soviet technology but also in enhancing the 'bargaining power' of India vis-à-vis the Western powers.

III. CONTRADICTIONS IN NEHRUVIAN APPROACH TO ECONOMIC DEVELOPMENT

Three mutually reinforcing and interrelated contradictions in the 'Nehruvian strategy' need to be noted. First, the State within the old economic policy regime had to simultaneously fulfil two different roles which were incompatible in the long-run. One it had to maintain growing expenditure, in particular investment expenditure, in order to keep the domestic market expanding. Two, the absence of any radical land redistribution meant that the domestic market, especially for industrial goods, remained socially narrowly-based; it had also meant that the growth of agricultural output, though far greater than in the colonial period, remained well below potential, and even such growth as occurred was largely confined, taking the country as a whole, to a narrow stratum of landlords-turned-capitalists and sections of the rich peasants who had improved their economic status. Under these circumstances, a continuous growth in State spending was essential for the growth of the market; it was the key element in whatever overall dynamics the system displayed. At the same time, however, the State exchequer was the medium through which large-scale transfers were made to the capitalist and proto-capitalist groups; the State, in other words, was an instrument for the "primary accumulation of capital." Through the non-payment of taxes (which the State generally turned a blind eye upon), and through a variety of subsidies and transfers, as well as lucrative State-contracts, private fortunes got built up at the expense of the State exchequer.

The contradiction between these two different roles of the State manifested itself, despite increasing resort to indirect taxation and administered price-hikes, through a growth in the fiscal deficit, i.e., the excess of total government expenditures, both revenue and capital, over government revenues. A persistent and growing fiscal deficit, under all circumstances, necessarily and inevitably undermines the State capitalist sector and strengthens demands for a rolling back of intervention. A fiscal deficit has to be financed through borrowing, i.e., through the private holding of additional claims directly or indirectly (mediated through the banking system) upon the State. If the borrowing is from abroad, then the building up of pressure for a change in the policy regime is obvious. If the borrowing is domestic then private wealth-holders may be willing to hold claims upon the State only after they have increased their holdings of other assets, such as urban property or consumer durables or commodity stocks, in which case the fiscal deficit has an immediate inflationary impact owing to this, and to keep inflation under check the State would have to cut back its expenditure which slows down the economy and eventually arouses capitalists' demands for an alternative policy regime. Even if private wealth-holders are willing temporarily to hold government debt without there being any inflationary pressures immediately, this only accentuates the inflation-proneness of the economy in the long-run with identical results. And finally at some point, both at home and abroad, the demand is raised that in lieu of claims upon the State, the private wealth-holders should be allowed to hold State property directly, i.e., for the privatization of the State-owned units. This is the sort of demand that we are witnessing in

India, namely that the State should cut down its fiscal deficit and its influence naturally was in the direction of adopting the Fund-Bank policy regime by "privatizing" several public sector units.

The second contradiction lay in the inability of the State to impose a minimum measure of "discipline" and "respect for law" among the capitalists, without which no capitalist system anywhere can be tenable. Disregard for the laws of the land, especially tax laws, was an important component of the primary accumulation of capital. The same disregard, the same absence of a collective discipline which a capitalist class imposes upon itself in any established capitalist country also meant that a successful transition could not be made from a Nehruvian interventionist regime to an alternative viable capitalist regime with State intervention, but of a different kind. After all the State is strongly interventionist even in a country like Japan, but it is interventionism based on close collaboration between the State and capital which simultaneously promotes rigorous discipline among the capitalists. Indeed many advocates of a retreat from Nehruvian dirigisme (economic control by the state) had talked explicitly of the Japanese "model" and had hoped for a new consolidation of Indian capitalism much in the way that Japanese capitalism had consolidated itself. They were, of course, being unhistorical, an important aspect of their unhistoricity was their refusal to recognize the inability of the Indian State to impose a measure of "discipline" on Indian capital.

The third contradiction had its roots in the cultural ambience of an ex-colonial society like ours. The market for industrial goods was from its inception, as we have seen, a socially narrowly-based one. Capitalism in its metropolitan centres, however, is characterized by continuous product innovation, the phenomenon of newer and ever newer goods being thrown on the market, resulting in alterations of life-styles. In an ex-colonial economy like ours, the comparatively narrow social segment in whose hands additional purchasing power accrues in a large measure and whose growing consumption, therefore, provides the main source of the growth in demand for industrial consumer goods is also anxious to emulate the life-styles prevailing in the metropolitan centres. It is not satisfied with having more and more of the same goods which are domestically-produced, nor is it content merely with expending its additional purchasing power upon such new goods as the domestic economy, on its own, is capable of innovating. Its demand is for the new goods which are being produced and consumed in the metropolitan centres, and which, given the constraints upon the innovative capacity of the domestic economy, are incapable of being locally-produced purely on the basis of indigenous resources and indigenous technology. An imbalance therefore inevitably arises in economies like ours between what the economy is capable of locally producing purely on its own steam, and what the relatively affluent sections of the society who account for much of the growth of potential demand for consumer goods would like to consume. This imbalance may be kept in check by import controls. But the more the imbalance between what is produced and what is sought to be consumed is kept in check through controls, the more it grows because of further innovations in the metropolitan economies. The result is a powerful build-up of pressure among the more affluent groups in society for dismantling of controls which would result in substantial sections of domestic producers going under, i.e., in a de-industrialization in the domestic economy, together with an accentuation of the already precarious balance of payments situation, which does not come in the way of such pressures being built up.

It is in this light that the new policy regime being instituted by the government has to be assessed. That regime has two components. First, it involves a set of measures aimed at "stabilization" or bringing the rate of inflation and the current account deficit on the balance of payments to acceptable levels. At the centre of that stabilization strategy is a reduction of the fiscal deficit on the government's budget through a cut in expenditures (principally subsidies) and enhanced resource mobilization, and a devaluation of the rupee aimed at raising the rate of growth of exports and curbing imports. Second, it involves a strategy of "structural adjustment" that, by liberalizing imports and subjecting domestic industry to the cutting edge of international competition, permitting the free inflow of foreign direct and portfolio investment, dismantling regulation of domestic and foreign private capital and privatizing the public sector, aims to "get prices right." This, it is argued, would improve the efficiency of domestic economic activity, reallocate resources to areas where India has a comparative advantage relative to its international trading partners, improve its export competitiveness, and raise the medium-term rate of growth on the basis of a stimulus provided by the international market. Export surpluses are now to take the place of State expenditure as the principal stimulus to growth.

From the point of view of international finance capital, this is a strategy which seeks to bring developing country's external deficits down to reasonable levels without adversely affecting the operation of transnational investment in their markets. It should be clear that this new regime is not so much an effort to overcome the constraints faced by the Nehruvian strategy, but aims to change strategy altogether. No more is metropolitan capital to be held at bay, but rather domestic capital would have to either compete with international capital or collaborate with it to obtain a foothold in either the domestic or the international market. Given the strength of the transnational monopolies that developed country governments nurture, protect and strengthen, there are limits to the ability of as-yet-underdeveloped economies to compete. This implies subordination as part of a strategy of growth. One cost of such subordination is, of course, the fact that growth depends on the willingness of transnational corporations to use India as a location for world-market-oriented production. The less that inclination in a world where all countries compete to attract foreign investment, the greater the extent of de-industrialization, the lower is the rate of growth of the system and the greater the burden heaped on the poor and the working people.

It is the belief that the extent of de-industrialization would far outweigh any gains from tethering a nation to the world economy that underlay the dirigiste regime (economic control by the state) which India opted for at independence. That regime was dictated by the perception that given the extreme external vulnerability characterizing the open economic regime that India was subject to under colonial rule, a degree of isolationism that curtailed the inflow of imports and displaced metropolitan capital in the domestic market was inevitable. If that strategy had not been adopted there was no reason to expect that India would have seen any departure from the economic stagnation that characterized the first half of the century.

IV.. MPACT OF NEW GLOBALIZATION ON NEHRUVIAN ECONOMIC IDENTITY

From an economic point of view, the new globalization may be perceived as a process of 'global marketization'. The two pillars of it are 'privatization' and 'liberalization'. From 1991 onwards, the politicians who assumed 'power' in India accepted this philosophy, even though the masses of the Indian people were averse to it.

In the management of the economy, 'planning' was pushed backward and 'market mechanism' was given the driver's seat. Public sector was pruned and displaced by disinvestment programmes. Private sector firms, including transnational corporations, started enjoying the privilege of assuming the 'commanding heights of the economy'. The exim sector was considerably liberalized. The service sector, including finance also was brought under liberalization.

Globalization integrated the Indian political economy with 'world capitalism'. This process could unleash 'dependent development', enabling India to achieve a relatively higher growth in GDP. India is now branded as an 'elephant', emerging as a 'global economic power'. But the vast majority of the people are still in the periphery of the economy. They are being marginalized, excluded and even exterminated. Poverty deaths and suicides have become regular occurrences.

Of late, globalization on a world scale, has started addressing its own limitations. The energy crisis, global warming, agri-flation, massive unemployment and mounting food insecurity all make globalization unpopular. The cradle of globalization, the American economy, is currently undergoing a severe recession. The sub-prime lending crisis triggered a vulnerable monetary and financial situation with which, many economists fear, the country is heading towards a depression similar to the one that happened in the 1930s. A number of Indian financial institutions like the ICICI lost huge amount in this crisis. The 'American Contagion' may affect India in many other fronts.

V. IS DE-GLOBALIZATION NECESSARY FOR INDIAN ECONOMIC IDENTITY?

Retrieval of the genuine Indian economic identity is essential for the sustainable human and social development of the Indian people. This 'identity' has to be a concern for all committed Indian people. We need a historical and interdisciplinary intellectual enquiry for rediscovering the true economic identity of India. We can start our intellectual journey from the Buddhist economics to the present times. This does not mean that we have to be fundamentalists. Rather, we must take history as a source of intellectual input.

Further, we need to identify our resource potential including traditional technology. India is a continental economy with a diversified resource base. We have to accept our vast population as an asset and political power has to be made accountable to the people. Then only would there be a true democracy.

The foregoing facts reveal that Jawaharlal Nehru attempted to formulate and implement a distinct economic identity for India. But it was betrayed mainly by neo-colonialism. However, there was a struggle between the Indian state and neo-colonialism on economic identity. But in this struggle, the Indian state was gradually defeated and new globalization was imposed on India which facilitated rapid economic growth. But globalization only enhanced the misery of the people of India. Hence 'de-globalization' is required for evolving a genuine economic identity of India.

REFERENCES

Audichya, Janardan *Economic Ideas of Jawaharlal Nehru*, by Jain Brothers, 1997, Jodhpur

Dantwala, M.L. (1964), 'Economic Ideology of Jawaharlal Nehru', *Economic and Political Weekly*, July.

Evolution of Nehru's Economic Thinking, *Economic Times*, May 26, 1974.

Haksar, P.N. (1986), Relevance of Jawaharlal Nehru, *'Mainstream'*, 24 May.

Hussain, S. Abid (1953), *Way of Gandhi and Nehru*, Bombay, Asia Publishing House.

Kapoor, P. Purnima (1985), *Economic Thought of Jawaharlal Nehru*, New Delhi, Deep & Deep Publications Pvt. Ltd.

Kurian, V. Mathew (1994), "Economic Policy Changes from Nehru to Narasimha Rao: What Lessons We Draw?", *Mainstream*, Vol. XXXII, No. 5 September 24, pp. 11-13.

Mathai, M.O. (1979), *My Days with Nehru*, New Delhi, Vikas Publication.

Moraes, Frank (1964), *Nehru: Sunlight and Shadow*, Bombay, Jaico Publication.

Nehru and Planning, Gyanchand, New Delhi, 1966

Nehru Abhinandan Granth, New Delhi, 1949.

The term 'globalization' may be viewed from three points of view: (a) as a programme, (b) as an ideology, and (c) as a process. As a programme it is by TNCs, for TNCs, and of TNCs. As an ideology it is 'neo-liberalism'. As a process, 'globalization' is as old as capitalism. Globalization is only the new phase of historical capitalism. See V. Mathew Kurian, *"Life and Death through Globalization: The Indian Experience"* in P. Jegadish Gandhi and K.C. John (ed.), Upon the Wings of Wider Enumerism (Delhi: ISPCK/Eec, 2006), pp. 223-35.

Radhakrishna, R. and Chandrasekhar, S. (2008), "Overview, Growth, Achievements and Distress" in R. Radhakrishna, (ed.), *India Development Report, 2008* (New Delhi: Oxford University Press), pp. 1-19.

Sachs, Jeffrey D. (2008), "Roots of America's Financial Crisis", *The Economic Times*, March 31, p. 15.

Tilak, Visi *et al.* (2008), "Will Wall Street's Flu Make India Sneeze?", *Tehelka*, February 9, pp. 38-41.

Tena, Bikram K. (2008), *"Did he do it?—Special Feature"*, 4 PS Business and Marketing, March 14-27, pp. 36-41.

12

Relevance of the Economic Thoughts of Jawaharlal Nehru in Present Times

M.M. GOEL

Nehru's vision for India's development was the economic well-being of the masses. In this pursuit, he set upon objectives and goals to be achieved as rapidly as possible. His own brand of socialism helped to devise various pro-poor economic policies and programmes. In the process, he laid the foundations of modern India. Areas of achievements of Nehru have been portrayed along with the gaps and cracks in the policies. For all the economic ills from which the country has been suffering is often attributed to Nehru by some opponents. This is indeed an unfair assessment. Nehru, not being an inflexible person, unyielding doctrinaire, would have greeted with affection the present day neo-classical economic policies designed by the GOI in 1991, had he been alive. Since Nehru's economic policies were not altogether unsuccessful, the processes of globalization need not to be practiced.

To imbibe the vision of Jawaharlal Nehru (Nehruji)—the first Prime Minister of India for the supply of dynamic element to society by the youth of present times, it is essential to understand, analyze and interpret the economic thoughts of the great mind of modern India which is the objective of the present paper. In fact, the present economic scenario calls for revisiting economic thoughts of Nehruji for making a room for continuous economic reforms in all times to come.

It is not necessary to know the person face to face, we can know even better by knowing the thoughts and actions of the same. It is relevant to know Nehruji's thought as he gave a vision to India. His thoughts must be grasped in proper perspective objectively, without any prejudices so that we can find its real relevance for the youth. His vision can be analysed in his own statement—

> "We have achieved political freedom but our revolution is not yet complete and is still in progress, for political freedom without the assurance of the right to live and to pursue happiness, which economic progress alone can bring, can never satisfy a people. Therefore, our immediate task is to raise the living standards of our people, to remove all that comes in the way of the economic growth of the nation. We have tackled the major problem of India, as it is today the major problem of Asia, the agrarian problem. Much that was feudal in our system of land tenure is being changed so that the fruits of cultivation should go to the tiller of the soil and that he may be secure in the possession of the land he cultivates. In a country of which agriculture is still the principal industry, this reform is essential not only for the well-being and contentment of the individual but also for the stability of society. One of the main causes of social instability in many parts of the world, more especially in Asia, is agrarian discontent due to the continuance of systems of land tenure which are completely out of place in the modern world. Another—and one which is also true of the greater part of Asia and Africa—is the low standard of

> living of the masses. India is industrially more developed than many less fortunate countries and is reckoned as the seventh or eighth among the world's industrial nations. But this arithmetical distinction cannot conceal the poverty of the great majority of our people. To remove this poverty by greater production, more equitable distribution, better education and better health, is the paramount need and the most pressing task before us and we are determined to accomplish this task. We realize that self-help is the first condition of success for a nation, no less than for an individual. We are conscious that ours must be the primary effort and we shall seek succour from none to escape from any part of our own responsibility. But though our economic potential is great, its conversion into finished wealth will need much mechanical and technological aid. We shall, therefore, gladly welcome such aid and co-operation on terms that are of mutual benefit. We believe that this may well help in the solution of the larger problems that confront the world. But we do not seek any material advantage in exchange for any part of our hard-won freedom."

To look forward and live forward by Indians, Nehruji projected India into the modern age. His dynamic thinking as a humanist will always bear the imprint on one and all in all times to come.

To honour the commitment of building up a strong and prosperous India free from disease, ignorance and poverty (DIP)—the commitment to posterity by Nehruji, the Indian youth needs to be human to be healthy, wealthy and wise (HWW). To reduce the misery and build up a better society, we must replace competition (particularly unhealthy) by cooperation as envisioned by Nehruji.

Nehruji's love for nature is not Byronic in the sense in which the great romantic poet confessed: "I love not man the less but nature more." With Nehruji it is other way round. He loves not nature the less bout man decidedly more. This attitude is crystallized in Robert Frost's famous lines from his poem *'Stopping by Woods on a Snowy Evening'*:

The woods are lovely, dark and deep,
But I have promises to keep,
And miles to go before I sleep,
And miles to go before I sleep.

Nature has a spell, a panacea for all ills. He has 'miles to go' before he sleeps—and yet the momentary charm of nature cannot withstood by him. Nehruji looked upon life as a glorious adventure offering new challenges and new possibilities at every step. Nehruji believed that we stand between past and the future, the past lights our path and the future beckons to us forward—a luminous vision of unique kind.

In economic growth he called the industries, dams and thermal plants, 'the temples of modern India'. He provided a free hand to our economists (this fact is also not much talked about in his favour). He was a far-sighted person, he talked for the trinity of India, China, and the USSR. He could be regarded as a responsible person, a good leader in today's context but he carries with him the burden of his failures. The early education of Jawaharlal Nehru influenced him in his later life. The influence was clearly visible on the economic policies adopted by the Government of India (GoI) after the country's independence in 1947. Nehru clearly favored a more socialist approach when compared to other South Asian economies. Nehruji was clearly thinking about his heady educational period in London when he promulgated the socialist ideology that influenced Indian government of the 1950s. The economy was treated with a mixed control. The Government of India was in control of the primary industries like electricity, mining and heavy engineering workshops.

The socialist leaning of Nehruji was apparent in the land redistribution programme announced by the Government of India in the middle of the 20th century. The rural sector was given importance. Nehruji correctly thought that since the majority of the Indian population lived in its villages, the rural sector should also get a lion's share of the country's economic resources. Dams were built. Canals were dug. The British education of Nehru is starkly visible in the promotion of fertilizers to increase the crop yield of the land.

The British education of Jawaharlal Nehru is also displayed in Nehruji's quest for independent energy sufficiency. Nehruji actively promoted the acquiring and development of nuclear energy. Hydro-electric power projects were also enthusiastically taken. The 'license raj' was also his creation.

The license raj was a unique byproduct of Nehru's combined social-liberal philosophy. The license raj was started with the view to help the Indian industrial sector. The intention led to limited success. Indian industries soon became unprofitable and became globally uncompetitive. The failure of the license raj led to its gradual scrapping by successive Indian governments from the 1980s.

Nehruji was the epitome of a resurgent India in the middle of the 20th century. The economic policies of Jawaharlal Nehru have been subject to much controversy in the past few decades. However, it is important to place Nehru's economic policies in context for a proper appreciation of his policies. Nehruji's commitment to the cause of India's development remains unquestioned, and it is no doubt that much of his plans and speculations were jeopardized by the unexpected partition that came along with the independence of India, which brought about an unprecedented fissure in the economic resources of the Indian mainland. Nehruji himself confessed that the partition brought about a large share of problems, including a great rift in the agricultural and the industrial sectors. A large portion of the most productive agricultural lands fell in Pakistan whereas the corresponding industries remained in Indian dominion. The problem faced by the jute industry soon after independence can be stated as a case in the point. The jute producing areas were in Pakistan whereas the jute processing factories remained in India, thereby affecting jute productions on both sides of the border.

Nehruji as the Prime Minister of independent India in 1947 immediately launched a number of economic reforms. Nehruji was a firm believer in State control over the economic sectors. His socialist ideals revealed themselves in the way he introduced laws for land redistribution in order to curtail the economic disparity in India among the landed and the landless classes. One of Nehruji's key economic reforms was the introduction of the Five Year Plan in 1951. It was introduced to determine the mode of government expenditure and grants in important development sectors like agriculture, industries and education.

Nehruji's economic policies have often been considered to be socialist in nature. It is no doubt that socialism did play a very important role in Nehruji s ideological make-up. But at the same time, it is also impo tant to consider that Nehruji himself denied any kind of overt Socialist tendencies in the economic policies adopted by him. Nehruji advocated a kind of mixed economy. Any kind of unquestioned ideological adherence to any form of economic tenet, or 'ism', he realized, would be detrimental to India's growth. He wanted a practical approach in framing the Indian economy, which would suit best the country's needs. On the one hand, as a devoted Gandhian, he had strong belief in the betterment of the rural economy. On the other hand, he had a strong belief that heavy industrial development would be the best way to serve India's economic interests.

Nehruji laid the foundations of modern India. His vision and determination have left a lasting impression on every facet of national endeavour since independence. It is due to his initiative that India now has a strong and diversified industrial base and is a major industrial nation of the world. The goals and objectives set out for the nation by Nehruji on the eve of independence, namely, the rapid agricultural and industrial development of our country, rapid expansion of opportunities for gainful employment, progressive reduction of social and economic disparities, removal of poverty and attainment of self-reliance remain as valid today as at the time. Nehruji first set them out before the nation. Any industrial policy must contribute to the realization of these goals and objectives at an accelerated pace. The present statement of industrial policy is inspired by these very concerns, and represents a renewed initiative towards consolidating the gains of national reconstruction at this crucial stage.

In 1948, immediately after independence, Government introduced the Industrial Policy Resolution. This outlined the approach to industrial growth and development. It emphasized the importance to the economy of securing a continuous increase in production and ensuring its equitable distribution. After the adoption of the Constitution and the socio-economic goals, the Industrial Policy was comprehensively revised and adopted in 1956. To meet new challenges, from time to time, it was modified through statements in 1973, 1977 and 1980.

The Industrial Policy Resolution of 1948 was followed by the Industrial Policy Resolution of 1956 which had as its objective the acceleration of the rate of economic growth and the speeding up of industrialization as a means of achieving a socialist pattern of society. In 1956, capital was scarce and the base of entrepreneurship not strong enough. Hence, the 1956 Industrial Policy Resolution gave primacy to the role of the State to assume a predominant and direct responsibility for industrial development. Nehruji wanted to create a balance between the rural and the urban sectors in his economic policies. He stated there was no contradiction between the two and that both could go hand in hand. He denied to carry forward the age-old city *versus* village controversy and hoped that in India, both could go hand in hand. Nehruji was intent to harness and fully exploit the natural resources of India for the benefit of Indians. The main sector he identified was hydroelectricity, and he constructed a number of dams to achieve that end. The dams would not only harness energy, but would also support irrigation to a great degree. Nehruji considered dams to be the very symbol of India's collective growth, as they were the platforms where industrial engineering and agriculture met on a common platform. Nehruji also considered the possibility of nuclear growth during his tenure as the Prime Minister of India.

The idea that the Mahalanobis Model had neglected agricultural progress either by design or by default is based on ignorance. If the plan's author had been aware of the role of agriculture as a source of demand for industry, he had also recognized early on that any expansion of agricultural supply required industrial inputs: think of cement for irrigation canals, steel for pumps, and mere brick-and-mortar for pump houses. Even these basic goods of industrial origin were in short supply as the capacity for their production was lacking. The Mahalanobis Model did not view industrialization as a rival to agricultural growth; on the contrary, it had envisaged it as complementary.

As evidence consider the fact that for the first time in the twentieth century the per capita production of grain began to rise in India. This is all the more striking as it occurred in the context of a substantial rise in the rate of growth of the population following the launch of the republic.

That the policies of the Nehru era were able to reverse the decline of agriculture that had plagued the first half of the twentieth century should be considered achievement enough.

The seed bed for the green revolution that was to follow from about the mid-sixties was at least partly laid by this policy regime. Specifically, the Nehru era witnessed the expansion of publicly-provided irrigation, the provision of an agricultural extension service in the form of the Community Development Programme, and the initiation of field trials within the rejuvenated Indian Council for Agricultural Research.

The central feature of the planned industrialization drive was that it was state-directed. This has by itself been the subject of much criticism. The point, however, is to judge this strategy, any strategy for that matter, by its results. For a state-directed scheme to be effective the state must have sufficient resources at its command. The public sector was an instrument conceived as an agent of resource mobilization.

Nehruji inspired the industrialists to provide a fillip to India's economy. However, he had strict reservations on the question of foreign investment. Nehruji was wary of foreign investment. Nehruji's nationalist ideals confirmed in him the belief that India was self-sufficient to bolster her own growth. Although he did not officially decry the possibility of foreign investment in direct terms, he did stress that the sectors of foreign investment would be regularized, and the terms and conditions of investment and employment would be strictly controlled by government rules in case there were possibilities of a foreign investment. Nehruji, moreover, emphasized that the key sectors will always be in government hand. This step of Nehruji is much criticized now. Yet, it cannot be denied that Nehruji aptly looked forward to long term investments for which he banked more on Indian industries. It is also often suggested that his endeavor to harness international support to develop India's infrastructural profile between 1947 and 1955 did not meet with much success. It, however, remains a fact that Nehruji's regime was not one of great economic growth for India. Although his economic policies are blamed for the failure of India to turn into a major economic force in the aftermath of independence, yet Nehruji was probably thinking on a more long term basis. It is often inferred that the economic liberation of the later years was possible only because of Nehruji's policies in the initial stages.

The most distinctive, and often debated feature of Nehruji's economic policies, was the high level of State and central control that was exercised on the industrial and business sectors of the country. Nehruji emphasized that the State would control almost all key areas of the country's economy, either centrally or on a state-wise basis. His socialist emphasis on State control somehow seemed to undermine his stress on industrial policies. The rigorous State laws and license rules put a great degree of restrain on the free execution of industrial policies. Even the farmers, along with the business personnel, found themselves to be at the receiving end of rigorous State control policies and high taxation. Poverty and unemployment were widespread throughout Nehruji's governance.

Nehruji's policy towards the rural economy of India was also significant. Nehruji felt for the rural self-development of India very strongly. He tried to boost India's cottage industries. Much on the lines of Gandhiji, Nehruji believed that the rural and cottage industries of India played a major role in the economic fabric of the country. But most of his cottage industry development programmes were meant as a part of community development. He was also of the belief that small scale industries and cottage industries were effective solutions to the massive employment problems that remained a perpetual issue of concern throughout his tenure.

The economic policies of Nehruji are often blamed for the poor economy of India in the subsequent years. However, it cannot be denied that his decisions were necessitated by the needs of the times. India needed to effectively harness its domestic means as well as strengthen its governmental control to lay the base for future privatization. It is often speculated that Nehruji would have embraced the economic reforms and economic liberalization of the late twentieth century if he was alive.

The future beckons to us. Whither do we go and what shall be our endeavour? To bring freedom and opportunity to the common man, to the peasants and workers of India; to fight and end poverty and ignorance and disease; to build up a prosperous, democratic and progressive nation, and to create social, economic and political institutions which will ensure justice and fullness of life to every man and woman.

We have hard work ahead. There is no resting for any one of us till we redeem our pledge in full, till we make all the people of India what destiny intended them to be. We are citizens of a great country on the verge of bold advance, and we have to live up to that high standard. All of us, to whatever religion we may belong, are equally the children of India with equal rights, privileges and obligations. We cannot encourage communalism or narrow-mindedness, for no nation can be great whose people are narrow in thought or in action.

According to Nehruji 'the most amazing and terrible thing about India is her poverty.' He believed India has enough or can have enough for all her children if an alien government and some of her own sons did not corner the good things and so deprive the masses of their dues. Nehruji used to quote Ruskin, "Poverty is not due to natural inferiority of the poor or the inscrutable law of God, or drink, but because others have picked their pockets."

Although it is now fashionable to attack economic thoughts of Nehruji from the free-market or environmentalist points of view, yet his views in this respect were not singular, but representative of a wide spectrum of intellectual and scientific opinion. Even the capitalist class was then behind the mixed economy—they thought the Government should invest in infrastructure, and protect them from foreign competition. In any case, those economic policies have not been altogether unsuccessful. They have built a decent industrial base, helped assure self-sufficiency in food, and created a pool of technically skilled manpower that has fuelled the recent software boom. Nehruji built on the inclusive idea of India framed by Tagore and Gandhiji before him.

In brief, there is a strong case for the continuous research on the relevance of economic wisdom of Nehruji in all times to come.

References

Sat Pal Anand (compiled and edited) (1973), Promises To keep (Selections from Jawarlal Nehru), Publication Bureau, Panjab University, Chandigarh.

http:www.indianembassy.org/indusrel/India_us/Nehru-congress_oct-13_1949 Source: Prime Minister Jawaharlal Nehru's speech in the U.S. House of Representatives and the Senate.

Ramachandra Guha (2005), *Verdicts on Nehru: The Rise And Fall of a Reputation* (Second V.K.R.V. Rao Memorial Lecture, Institute of Social and Economic Change, Bangalore, 20 January 2005.)

Government of India, Ministry of Industry: Statement on Industrial Policy, New Delhi, July 24, 1991.

Pulapre Balakrishna (2008), "Nehru's Economic Legacy" in *Business Line*, dated 26/1/08.

Jawaharlal Nehru (1956), *The Discovery of India*, Meridian Books Ltd., London.

13

Socialism in the Works and Thoughts of Jawaharlal Nehru

RAJAN KUMAR SAHOO

This paper places importance to Nehru's ideas of socialism or what one may dub it as 'Nehruvian socialism'. His typical brand of socialism is not based on coercion, but on democracy. The two evils of the Indian society—poverty and unemployment—could be removed only through Indian variety of socialist planning. The paper also addresses Nehru's land reform programmes and industrialization policy.

I. INTRODUCTION

Pandit Jawaharlal Nehru—an India born English educated, prolific writer—is ever remembered as the first Prime Minister for his contribution towards socialism in an underdeveloped nation like India. He was a cosmopolitan leader, a voracious reader and a profound scholar. His works bear an ample testimony to his dynamism, understanding, originality and clarity of thought. As the first Prime Minister and the builder of free India, he has the unique opportunity to give a practical shape to his ideas. His economic and social ideas are understood from his address that he has made to the nation at the stroke of midnight hour of 14th August 1947. The address was a testament of his faith, vision and life's mission. With a voice buoyant and vibrant Jawaharlal said,—"Long years ago we made a tryst with destiny, and now the time comes we shall redeem our pledge.... a pledge of dedication to the service of India and her people and still larger cause of humanity..... The service of India means the service of the millions who suffer. It means the ending of poverty and ignorance and disease and inequality of opportunity. The ambition of the greatest man of our generation has been to wipe every tear from every eye. That may be beyond us, but so long as there are fears and suffering, so long our work will not be over. ....To the people of India whose representatives we are, we make appeal to join us with faith and confidence on this great adventure. This is no time for petty or destructive criticism, no time for ill will or blaming others. We have to build the noble mansion of free India where all our children may dwell."

In this eloquent and passionate address Jawaharlal Nehru presented a vista of the future. Freedom for which he made a valiant fight was not the end, only the means to an end. His vision for the nation, and concern for wiping the tear from the eyes of countrymen and pledge for ending poverty, disease and establishing equality presents a glimpse of his socialistic ideals which is to be unfolded at this juncture. Realising various aspects in his thought and action it was felt appropriate to make deeper analysis on his ideas and actions.

Objective of the Study

The study is planned with the following objective:

1. To study the ideas of Nehru on socialism and to make a deeper analysis of its basic features

II. NEHRU'S IDEAS ON SOCIALISM

Jawaharlal Nehru, when he was a student in London was particularly moved by the idea of Fabian Socialism. His early ideas were not based on any practical experience. They were vague humanitarian and utopian rather than scientific. In later years he developed some concrete ideas on socialism.

Nehru's ideas on socialism were deeply influenced by Russian socialism. During his visit to the Soviet Union in November 1927, his socialist urge was stimulated seeing the establishment of a classless society based on equity. No doubt, he disliked the violence, ruthlessness, and wholesale regimentation practiced by the Soviet system.

Nehru was also deeply influenced by the Marxist philosophy which could be worked in to practical shape. Nehru accepted monism and non-duality of mind and matter, the dynamics of matter and the dialectic of continuous change by evolution as well as a leap, through action and interaction cause-and-effect thesis, anti-thesis, and synthesis.

Nehru admitted that communist philosophy of life gave him comfort and hope. Like Marx, he believed in scientific approach to social problems and appreciated the role of technological forces. Though he deeply appreciated Marx but he remained a socialist and not a communist. M.N. Das has rightly commented,—"The Marxian diagnosis of the ills of Modern society made a deep impression on Nehru's socialistic ideas. He resolved the prophecies of Marx to understand more deeply the fundamental causes of the socio-economic conflicts which affilicted the world."

Nehru did not want to introduce the foreign brand of socialism in India. Socialism was to grow out of Indian conditions. Hence socialism was to be practical and indigenous. Under Nehru's leadership at the *Avadi* Session in 1955, the Indian National Congress accepted the ideal of a socialistic pattern of society. Nehru believed that socialism was the panacea of all human ills. It was only through socialism that poverty, unemployment and economic miseries could be removed. Socialism was a means to change the political and social structure.

III. BASIC FEATURES OF NEHRUVIAN SOCIALISM

The following are the basic features of Nehruvian socialism:

1. Democratic Socialism

Nehru detested Nazism and Facism because they indulged in physical acts of aggression, brutality, and vulgarity. Similarly, the dictatorial ways of the communists, their aggressive methods and intolerance of any opposition were resented by him. Hence he went for democratic socialism, which will be based on political liberty, equality and tolerance. Under democratic socialism, we could maintain individual freedom and initiative with centralized social control and planning of the economic life of the people.

2. Peaceful Methods

Nehruvian method of democratic socialism is based on discussion, argument and persuasion. He rejected the idea of class war. He was in favour of consent, and compromise and not conflict.

3. Mixed Economy

Nehru was fully aware of the inherent defects of capitalism—its acquisitiveness, rapaciousness and violence. He was also against the regimentation and intolerance of totalitarian socialism. Hence he evolved a system of mixed economy as an alternative to both the rival systems, drawing the positive aspects of each and rejecting their negative aspects. It would be a combination of free private enterprise and state-controlled economy.

Nehru favoured a positive role for the private sector, which called for effective state regulation and control. The basic, heavy and defence industries would be in the public sector. Large scale industries which needed huge capital investment would also be in the public sector. Nationalism was advocated to gain state control over key industries. According to him, nationalism was not synonymous with socialism.

4. Science and Technology

Nehru had tremendous faith in science and technology. A modern society cannot be built without science and technology. Most of the developed countries have attained success due to the improvement in science and technology. If science and technology are applied in the field of agriculture and industry, there can be great improvement in productivity Nehru once observed that we cannot solve the problem of poverty and hunger and improve the effective utilization of resources without science and technology. That is why he established a number of scientific institutions to create a scientific base for the economy and scientific temper among the people. These scientific institutions have made immense contribution for the development of the economy and for the improvement of a modern outlook.

5. Priority to Planning and Socialism

Nehru was greatly influenced by the planning process of Soviet Russia and wanted to introduce planning in India to increase the pace of economic development and allocate scarce resources to priority sectors to meet the essential requirements of the country. Jawaharlal observed—"Planning was the application in an organised way of intelligence to the solution of a problem. There had to be a certain strategy because planning did not become an exercise for a year or five years. It was a continuous process. We have to think in terms of not one plan but of several plans ahead, fifteen years, twenty years or more, whatever subject we might take up."

Further he proposed to establish a socialist pattern of society through planning, "where the principal means of production are under social ownership or control, production is progressively speeded up and there is equitable distribution of national wealth." With regard to economic policy, "The public sector must play progressively a greater part, more particularly on the establishment of basic industries." This does not mean that he was opposed to private sector or individual freedom.

P.C. Mahalanobis writing on Nehru's socialist planning points that it can be called the middle way. It is an attempt to achieve rapid economic progress in a manner in which political and economic democracy would be reconciled. This is clear from what he wrote to the Chief Ministers on 15th September 1954. In his letter, he says, "I take it that our objective is to have ultimately a socialist economy. I am not using the word in any doctrinaire sense, but in its broad meaning. That economy as well as any planning requires an organized approach based on adequate data with definite targets. It requires various kinds of control at least at strategic points. It is clear that we cannot proceed along authoritarian lines, such as in the Soviet Union or even as in China. The problem for us, therefore, is how far we can achieve our objective through democratic planning without too much compulsion. It may be that this kind of planning does not yield those spectacular results which might be obtained by an authoritarian approach to this question and a great deal of compulsion. Even so, we prefer the democratic approach because of certain values and standards we cherish."

While replying to critics, Jawaharlal once said, "I have hardly mentioned socialism except incidentally, but I have laid stress on the amazing poverty of our people, the vast unemployment of our peasants, workers and middle class, on the progressive deterioration of all classes except the handful at the top. That has been my sin in the eyes of that handful. But there is the only future that comes before my eyes when I think of India, I cannot rid myself of it, try as I may. It is not a pleasant picture. I do not like it and as I see it, sometimes my blood freezes within me and sometimes it boils with indignation that such things should be." (*The Tribune*, June 1956). This shows that Nehru was advocating socialism to eradicate poverty and unemployment

His socialist planning therefore does not exclude private sector. We require both public sector and private sector to increase the pace of growth. Private sector has, of course, to work under certain rules and regulations. It should not lead to monopoly or concentration of wealth. All this shows that he was in favour of a mixed economy. Public sector should make investment in basic and heavy industries, defence industries and large scale industries where large investments are necessary and social sector like education, health, sanitation where private sector is not likely to make investment since the rate of profit in such sector is very small.

6. Agrarian Reforms

The land problem in India had been a dominant issue during the 19th century. The prevalent land tenure systems in India led to exploitation, insecurity of tenancy rights, poverty, vast army of landless labourers, sub-division and fragmentation of holdings and intermediaries between the state and the peasants. Nehru in his Presidential address at the Lahore Congress session in 1929 said, "Real relief can only come by a great change in the land laws and the present system of land tenure." In 1936, during the Lucknow Congress session, Nehru suggested to draw an agrarian programme to meet the land problem. After independence under the active leadership of Nehru, Zamindari System was abolished. Legislations were enacted for consolidation of holdings, fixity of rent and redistribution of surplus land to the landless. Nehru was also an advocate of co-operative socialism as well. In January 1959 at Nagpur AICC session, Nehru insisted on co-operative joint farming, state trading in food grains and labour co-operatives.

7. Industrialization

In Nehru's socialist pattern of development, greater emphasis was given to heavy industries to accelerate the process of change. Nehru thought that unless heavy industries like steel, cement, machine tools, heavy electrical, etc., are developed there cannot be any substantial change in the economic set-up of India. A strong industrial base is necessary for modernization of the economy.

But while emphasizing heavy industries, Nehru did not neglect agriculture or small scale industries. He emphasized the improvement of agricultural productivity through the help of mechanization. Traditional way of agriculture cannot increase productivity. Therefore, industry and agriculture are inter-related. Increase in productivity of agriculture will not only provide adequate amount of food and raw materials to meet the basic requirements of the country but also increase employment opportunities for those who are dependent on agriculture.

In Industrial Policy statements of 1948 and 1956 for the improvement of rural economy, great emphasis was laid on the small scale and cottage industries, including Khadi. It was thought that agriculture alone cannot provide sufficient employment and income to all those who are dependent on agriculture. Along with the development of agriculture if such small scale and cottage industries are developed, scope for greater employment and income will be generated in rural areas.

Nehru continually stressed the need for decentralization and delegation of executive powers and responsibilities. The main purpose of his programmes is to change the entire social and economic structure of India and participation of people is an essential part of his programme of action.

CONCLUSION

Nehru stood for sanity and peace in the critical moments of human history. If one examines carefully the foreign policy of Nehru, one can see that he was trying to work out a synthesis between our cultural heritage and economic requirements of the people. Though he could not succeed all that he wanted to achieve, we cannot blame him for this failure. One has to judge the man, the efforts that he makes to fulfil the objectives he plans to achieve. Once he said, "We are little men, serving a great cause, but because the cause is great something of that greatness falls upon us also. Mighty forces are at work in the world today and in India and I have no doubt that we are ushering in a period of greatness for India. The India of geography, of history and tradition, the India of our minds and hearts cannot change." Actually he was more an idealist than a pragmatist. He was a humanist and was a strong advocate of human values and dignity. No doubt, he was a supreme leader of post-independent India. He evolved an ideology which was rooted to Indian traditions and was enriched by the Western liberalism and Gandhian thought. The posterity would ever remember him as the builder of modern India.

References

Gopaḷ Sarvepalli (1975), *Jawaharlal Nehru, A Biography*, 3 Volumes, Oxford University Press.

Mishra, Baidyanath (1999), *Pandit Jawaharlal Nehru's Economic and Social Ideas*, in Mishra Bidyanath, Comparative Economic System, Kitab Mahal, College Square, Cuttack, pp. 284-90.

Moraes, Frank (1956), *Jawaharlal Nehru*, Asia Publishing House.

Mukherjee, Hirendranath (1964), *The Gentle Colossus, A Study of Nehru.*

Nehru, Jawaharlal (1962), *An Autobiography*, Allied Publishers, New Delhi.

Nehru, Jawaharlal (1961), *The Discovery of India*, Asia Publishing House.

Sen, K.K. (1964), *Socialist Thinking of Paṇdit Jawaharlal Nehru* in Sen K.K., Comparative Economic Systems, Sultan Chand and Sons, 23, Daryaganj, New Delhi, pp. 6.24-6.29.

Zakaria, Rafiq (Ed. 1959), *A Study of Nehru*, A Times of India Publication.

14

Nehru and Indian Economic Planning with Special Reference to the Second Five Year Plan

SUBODH KUMAR SINHA AND RAJESH KUMAR

Nehru's ideas about economic planning to be practiced in this country to lift the Indian economy from the morass of underdeveloped, backward agrarian economy to a vibrant self-reliant economy with greater emphasis on heavy and basic industries has been analyzed in this paper. Special attention has been given to the 4-sector Mahalanobis Plan model as well as Nehru's approach towards full employment.

I. INTRODUCTION

In fact, Jawaharlal Nehru was the builder of modern India and the architect of Indian planning. Nehru was a man of rare dedication, who devoted himself to his country for socio and economic development of India. He was always in favour of social justice. Nehru's ideas and approach to economic and social issues are more relevent now than even in his time.

II. NEHRU AND INDIAN PLANNING

Without recall of Nehru we can't complete discussion of Indian economic planning till Third Five Year Plan. So that no one can deny that the introduction of planning in the Indian economy was solely due to the initiative of Jawaharlal Nehru, nor can it be disputed that during the long period of his chairmanship of the Planning Commission from March 1950 to the day of his death in May 1964, his was the most dominant influence not only in shaping the recommendations of the Commission but also in acquiring for them the support of the people and the Parliament of India. The National Planning Committee worked for a number of years in dealing with different aspects of the economic development of the country. It helped a great deal in popularizing the idea of planning in the country.

Nehru had very definite ideas on what constituted planning, its objectives, its approach, and its strategy; and to a large extent he succeeded in stamping his ideas on India's first three Five Year Plans.

In March 1950, the Government of India appointed a Planning Commission with the Prime Minister as the Chairman in July 1950—a five year plan for the country, to be placed before the Commonwealth Consultative Committee, was prepared. This Plan was later incorporated in the Colombo Plan with the desire to enlist the cooperating of the Commonwealth and the other countries in the process of economic development. After the preparation of the Colombo Plan, the Planning Commission continued its efforts to formulate a detailed National Plan for the country in consultation with the representatives of the Central and State Governments and private enterprises. It published the draft outline of the First Five Year Plan in July 1951 opening a new chapter in the course of economic history.

The Planning Commission has invited criticisms and constructive suggestions on the Plan. But it had received either faint praise or destructive criticism. Two of Prof. C.N. Vakil's close associates Prof. J.J. Anjana and Dr. K.S. Krishnaswamy were in-charge of the formulation of the First Five Year Plan. This gave an occasion to Prof. Vakil to put out a book entitled *Planning for a Shortage Economy, The Indian Experiment* (1952) along with P.R. Brahmananda. The object of the book was to emphasize the essential soundness of the plan so far as its realistic approach was concerned and to critically examine the various problems and proposals with a view to making constructive suggestions.

III. NEHRU AND THE SECOND FIVE YEAR PLAN

The Second Five Year Plan is known as the Nehruvian Model. Many economists belive that the Second Five Year Plan which gave high priority to heavy Industry was one of the major contributions of Nehru. The Mahalanobis heavy industry model has also been a matter of intense debate. The main critique of Nehru's model are: Vakil, Brahmananda and B.R. Shenoy.

In the process of Second Five Year Plan formulation, a panel of economists had been set-up in January 1955 with C.D Deshmukh, the Finance Minister as Chairman, D.R. Gadgil as Vice-Chairman and twenty leading economists of the country as members.

Mahalanobis model was not only a theoretical model for academic discussion but it was an Operational Research Model for development of the Indian Economy. Mahalanobis had prepared his model with the help of planning experts of the world, under the overall guidance of Nehru. Vakil and Brahmananda were not opposed on his view about large size of investment, i.e., 10 per cent to 11 per cent of the national income per annum, but were opposed about his view on resource allocation pattern and by that neglect of wage goods sector, which would ultimately aggregate the problem of unemployment and price rise.

Mahalanobis had prepared the four sector model for his Second Five Year Plan of India. The model was the extension of the one sector and two sector model into four sector model = capital goods sector (basic Investment goods), C_1 = factory producing consumer goods, C_2 = Household industries (including agriculture), C_3 = service (e.g., education, health, etc.), sector.

While the earlier models were growth models, this

model should properly be called on allocation or decision model. Mahalanobis was of the view that the k sector plays a vital role in economic development. The rate of development over a long period would be intimately connected with the pattern of investment. So capital goods sector should be developed.

Mahalanobis allocated the investment proportion for different sectors separately.

$$\lambda\kappa + \lambda_1 + \lambda_2 + \lambda_3$$

Mahalanobis calculated incremental net output investment ratio for different sectors separately :

$$\beta\kappa + \beta_1 + \beta_2 + \beta_3 .$$

A set of parameter was also introduced giving the investment required for per engaged person (i.e., capital-labour ratio) in the four sectors respectively, as

$$\theta\kappa + \theta_1 + \theta_2 + \theta_3$$

Mahalanobis model was to get a consistent solution to obtain a desired rise in national income as a result of given amount of investment and at the same time creating a desired volume of employment. It was necessary to use such a model to get the broad sector allocations of investment in the draft plan frame for the Second Plan prepared by Mahalanobis; the actual situation before the preparation of the plan frame was somewhat like this ;

Yq	=	Initial national income = Rs. 10,800 crore
A	=	Total investment fund = Rs. 5,600 crore. 10 per cent to 11 per cent of national income
n	=	Rate of increase of national income = 5% per year
N	=	Total new employment to be created
	=	110 lakhs (=11 million)
K	=	Proportion of investment to industries producing investment goods = 33% settled from consideration of growth over a long period

The capital and labour requirements per unit of increase in national income differ among these four sectors. The basic problem of economic planning was then how to distribute a given amount of available investment funds among these sectors so as to achieve both the target for the rate of increase in national income and full employment of the labour force.

In distributing investment funds, sector K was given special priority of total funds for new investment. One-third was allocated to sector K. This allocation was arrived at from consideration of long-run point of view.

Mahalanobis settled parameters of capital-output ratio and capital-labour ratio for different sectors (per one million rupees of income).

On the basis of parameters, Mahalanobis calculated income and employment position for the whole Second Plan period. (Table 1)

TABLE I

Parameters of Capital-Output and Capital-Labour Ratios for the Second Plan

Sector	*Description*	*Capital (Rs. Million)*	*Labour (manpower*
K	Basic Investment goods	β_K–5.00	θ_K–250
C_1	Factory Consumer goods	β_1–2.86	θ_1–327
C_2	Agriculture and Household Industries	β_2–0.80	q_2–320
C_3	Service Sector	β_3–2.22	q_3–593

Source: Komiya, R. : A Note on Professor Mahalanobis Model of Indian Economic Planning in Wadhva, C.D. (Ed) *Some Problems of India's Economic Policy*, Tata McGraw-Hill Publishing Company Limited. New Delhi. 1985, p. 33.

Mahalanobis was of the view that 33 per cent of total investment in the capital goods sector contributes only 12.76 per cent of toal income and 8.18 per cent of total employment meaning that productivity of capital in K sector is less than that in other sectors while the capital-labour ratio in this sector is very high. The target values of income and

TABLE 2

Income and Employment Estimation for Second Five Year Plan

Sector	*Investment (A) (Rs. Crore)*	*Increase in income (E) (Rs. Crore)*	*Employment (N) (Million)*
K	1850	370	0.9
C_1	980	340	1.1
C_2	1180	1470	4.7
C_3	1600	720	4.3
Total	5610	2900	11

Source: Bose, P.K. and Mukherjee, M., P.C. Mahalanobis papers on planning, Statistical Publishing Society, Calcutta, 1985, p. 95.

employment were fixed in such a way as to satisfy the requirements of prospective and also to confirm to the needs of a capital poor and welfare conscious economy thus instruments were the proportions of distribution of total investment between sections. Though C_1 Sector was quick-yielding but Mahalanobis was of the view that. K Sector was essential for the sound development of the country in the long-run. 17 per cent of total investment in a sector contribute 11.72 per cent of total income and 10.00 per cent of total employment. C_2 sector, that is agriculture and household industries sector needs only 21 per cent of total investment to contribute 50.69 per cent of total income and 42.73 per cent of total employment. In spite of the capital labour and capital-output ratio, Mahalanobis allocated 50 per cent of the investment outlay for K and C_1 sector in view of long-term interests.

IV. LIMITING FACTORS OF PLAN DEVELOPMENT

Mahalanobis was very serious about the obstacles, i.e., limiting factors in the way of planned development efforts.

In the Mahalanobis approach, the strategy was to balance the increase in demand created by investments in the heavy capital-intensive industries and expenditure on service by adequate production of consumer goods at first through small and household industries. The rate of development would be determined by the amount of surplus consumer goods which can be actually produced. The production of enough consumer goods in the small and household industries of strategic importance might constitute a limiting factor.

The capacity of investment in any given year is determined by the pattern and volume of productions of capital goods in the previous year. The rate of expansion of the basic industries, therefore, sets a limit to the rate of growth of the economy as a whole and might constitute a second limiting factor.

The possibility of planning to the proposed scale would depend on raising adequate financial resources which might constitute a third limiting factor.

The capacity to increase both production and the flow of service would depend on the rate at which technical personnel of the required type can be trained, lack of trained personnel might be a serious bottleneck. The rate at which training could be provided would thus constitute a fourth limiting factor.

Inadequate administrative machinery might form a fifth limiting factor. Mahalanobis was aware with these limiting factors. Any one of the five limiting factors could retard progress. But Mahalanobis was of the view that so far as plan making was concerned (as distinguished from plan implementation) all that could be demanded was internal consistency, valid technical reasoning, and correct appreciation of soical needs which his model had and there was no alternative plan which was more satisfactory to eliminate unemployment and poverty more quickly and more effectively and at the same time, lay the foundations for a continuing increase in the level of living in future. Therefore, he suggested to implement his model.

Initiating the debate on the Secnd Plan in the Lok Sabha in May 1956, Nehru returned to the theme of what planning meant. He said:

> The essence of planning is to find the best way to utilize all resources of manpower, of money, and so

> on... We want to arrive at stage when we can assess accurately what the next stage is going to be, visualize our problems in advance, and take appropriate action before events force our hands. That is, after all, the objective of planning... There is no other way but planning for an underdeveloped country like ours.

Nehru while speaking at the National Development Council in 1956, said about the long-term aspect of planning: "We can then see whether what the country does in the next five years fits in with our objective of ten or fifteen years hence. It is not enough merely to test it by some broad concept of socialism. It is most neccessary that we must have a clear idea of what we hope to achieve in fifteen years time. Then we can come to the shorter plans which must fit in with the broad general scheme, and then to the shortest plan, the One Year Plan or the Annual Plan, which must also fit in with the larger scheme. The five year plan should be a broad framework, subject to suitable changes, not only in keeping with our resources, but also of the ultimate long range picture that we may develop. It would be easier to adopt the shorter plan when we have the fifteen years objective before us."

No dubt, Nehru had in his mind about the fifteen year's objectives. The most important, of course, was the removal of mass poverty. It was not enough to increase the national income or the per capita income, it was also important to ensure minimum levels of living to the vast masses who were living under sub-standard levels.

V. NEHRU'S APPROACH ON FULL EMPLOYMENT (IN THE LIGHT OF THE SECOND FIVE YEAR PLAN)

For effecting economic planning, it was neccessary to ensure full employment and so employment figures with the largest frequency in all his speeches on planning and the plans.

Answering the question "What are our objectives", Nehru told the Lok Sabha in December 1954: We may define them in many ways, but perhaps one way which is more important than other is to find progressively fuller employment till we reach full employment through increased production.

Eariler in 1953, he had said, "Every modern economic theory today bases itself unlike the previous ones, on full employment in the country. We cannot produce employment by legislation. Our economic approach must be such that we reach the stage of full employment within a measurable period of time.

Reverting to the subject in his speech to the Lok Sabha in May 1956, he stressed the fact that full employment did not mean just giving some kind of occupation without reference to productivity.

That would be a completely wrong approach to this problems. Employment comes through newer and more effective means of wealth production. The whole experience of the past two hundred years shows that it comes with the growth of technological methods. It is true that technological growth often leads to human misery. But precautions can be taken. Do not imagine that minus technological progress we are going to deal with the problem of unemployment. Every country which boasts of full employment today is a country which is technologically advanced. Even country which is not technologically advanced has unemployment or under-employment. Therefore, if India is to advance, India must advance in science and technology and India must use the latest techniques, always keeping in view no doubt, that in doing so, the intervening period, which always occurs, must not cause unhappines or misery.

CONCLUSION

Nehru was always emphatic on science, technology and large scale industries as part of the strategy for promoting not only fuller but also more productive employment. Nehru was aware that industrialization and technology meant foreign aid. He was prepared to take it but he did not want it to continue indefinitely. On the contrary, he wanted the pattern of economic development to be such that dependence on foreign sources was terminated as early as possible.

He wanted the economy to become self-relient and develop within itself the seeds of self-acceleration. Hence, his emphasis on heavy industres, on iron and steel, on coal and oil, on chemical industries, and on technical education.

Nehru was thus all the time laying stress on production. But he was not unaware of the importance of distribution and of the larger social objective that lay behind all his enthusiasm for planning. He wanted equality of opportunity and he wanted substantial reduction in inequalities of income and wealth. Extension of the public sector, fiscal and other controls on large incomes, and vast extension of social services, these were part of the strategy he advocated for achieving the social objectives behind socio and economic development planning.

References

Ajit K. Sinha (2004), Wage Goods Model for India: A Viable Alternative, Great Indian Economists, Vol. 4, Dr. D.K. Das, Deep & Deep Publication, Pvt. Ltd., New Delhi.

Brahmananda, P.R., Jawaharlal Nehru: A Centennial Appraissl of an Economist, *Southern Economist*, Vol. 28, Numbers 13-14, Nov. 1-15, Bangalore.

C.N. Vakil and P.R. Brahmananda (1956), *Planning for an Expanding Economy*, Vora and Co, Bombay.

C.N. Vakil and P.R. Brahmananda (1978), *Investment Pattern of Second Five Year Plan, Poverty, Planning and Inflation*, Allied Publication Private Limited, Bombay, pp. 52-64.

C.N. Vakil and P.R. Brahmananda (1952), *Planning for a Shortage Economy, The Indian Experiment*, Vora and Co. Publishers Ltd., Bombay.

Mahesh, P. Bhatt (1996), Planned Progress or Planned Chaos? (Selected Prophetic Writing of Prof. B.R. Shenoy), East-West Books (Madras) Pvt. Ltd.

P.C. Mahalanobis (1963), *The Approach of Operational Research to Planning in India*, Asia Publishing House, Calcutta, pp. 7 and 143.

Sanjeev K. Mishra (1994), *Mahalanobis Approach to Planning in India*, Deep & Deep Publication, New Delhi.

Subodh K. Sinha (1994), Contribution of C.N. Vakil to Indian Economic Planning, Deep & Deep Publication, New Delhi.

V.K. R.V. Rao (2005), Nehru and Indian Planning, *Mainstream*, Vol. XLIII No. 47. pp. 13 to 16, New Delhi, Nov. 12.

15

An Assessment of Role of Economic Thoughts and Basic Philosophy of Jawaharlal Nehru over Growth and Development of India

DEBDAS GANGULY AND PANKAJ BASU

Though Nehru's early life was spent in England, he made a balance between industrial civilization and agricultural civilization—latter being the root of Indian culture. Nehru's economic policies and actions have been presented in the first section of the paper. Nehru had deep regard for socialism but when he applied it on the Indian soil on the Gandhian lines, it turned to something like a 'socialistic pattern of society' —a paraphrase used by Nehru himself. Nehru's blueprint of economic planning was based on democratic socialism. All these issues get reflected in this paper in a rather critical way.

I. INTRODUCTION

Many of the Indian nationalist thinkers and leaders rejected the doctrines of the English classical school, who emphasized welfare of the individual, personal profit motive, competition among producers and consumers. These leaders wanted the Government of India to take positive and constructive measures to help the process of agricultural and industrial development in the country. Those nationalist thinkers and leaders while believing in private enterprise, wanted at the same time the state or government to help Indian entrepreneurs in bringing about a transition of the country from agrarian to industrial economy.

Indian nationalist thinkers envisaged state's paternalistic role under the protection of which Indian private enterprise and capital were expected to emerge, develop, prosper and in course of time, bring about industrialization and economic development of a country.

The point to be noted, however, is that Indian nationalist thinkers and leaders while pleading for state interventions or role of the state in the economic activities of the people of the country were not at all thinking in term of socialism and its concomitant economic planning. They had in mind development of indigenous capitalism which they felt had been arrested because of the British rule over the country and unequal competition which agricultural India had to face with a highly industrial country like England.

In the background of such opinion and expectation, the economic thoughts and basic philosophy of Jawaharlal Nehru, the first Prime Minister of India after independence, had a significant role over the formulation of policies and principles of growth of new India.

Jawaharlal Nehru who was educated at Cambridge in England was highly influenced by the English ideas and institutions. He became a firm believer in personal freedom and democracy—ideals those he tried to establish in India when he assumed leadership of independent India.

Pandit Nehru visited Soviet Union in 1927. Karl Marx made a deep impression on him and he was prepared to accept some of the tenets of Marxism or communism. He was highly impressed by the achievements of Soviet Planning and Technique of rapid economic development through development of capital goods industries.

The Fabian society had a great impression on Nehru

and he accepted many of the tenets of Fabian socialism. Pandit Nehru accepted the Fabian tenet of gradual transformation of a capitalist society into a socialist society, collective ownership of basic and heavy industries, equitable distribution of income, wealth, and preparing the people through education and persuasion for gradual and peaceful transformation of capitalist economy into democratic socialism..

II. NEHRU'S BASIC PHILOSOPHY AND OUTLINE OF ECONOMIC THOUGHT

Since an individual is greatly influenced by the fundamental principles, which he holds dear to his heart, it requires knowing the basic philosophy or fundamental principles that motivated Pandit Nehru's policies and actions in the economic sphere. As a young man, Jawaharlal Nehru spent many years of his life in England and accordingly English values and institutions had a deep impact on him. He developed deep faith in individual freedom and democratic institutions. Pandit Nehru believed in peaceful and harmonious living both for every individual and for the society as a whole. He wanted to bring about development of every individual in society as that alone would enrich social life. For Pandit Nehru, welfare of all people in the community was of primary importance. He had deep faith in democracy and democratic process and institutions. Jawaharlal Nehru developed a systematic approach, combining good features or aspects from all possible solutions to a problem. According to him, India need the synthesis of the past and the present, of the old and new. In India, the march of industrial civilization cannot be resisted, though it is an attack against and an upheaval of so much that is old—that is agricultural civilization. He was fully aware of the deep roots of Indian civilization and culture and basic aspects of those. He was in favor of striking a balance between the two extremes.

Jawaharlal Nehru may be said to be one of the earliest nationalist leaders to advocate economic planning to bring about rapid economic development of the country and eradication of mass poverty.

As early as 1929, the Indian National Congress passed a resolution at his initiative to the effect that, "...in order to remove poverty and misery of Indian people and to ameliorate the condition of the masses, it is essential to make revolutionary changes in the present economic system of society and to remove gross inequalities."

As a result, mainly at the initiative of Pandit Nehru, a resolution was passed in 1931 at the Karachi session of Indian National Congress to the effect that, "...the state shall own or control key industries and services, mineral resources, railways, waterways, shipping and other measures of transport."

The National Planning Committee with Jawarharlal Nehru as Chairman was set-up in 1938 and thereby giving a decisive turn to his thinking on economic problems confronting the country.

In the very first note submitted to the National Planning Committee, Pandit Nehru pointed that, "although the Congress desired to support village and cottage industries, it was not against large scale industries. It was open for the National Planning Committee to take up the question of large scale industries in India." Pandit Nehru emphasized, "There can be no planning if such a planning does not include big industries."

According to Pandit Nehru, the state was to own or control basic and heavy industries with the possibility of extension of the public sector to some additional large-scale industries. It emphasizes that there was not to be nationalization of existing large-scale industries and in case circumstances necessitated their nationalization in particular individual cases, fair compensation to be paid to the private enterprise, which was to be taken over by the state. Cottage and small-scale industries were to be promoted and encouraged and as far as possible competition between large scale and small scale industries was to be prevented.

Pandit Nehru was never dogmatic, though he was wedded to the idea of socialistic pattern of society. He proclaimed that orthodox Marxism was out of date in modern world and orthodox communism was unsuitable to Indian conditions. Pandit Nehru, therefore, advocated and subsequently adopted The Middle Way in which private as well as public sector could exist and function side by side as a matter of principle. In this middle way, he tried to combine the virtues and advantages of capitalism and communism, avoiding at the same time, the disadvantages and evils of both the systems.

Pandit Nehru expressed his considered thinking on socialism in 1958 in the following words, "...The state is very powerful politically. If you were going to make it economically very powerful also, it would become a mere conglomeration of authority. I should, therefore, like decentralization of economic power. We cannot, of course, decentralize iron, steel, locomotives, and such other big industries, but you can have small units of industries as far as possible on cooperative basis with state control in a generai way.

Pandit Nehru thus emerged as not only a fervent advocate of economic planning in India but he also provided an ideological foundation and direction to India's Five Year Plans and helped to mould administrative and political institutions essential to execute five year plans.

It would be correct to say that Jawaharlal Nehru directed the course of economic planning in India during his tenure of Prime Ministership of the country.

After the end of the First Year Plan (1951-52 to 1955-56), Pandit Nehru strongly supported the approach of the Second Five Year Plan (1955-56 to 1960-61) based on approach of rapid economic development of the country through the strategy of development of capital goods industries. In this, Pandit Nehru was influenced by the rapid economic development brought about in erstwhile Soviet Russia by that strategy (i.e., economic development through development of capital goods industries, instead of development through development of consumer goods industries or through development of agricultural sector). Also Pandit Nehru understood the danger of dependence on other countries, especially on western countries in regard to essential goods like machinery, spare parts and defense goods and armaments. It was his desire to make India self-reliant in respect of essential goods and services that resulted in his advocacy of rapid industrialization of the country, especially development of basic and heavy industries. Pandit Nehru may be said to have laid the foundation of modern industrialization in India.

III. JAWAHARLAL NEHRU'S FAITH UPON SOCIALIZATION

Jawaharlal Nehru was a socialist and had a deep faith in democratic socialization and equitable distribution of income and wealth. He used to disclose that he was a socialist, and also republican and no believer in kings and princes.

Pandit Nehru may be said to be the first to introduce the ideal of socialism in Indian administrative system as the first Prime Minister of India. He believed that "The only key to the solutions of world's problems and India's problems lies in socialism, and when I use the term I do so not in vague humanitarian way but in scientific economic sense." For Pandit Nehru, socialism was something more than an economic system or doctrine; for him it was philosophy of life. He saw socialism as the only possible way or remedy for ending poverty and vast unemployment. Nehru believed not in revolutionary transformation of capitalistic society into a socialistic society as in the erstwhile Soviet Union but only by a gradual transformation of the former into the later. It was only education that would lay the firm foundation of a socialistic society; violence cannot be the basis of such a society.

Pandit Nehru was opposed to capitalism because, according to him, the system bred monopoly, violence, and concentration of wealth in a few hands making the basis of such society extremely unstable. He made it clear that it is not large-scale industry that brings any injustice and violence but misuse of large scale industries by private capitalists and financiers that were responsible for those serious evils. He maintained: though big machine is multiplying the power of a man exceedingly both for construction and destruction, it is possible to eliminate the evil use and violence of big machine by changing the economic structure of capitalism and replacing it by socialism with state or public ownership of big machines to be used not for private profits and gain but for increasing the welfare of society.

Jawaharlal Nehru emphasized, "Our economic programmes must be based on a human outlook and must not sacrifice men to money." He was empathatic that if workers in an industry or land have not enough to eat, then the intermediaries who deprive them of their full share must go and will have to go. He emphasized that that the least that every worker in field or factory is entitled to a minimum wage which will enable him to live in moderate comfort and human hours of labor which would not break his sprit and strength.

"Obviously, this cannot be attained unless we produce the wherewithal to have the standards that a good life implies. We have, therefore, to lay great stress on equality, on the removal of disparities and it has to be remembered that socialism is not the spreading out of poverty. The essential thing is that there must be wealth and production."

IV. JAWAHARLAL NEHRU AND ECONOMIC PLANNING

It was Pandit Jawaharlal Nehru, who made the concept of economic planning popular in India as a means to solve her various economic problems such as poverty and mass unemployment. It was mainly at his instance that the planning era commenced in India in 1950 and five year plans became an important part of economic strategy to deal with the country's socio-economic problems.

According to Pandit Nehru, there were many other obstacles—our social backwardness, customs and traditional outlook—but they had to be in any event faced. Pandit Nehru made it clear that economic planning thus was not so much for the present times as for an unascertained future. "...If we could collect the available material, coordinate it and draw up blueprints, we would prepare grounds for the real effective future planning. ...The attempt to plan and see the various activities—economic, social, cultural—fitting into each other, had also highly educative value for ourselves the general public."

Pandit Nehru declared that, "Planning in a large sense

is thus an integrated way of looking at the nation's manifold activities. ...In view of the fact that we function under a democratic set-up which we have deliberately adopted and enshrined in our constitution....any planning that we do must naturally be within that set-up."

V. CRITICAL ASSESSMENT OF PANDIT NEHRU'S CONTRIBUTION TO INDIAN ECONOMIC THOUGHT

Jawaharlal Nehru, as a longstanding leader of the Indian National Congress Party (which eventually came to power after India became independent) and as Prime Minister of the country for almost seventeen years from 1947 until his death in 1964, has left strong impact on India's economic policies.

It was Pandit Nehru who made the concept of socialism popular and widely acceptable in India and it was at his initiative that the objective of socialistic pattern of society as the main objective of India's economic policies and her five year plans came to be accepted.

Pandit Nehru's deep concern for the vast poor Indian masses came to influence India's economic policies. Pandit Nehru, being both a socialist and a democrat, his concept of 'democratic socialism' which come to be accepted as one of the group of India's economic policy, may truly be said to be his unique contribution to Indian economic thought.

It was Jawaharlal Nehru, who introduced economic planning in India and made democratic economic planning popular and an essential part of India's economic policy—whatever the political party in power and whatever the variations there might be in the objectives of such economic planning.

Being essentially a democrat with deep faith in democratic philosophy and democratic institutions, Pandit Nehru had great abhorrence for the highly centralized dictatorial type of economic planning of the Russian type as also the Soviet method of implementation of five year plans. Pandit Nehru believed in consensus approach to planning and people's participation in both the formulation and implementation of five year plans. Accordingly, he advocated democratic and decentralized type of economic planning.

Another contribution of great significance of Pandit Nehru was that with the Second Five Year Plan (1955-56 to 1960- 61), he laid the foundation of rapid induatrialization of the country so that within a quarter of a century after its independence, India became one of the highly industrialized countries of the world.

While emphasizing modern large-scale industries, Pandit Nehru laid special emphasis on the development of basic and heavy industries. This was because he had experienced the political pressure (especially by the United States and United Kingdom) brought on India during the days of difficulties when she was dependent upon them for defence materials, capital goods, spares and food grains. If India today is more or less self-reliant and self-sufficient in respect of production of defence goods, heavy and light engineering goods, spares and food grains a substantial amount of credit must go to Pandit Nehru's vision and steps.

Pandit Nehru's deep impact can also be seen in the expanding public sector in India. Pandit Nehru was opposed to private monopolies and prevailing extreme inequalities in the distribution of income and wealth. He, therefore, advocated that basic and heavy industries and public utilities as also big financial institutions should be in the public sector.

This shows that Pandit Nehru was a believer in democratic planning that is discussed and adopted by the representatives of the people and not in favor of totalitarian planning of the Russian type. According to Jawarharlal Nehru, "Planning consists essentially balancing between industry and agriculture, the balancing between heavy industry and light industry, the balancing between cottage industry and others. If one of these goes wrong, then the whole economy is upset. If you concentrate too much on industry, leaving agriculture, the country goes into difficulties."

At the time of the adoption of the First Five Year Plan, Pandit Nehru said, "This is the first attempt in India to integrate agricultural, industrial, social, economic and other aspects of the country. It is a very important step.... It has made people think of this country as a whole.

The above opinion of Pandit Nehru gives an idea as to how he looked on five year plan not only as instrument to remove the evils of unemployment and poverty, but also an important instrument that would make Indians from different parts of the country take interest in the economic progress of the country and thus bring about emotional unity in the country. He felt that five year plans or economic planning would be an effective instrument to integrate economics of different regions of the country and thus help bring about both economic and emotional unity, which is fundamental to the overall unity of the country like India.

Jawaharlal Nehru was aware that economic planning by itself was not going to solve all the problems; it was the objective or various objectives of planning as also effective implementation that mattered. According to Pandit Nehru, "The idea of planning and a planned society is accepted now in varying degrees by almost every one. However, planning by itself has little meaning and need not necessarily lead to good results. Everything depends upon the objectives of the plan and the controlling authority, as well as of course on the Government behind it. An attempt to preserve old established and vested interests cuts at the very root of planning. If planning is largely controlled by big industrialists it will be naturally envisaged within the framework of the system they are used to and will be essentially based on the profit motive of an acquisitive society."

Pandit Nehru was fully aware of the limitations of economic planning—it is the objective or direction into which planning takes the country that is of utmost significance.

VI. NEHRU ON INDUSTRIALIZATION, SCIENCE AND TECHNOLOGY

Jawarharlal Nehru was a fervent advocate of modern large-scale industries, especially development of basic and heavy industries. While he appreciated the importance of agriculture in the nation's economy, he at the same time, was in favor of rapid industrialization of India. He believed that only large-scale industrialization would be in a position to provide increasing employment opportunities to country's population and would help produce wealth in increasing qualities and thus help remove mass poverty. He believed that poverty in India cannot be removed without rapid industrialization. It is Pandit Nehru who laid the foundation of industrialization of the country.

Jawaharlal Nehru also favored industrialization and especially development of key and basic industries because he was keenly aware of the dangers of dependence on other country, especially western capitalist and imperialist countries for vital goods like defence equipments and industrial machinery and spare parts. Pandit Nehru, therefore, favored self-reliance both in respect of essential consumer goods like food grains and also in respect of all the vital industrial goods and services.

Regarding the relationship between industrialization and defence of a country, he was beyond the conventional view. According to him, defence in a country is being industrially prepared for producing goods and equipments of defence.

Jawaharlal Nehru was not against introducing large machineries if the machineries had taken care for creating instead of eliminating meaningful employment opportunities. According to him, "....Foolish comparisons are made between man-power and machine power; of course, a big machine can do the work of a thousand or ten thousand persons. But if those ten thousand persons sit idly by or starve, the introduction of that machine is not a social gain, except in the long perspective, which envisages a change in social conditions. It is a net gain both from the individual and national point of view to utilise man-power for production. There is no necessary conflict between this and introduction of machinery on a large scale, provided that machinery is used primarily for absorbing labor and not for creating unemployment." Thus, in the long-run Pandit Nehru saw no conflict in the introduction of big machineries and increasing employment opportunities for labor while countries where machineries are scarcely used are the countries with a vast amount of unemployment.

Jawaharlal Nehru declared, "I am a great admirer of

the achievements of modern civilization, of the growth and application of science and technology. Humanity has every reason to be proud of them." He was also of opinion, "Technical achievements of science are enough and its capacity to transform an economy of scarcity into an abundance is evident." According to Jawarharlal Nehru, the world problem can inevitably be solved through the means of science and not by discarding science.

Jawarharlal Nehru repeatedly emphasized importance of modern science in which the economic salvation of countries like India lies. He observed, "It was science alone that could solve problems of hunger and poverty, of insanitation and illiteracy, of superstitions and deadening customs and traditions of vast resources running to waste of a rich country inhabited by starving people." He was of the view that "a country can survive today if it has enough of scientific and technical personnel."

CONCLUSION

Pandit Nehru was a great admirer of modern science and technology. He aimed at modernization of traditional-based feudal Indian economy and society with the help of modern science and technology. Pandit Nehru advocated modernization of Indian agriculture (His one failure in this sector was in the sphere of large-scale cooperative farming which he persistently advocated.) and industries based on advance modern sciences and technology. To introduce modern technology and for advancement of various sciences, Pandit Nehru favored collaboration, provided such collaboration agreements were in India's interest and led to training of Indian personnel which subsequently were to substitute foreign technicians, scientists and experts.

According to Pandit Nehru, under capitalism with vast unemployment and economic insecurity for large number of people there is personal freedom in name only; for a person who is unemployed, freedom as a consumer and as a producer appear meaningless though capitalism formally guarantees such freedom to all citizens. According to Nehru, socialism guarantees to every individual the minimum essential standard of living, people have a better chance and opportunity to exercise their personal freedom.

India, after independence, is being transformed towards the vision and the direction provided by Jawarharlal Nehru. If there have been some shortcomings and failures, the fault is not entirely Pandit Nehru's who wanted to rebuild Indian economy in a democratic way and within the framework of the Indian Constitution adopted in 1950.

References

A Bunch of Old Letters, 1958.
Autobiography, 1936.
Glimpses of World History, 1934.
India and the World, 1936.
Soviet Russia, 1929.
Speeches (1949-53), 1954.
Speeches (1953-58), 1958.
The Discovery of India, 1946
The Unity of India, 1944.

16

Economic and Technological Co-operation with Resurgent Africa: An International Vision of Nehru

A.K. JHA, BHAVNA JHA AND GIRISH CHANDRA MISHRA

India's economic and technology co-operation with the developing world (South-South co-operation), especially the African continent is the essence of Nehru's foreign relations. If such co-operation is guaranteed, the world may see then the peaceful coexistence of all nations endowed with different socio-political systems and the state of economic conditions. Nehru highlighted "people-to-people" co-operation between India and Africa. Such collaboration was indeed Nehru's brainchild. From a modest journey during Nehru's tenure, today most of the African nations rest on India's shoulders as she cooperated, supported and assisted in diverse fields of political freedom, agriculture, industry, education, military, and what not. All these aspects have been accommodated in this paper.

I. FROM BANDUNG CONFERENCE (1955) TO BELGRADE SUMMIT (1961)

India's economic and technology cooperation programme with the developing world, notably with the countries of the African continent, has now taken a firm shape, earning worldwide acclaim. It should, however, not be forgotten that Prime Minister Jawaharlal Nehru was the architect of this programme, aware as he was of the similarities obtaining in Indian and Africian political, social and economic situations.

Circumstances were such that in most African countries the colonial powers, white settler elements, and transnationals had squeezed Africa dry in the literal sense of the word. This had kept millions of hapless Africans in unparalleled conditions of illiteracy, poverty and degradation. Indians had also suffered from the economic onslaughts of colonialism, but in historical perspective, it had a sound rural economic base comprising successful agriculture, cottage industries and economic base and elementary skills. In the nineteenth and twentieth centuries, some Indian entrepreneurs had set-up a few medium and large industries, (steel, textiles, sugar, cement and paper, in particular) although borrowing heavily from British technology. Education had also made some headway in pre-independence India. On the eve of its independence, India had about 30 universities, some medical and engineering colleges and thousands of primary, secondary and post-secondary educational institutions all over the country. India was, thus in a slightly advantageous position than the countries of Africa.

While India was actively assisting the process of decolonization in Africa and was watching with great interest the emergence of new countries in the fifties and the sixties, Nehru kept on emphasizing that India's friendly relations with the neighboring continent of Africa could be and should be strengthened through economic and technical cooperation. Even at that time Nehru realized that economic co-operation among the developing countries was a must for the gigantic effort to overcome poverty, hunger and underdevelopment. He was an advocate of North-South cooperation, but he felt that economic self-reliance, meaning thereby South-South cooperation, was more important for the developing world.

Political independence is no doubt important, but it is well recognized that economic strength is a must to safeguard that independence. Gandhiji and Nehru always emphasized that freedom did not connote mere political independence, but must be accompanied by an economic base. Economic independence was also looked upon as an essential precondition for the success of an independent foreign policy.

Even in his famous speech of September 7, 1946, Nehru took pains to reiterate that India proposed to achieve independence in action both in "our domestic affairs and our foreign relations." He added: "We shall take part in international conference as a free nation with our own policy and not merely as satellite of another nation. We hope to develop close and direct contracts with other nations and to cooperate with them in the furtherance of world peace and freedom."

Cooperation in all fields was a favorable exercise with Nehru and this could be possible only among independent nations. In the early years of Indian independence, Nehru was yet to evolve a clear vision of the structure of such cooperation but, he said in a speech in the Constituent Assembly, this could be entirely within the scope of the Charter of the United Nations. Even his note on a "Foreign Policy of India", written in 1927, speaks of the similarities of the problems faced by Indian and other colonial countries, and suggests that "it must be to the advantage of both of us to know more of each other and to cooperate wherever possible."

At the 1955 Asian-Africian Bandung Conference, Nehru and other participants took time off from political matters to talk of economic development and cooperation. In his speech, Nehru said:

> "All of us are passionately eager to advance our countries peacefully. We have been backward. We have been left behind in the race, and now we have a chance again to make good. We have to make."

The final communiqué of the Bandung Conference marked an important milestone in the ongoing movement of fruitful economic cooperation between the developing countries of Asia and Africa. Spelling out the strategy and the policy framework to govern such mutually beneficial cooperation, the document says: "The Asian-African Conference recognized the urgency of promoting economic development in the Asian-African region. There was general desire for economic cooperation among the participating countries on the basis of mutual interest and respect for national sovereignty. The proposals with regard to economic cooperation within the participating countries did not preclude either the desirability or the need for cooperation with countries outside the region, including the investment of foreign capital. It was further recognized that assistance being received by certain participating countries from outside the region through international or under bilateral arrangements had made a valuable contribution to the implementation of their development programmes. The participating countries also agreed to provide technical assistance to one another to the maximum extent practicable, in the form of experts, trainees, pilot projects and equipment for demonstration purposes, exchange of know-how and establishment of national and, where possible, regional training and research institutes for imparting technical knowledge and skills in cooperation with the existing international agencies."

The Asian-African Conference recommended: "The early establishment of a special United Nations fund for economic development; the allocation by the International Bank for Reconstruction and Development of a greater part of its resources to Asian-African countries; the early establishment of an international finance corporation which should include in its activities the undertaking of equity investment; and encouragement of the promption of joint ventures among Asian-African countries in so far as this will promote their common interest." The Asian-African Conference recognized the vital need for stabilizing commodity trade in the region.

The Asian-African Conference also recommended that collective action be taken by participating counties for stabilizing international prices of and demand for primary commodities through bilateral and multilateral arrangement, and that as far as practicable and desirable they should adopt a unified approach on the subject in the United Nations permanent advisory commission on international commodity trade and other international forums. The Asian-African Conference attached considerable importance to shipping and expressed concern that shipping lines revised from time to time their freight rates, which were often to the detriment of participating countries; it recommended a study of this problem and collective action thereafter to induce the shipping lines to adopt a more reasonable attitude. It was further suggested that a study of railway freight of transit trade may be made.

The first non-aligned summit in Belgrade in 1961 picked up the threads. Although politics continued to dominate the sessions, the anxiety to promote greater economic cooperation among the countries of the developing world received ample expression. Stating that freedom was essential for building up their societies, Nehru wanted the delegates to devote more attention to the problems of economic and social development and sought the cooperation of the developed countries also. "It is right and proper that the affluent countries should help in this process. They have to some extent done so. I think they should do more in this respect but ultimately the burden will lie on the people of the countries themselves." Nehru was obviously referring to the need for North-South and South-South cooperation concepts which have received greater currency lately. Taking the cue from Nehru, the final declaration of the Belgrade summit spoke of active international cooperation in the field of material and cultural exchanges among peoples as an essential means of strengthening of confidence in the possibility of peaceful co-existence among states with different social systems:

The participants in the conference consider that efforts should be made to remove economic imbalance inherited from colonialism and imperialism. They consider it necessary to close, through accelerated economic, industrial and agricultural development, the ever-widening gap in the standards of living between the few economically advanced countries and the many economically less-developed countries. The participants in the conference recommend the immediate establishment and operation of a United Nations Capital Development Fund. They further agree to demand just terms of trade for the economically less-developed countries and in particular, constructive efforts to eliminate the excessive fluctuations in primary commodity trade and the restrictive measures and practices which adversely affect the trade and revenues of the newly developing countries. In general, to demand that the fruits of the scientific and technological revolution be applied in all fields of economic development to hasten the achievement of international social justice.

The participating countries invite all the countries in the course of development to cooperate effectively in the economic and commercial fields so as to face the policies of pressure in the economic sphere, as well as the harmful results which may be created by the economic blocs of the industrial countries. They invite all the countries concerned to consider to convene, as soon as possible, an international conference to discuss their common problems and to reach an agreement on the ways and means of repelling all damages which may hinder their development; and to discuss and agree upon the most effective measures to ensure the realization of their economic and social development.

The countries participating in the conference declare that the recipient countries must be free to determine the use of the economic and technical assistance which they receive, and to draw up their own plans and assign priorities in accordance with their needs.

It was during Nehru's time that the developing countries organised themselves into an operational force for multilateral negotiations on economic issues with the creation of the Group of 77 in 1964. This Group expressed strong support for cooperation among the developing countries. It also enhanced their negotiating power with the developed countries. No wonder, in the post-Nehru period, the Group of 77 came to be recognized as the authentic voice of the poor and depressed. They represented three-fourths of world's humanity.

II. PEOPLE TO PEOPLE CO-OPERATION

After the attainment of India's independence while Nehru was helping to hasten the process of decolonization in Africa, he was trying to promote in a modest way the economic stability of the continent. With its limited resources, whatever little contribution India could make or is making towards the well-being of Africa stemmed from Nehru's genuine desire to strengthen the roots of their hard-won independence. In looking at India's economic assistance, Nehru's fundamental approach was that India desired to appear as a friend and ally and not as an exploiter. Nehru was eager to share and exchange knowledge and experience. He had no desire to take part in what Julius Nyerere described as "second scramble for Africa."

Both for India and for the other developing countries, especially in Africa, Nehru prescribed the evolution of their own models of economic development. There could be no wholesale import of such models from the West. Each developing country must look into its own national conditions, genius and ethos. He would have unhesitatingly endorsed the latter day observation of Nyerere.

When we ask for technical assistance we are almost always offered very high-powered expert advisers with the very reasonable condition that we should provide a "counterpart who will absorb the wisdom made available to us. The trouble is that we do not desperately need exceptionally clever people, save in very rare and special cases. What we do need very badly are practical people who know their job and who will come and work with our people while they train them, and who are willing to take executive responsibility under the direction and control of our government where necessary. The world-renowned expert is often an embarrassment to us."

It was to encourage this type of "people to people" cooperation that the Nehru Government started sending small numbers of teachers, doctors, engineers and other professionals to Africa. He was against their living in ivory towers and always impressed on them to mix the people and be part of them.

It was Nehru's foresight that what Africa needed most urgently was trained and educated manpower. He was aware that educational facilities in most African countries were meagre and they would not be able to build a trained, technical and bureaucratic infrastructure with their limited resources and training facilities. Soon after the independence, Jomo Kenyatta, in his role as the leader of his people, approached Nehru with a request for providing facilities for education and technical training to students from Kenya. Nehru had no hesitation in responding to this request. He did not waste a minute in drawing up a schedule of such training, though in a modest way. African students from Kenya and later from other countries started coming to India for studies in medicine, engineering, law and liberal arts. Nehru was happy that by mid-fifties India had trained a few dozen Africian students who, on returning home, began rendering yeoman service. Apart from holding important bureaucratic positions, African graduates who had studied in India, began occupying important political positions. In late fifties, there were as many as seven India-trained scholars who were members of the Kenyan Parliament, while at one time five Indian-trained African "boys" were members of the Hastings Banda Government in Nyasaland (Malawi).

Nehru spoke proudly of this at a Press Conference in London in 1953: "We have nearly a hundred Government of India scholars from Africa in India and the number is likely to increase. Their hunger for education is tremendous. Thousands and thousands of schools are being started in East Africa from the pennies of other people. Whether the schools are good or bad is immaterial, but it shows their hunger for education."

It was in Nehru's knowledge that due to racial discrimination, the Indians in South Africa did not get enough facilities for higher education. He, therefore, paid special attention to the educational needs of Indian students coming from South Africa. In East Africa, there were medical and engineering colleges for Indian students.

There was one interesting development which clearly showed the deep and abiding interest Nehru evinced in ensuring the welfare of the African students. He desired that

African students, especially those joining Indian medical and engineering colleges, did not have to pay heavy capitation fees which were in vogue in a number of Indian States. Nehru also did not relish the idea of the Madras Medical College charging tuition fees at the normal rates for students from Africa. He wrote a special letter to the Chief Minister of Indian States on April 4, 1948.

Jawaharlal Nehru's lasting contribution, not only to India but also to all developing countries in the world, is the instrument of planning for economic development. Indian planning took an overall view of the needs of the country so as to bring about a balanced development, which would ensure a rising national income and a steady improvement in the living standards over a period of time. Since in the early fifties India was importing food grains on a large scale and this brought about inflationary pressures on the economy, Nehru accorded the highest priority to food and agriculture, including irrigation and power project in Indian planning.

Whenever the Indian Prime Minister met any African leader, Nasser, Nkrumah, Emperor Haile Selassie, or even some visiting African ministers and officials, he would lecture them at length on the beneficial aspects of planning. He would suggest to the African leaders to send their experts to India so that they could study Indian planning in detail. He even offered to send Indian planning experts to their countries. Nehru also urged the African leaders to accord to highest priority to agriculture in their respective plans.

Nehru told the visiting Prime Minister of Somalia, Dr. Abdirashid Ali Shermarke, on August 12, 1963, the story of India's programme of planned development and his desire to cooperate with the country of Africa. He said:

> "Ever since our freedom, we ourselves are engaged in the big adventure of building up a new India. Not wholly new, because we are very old and we value our past and cherish it. Nevertheless, we have to put on a new garb, understand the new world and function in it, the world of science which brings with it opportunities of development, of welfare for all our people, because ultimately freedom means for the people not only political freedom but economic freedom."

We are engaged in this task of developing India and trying to give the fruits of freedom to hundreds of millions of our people. It is a tremendous and very difficult task, but I think we have made good to some extent, laid the foundations for it, and we have every hope and belief that we will go along this path progressively, succeeding in our endeavors. I have every hope and belief also that the countries of Africa too will develop and increase the welfare of their people.....We believe in each country developing according to its own light and genius, But because there are common problems, there can be a great deal of cooperation and help and we believe that this will take place. At any rate, so far as we are concerned, we shall certainly endeavor to the best of our abilities to cooperate with the countries of Africa and your country, Mr. Prime Minister, and give it such cooperation and help as may be beneficial to both countries—yours and ours.

Economic cooperation with the developing countries was for Nehru not merely a policy but a firm commitment. It was because of this that India had been playing a prominent role in sponsoring economic cooperation as an integral programme among the nonaligned countries and in the Group of 77. Finding the response from Africa positive, economic cooperation with Africa during the Nehru era became a strong underlying theme with India in its relations with that continent.

III. THE TRINITY OF INDO-AFRICAN CO-OPERATION

In concrete terms, India under Nehru's leadership, conceived economic cooperation with the countries of Africa in a broad three-tier set-up—balanced trade, technical assistance, and joint ventures. Barring a few countries like Egypt, Sudan, Ethiopia and of the sixties, India's economic cooperation programme could not take a firm shape with the rest of the continent in his life time.

The basis of fruitful cooperation is, of course, exchange of commodities. International trade thus plays a vital role in getting together countries geographically apart and creating in them a sense of belonging.

The mutuality of interest generated by close and increasing trade exchanges tends to influence countries to work in cooperation in other fields as well. For confining the exchanges between independent countries to the field of trade alone may prove unequal at times. If, however, on this foundation the growing super-structure of technical assistance and join collaboration is also built up, what results is an integrated pattern of relationship, strong enough to sustain short-term strains, and yet dynamic enough to propel an ever-widening area of close inter-dependence, a feeling of partnership. That is what India is trying to achieve with the friendly countries of Africa. Signing of trade agreements with a number of African countries bears testimony to the desire of mutual cooperation. The dimension of commercial exchanges between India and Africa is steadily widening, although it started in a modest way. India started as an exporter of old traditional items; but in the later years Africa had been importing from India sophisticated manufactured goods also. Today, India imports from Africa are limited in numbers and quantity and are mainly precious and semi-precious stones, phosphates, copper, raw cashew and edible oil. All these are crucial items and any reduction in their imports is likely to cause a slow-down in India's major trading partners—the English and Arabic-speaking countries of Africa. It is a cause for concern to India that its trade with the Francophone countries is almost negligible. It is rather odd that while Indian ships have been sailing in the Indian Ocean for centuries together, the present shipping facilities between India and Africa are rather inadequate.

All the initiatives taken by Nehru to promote trade exchanges between India and the African countries did result in their gradual increase. A booklet issued in 1960 by the federation of the Indian Chambers of Commerce and Industry, New Delhi, pointed out that out of the total imports of India in 1960 amounting to Rs. 10,000 million, the share of the countries of the Afro-Asian region amounted to Rs. 2,795 million, nearly 28 per cent. The percentage share of the African countries was 7.5. As far as India's exports were concerned, of the total value of Rs. 6,370 million in 1960, the off-take of the African countries amounted to Rs. 1,731 million about 27 per cent.

While trade is recognized as an important link in the economic cooperation programme, India also recognizes the need for cooperation with the friendly countries in the matter of setting up joint ventures and sponsoring of mutual collaboration. During Nehru's time, the policy framework and scope for such ventures had been formalized; but most of the join ventures in Africa, now numbering over a hundred, came up during the post-Nehru period.

The most prominent joint venture that came up during his time was textile mill in Addis Ababa in 1959. It was collaboration between the Birla group and the Ethiopian Government. The Ethiopian Government owned 51 per cent of the shares, while the remainder went to the Birlas and to some private Ethiopian citizens. The textile mill made sound contribution towards the needs of the Ethiopian masses, but after the downfall of the Emperor in a military coup in 1974, the socialist government nationalized it.

Undoubtedly, joint ventures have played a major role in stepping up two way cooperation, thus, to some extent, paving the way for the much desired self-reliant industrial development. Africans are now beginning to realize and accept that economic and technical cooperation among developing countries (ECDC and TCDC) is an extremely beneficial way of boosting economic development, for it provides an opportunity of transfer and assimilation of modern technology best suited to the needs and genius of the developing countries.

In the ultimate analysis, India is largely motivated by the desire to share its experiences of development. Significantly, therefore, the scope for overseas ventures is slowly but steadily expanding. Some of these projects are even on turnkey basis.

As early as in 1948, when India was still feeling the birth pangs of freedom, it instituted a modest programme of scholarships for African boys and girls to study in India. Since then thousands have come and gone and are still pursuing studies in Indian's centers of higher learning.

The need for Indian technical and professional personnel in Africa and to train African personnel in India led to the establishment of the Indian Technical and

Economic Cooperation (ITEC) programme with a view to sharing India's technical experience with the developing countries. The thrust of this programme has been in the African continent.

The main forms of technical assistance are providing training in India, deploying experts abroad for short or long-term period, undertaking feasibility and techno-economic studies, organizing technical workshops and supply of equipment. The field of cooperation is extensive.

Training facilities have been provided in such diverse field as development of water resources, foreign trade promotion, rural development, small-scale industries, standardization, journalism, veterinary science, railways, constitutional and parliamentary studies, etc. The Indian experts have been in the field of medicine, civil engineering, architecture, geology, agriculture, transportation, animal husbandry and telecommunication. Equipment supplied has been mainly in the areas of scientific laboratories, agriculture and engineering. Assistance in setting up of industrial estates and technical training institutes has been warmly welcomed by many in African countries, especially Tanzania, Kenya and Mauritius.

The ITEC programme is multi-dimensional and covers a large number of countries. It is a major programme today, constituting a considerable portion of what has come to be known as India's economic diplomacy. It has been observed that lately assistance to Africa in the field of food and agriculture occupies a lot of attention of the Indian authorities handling ITEC programme. This is what Nehru wanted it to be and what Africa needs.

The spectacular growth of small-scale industries in India has attracted world wide attention. The expertise India has developed is being sought by African countries where the growth of small industries is crucial. National Small Industries Corporation of India is, therefore, playing a stellar role in many African countries. The work of TITES and IRCON in developing African railways is a post-Nehru phase. India is also in co-operation with the UN Economic Commission for Africa and African Development Bank in promoting the continent's growth.

Besides the ITEC programme, India also participates in other programmes of cooperation such as the Colombo Plan and the Special Commonwealth African Assistance Plan. Under the Colombo Plan India has so far provided technical assistance by way of training places and making available the services of experts to various member-countries, a number of them from Africa.

The Commonwealth African Plan, in the formation of which Nehru took a keen interest, was inaugurated in 1963. It provides for training places and deputation of experts to Ghana, Nigeria, Sierra Leon, Gambia, Kenya, Tanzania, Malawi, Zambia, Zimbabwe, Uganda and Mauritius.

India also introduced a general Cultural Scholarship Scheme in 1949, under which more than 400 scholarship have been awarded annually to nationals of African countries, including those from South Africa and Namibia, for post-matriculation studies in arts, humanities and science. There is hardly any field of study in which African students are not to be found.

Thousand of African students also pay their way for education in India's places of learning, because they find education in India economical, while being eminently suited to the needs of their respective countries. A number of African governments also provide scholarships to their nationals for studies in India. An estimated 25,000 African students are in colleges and universities all over India, the bulk of them coming from Mauritius, Kenya, Tanzania, Zambia, Ethiopia, Sudan and Nigeria. New Delhi, Chandigarh, Lucknow, Aligarh, Pune, Bombay, Kolkata, Hyderabad, Bangaluru and Chennai are Indian cities preferred by self-financing African students. It is common knowledge that many students from Africa have returned home disappointed because they fail to get placement.

In the early fifties, when India's programme for economic cooperation was taking under Nehru's guidance, there were just about three independent African countries, namely, Egypt, Ethiopia and Liberia. In view of India's old friendly ties with Ethiopia and Egypt, it was but natural that these two countries received greater attention under this programme.

Emperor Haile Selassie of Ethiopia, who always acknowledges India's support for the freedom of Ethiopia from Italian colonial rule, had great regard and respect for Jawaharlal Nahru. A very little known fact is that in 1951 the Ethiopian Emperor sent to India an aid of 500 tonnes of wheat, when India was facing acute food shortage. It is somewhat tragic that this one time donor of food to India, Ethiopia was compelled to receive large food aid from India during the worst famine of its history in the eighties.

Among the Indian settlers in various African countries, it was those in Ethiopia who were the first to respond to Nehru's advice that they should identify themselves with the interests of the people of the land of their domicile. Nehru was very happy to learn that the Indian community in Addis Ababa had risen about Rs. 350,000 for the setting up of a hospital in the Ethiopian capital while the Indian Mission laid the foundation stone of this building, the Government of India also made a token grant towards this project.

The Ethiopian Monarch was keen to cooperate with India in as many fields as possible, one such was in the field of agriculture. Under a scheme formulated by the Ethiopian Government for the permanent settlement of Indian peasant families reached Ethiopia, the first batch of eight Indian peasant families reached Ethiopia in October 1953. The Ethiopian Government had allotted about 96 acres of land per family and also gave them some facilities. Some more farmers followed, but not much was heard of the scheme in later years.

A team of seven Indian experts were sent to Ethiopia to help the country in implementing its community development scheme that was akin to India's. Ethiopian officers also came to India in 1960 to be trained in this field.

The state visit of the Ethiopian Emperor to India in October 1956 brought the two countries closer to each other. In a joint statement Emperor Haile Selassie and Prime Minister Nehru reaffirmed their opposition to colonialism and racialism. They expressed the resolve of the two countries to strengthen their friendship by promoting economic and cultural ties. During his visit to India, the Emperor made several donations to India in situations and funds including the Prime Minister's Flood Relief Fund. The Emperor expressed his desire to recruit Indian technical personnel and more teachers for Ethiopian schools. Indian teachers in the rural areas of Ethiopia are loved and respected even today.

A major offshoot of the Emperor's visit was close collaboration between the two countries in the field of defence. Ethiopia had sought India's assistance in the establishment of a military academy in Harare. An Indian was made the Commandant of the Academy when the Emperor inaugurated in October 1958. India's Chief of Army Staff General K.S. Thimayya was a special invitee at the first graduation ceremony of the Academy in October 1960. Meanwhile, Ethiopian police officers and naval cadets started coming to India for training. From 1957 onwards, a number of Ethiopian defence service delegations came to India for an on-the-spot study of the various training establishments.

The new Egyptain military leadership was keen on cooperating with India in various fields but it attached special importance to cooperation in military training. At India's invitation, an Egyptian military mission paid visits to important Indain training establishments and military installations in January 1954.

Prime Minister Gamal Abdul Nasser's visit to India in 1955 and two visits by Nehru to Egypt around that time, paved the way for closer relations between the two countries. A Treaty of Friendship was signed at Cairo on April 6, 1955. The Treaty *inter alia* provided for the conduct of commercial and industrial relations as well as those pertaining to customs, navigation, civil aviation, and cultural affairs.

There was emphasis on cooperation in industrial and agricultural field. An officer of the Planning Commission of Egypt visited India and studied the working of the Planning Commission and the implementation of India's five year plans. Students from Egypt started coming to Indian educational institutions.

A cultural agreement was signed between India and the United Arab Republic (merger of Syria and Egypt) in September 1958. This envisaged exchange of teachers, a ward of scholarships and training of each other's nationals in scientific, technical and industrial institutions.

India maintained a contingent of the UN Emergency Force in Gaza for many years. Later, General P.S. Gyani of India was appointed Commander of the UN Force in Gaza. Nehru paid a visit to Gaza in 1960 and met the Indian contingent.

The exchange of military delegations between the two countries led to India participating in the Military Training Programmes in Egypt. A team of Indian Air Force officers was training Egyptian officers and cadets in their Air Force Academy in the late fifties.

An agreement for collaboration in the manufacture of supersonic Mach II Combat Aircraft was signed in 1964. UAR was to assist in developing the engine, while India had been developing the airframe. The agreement aimed at "marrying the two into an advanced fighting machine."

There had been exchange of visits by nuclear scientists of the two countries. In September 1962, India and the UAR concluded an agreement for cooperation in the development of atomic energy for peaceful purposes. The agreement covered exchange of unclassified information and documents, exchange of facilities for the purchase of nuclear material and equipment required by either country, or the training of UAR scientists in India. Economic cooperation between India and Sudan had a promising start during Jawaharlal Nehru's life time. Of all the African countries, Sudan had perhaps the maximum number of Indian experts working in different departments in the initial phase of post-independent Sudan's history. As Sudan was nearly to its independence, an Agro-Egyptian agreement provided for the establishment of an international election commission of seven members with an Indian chairman. At the invitation of the British and Egypt Government, India's Chief Election Commissioner Sukumar Sen was sent in 1953 to head the Commission. The work of the Commission came in for commendations from all shades of opinion in Sudan. As a self-governing territory, Sudan sought in 1954 the services of Indian judicial and other officers to assist the government. The Indian community in Sudan offers two scholarships to Sudanese students for study in India. With Sudan becoming a sovereign republic on January 1, 1956, and with the conclusion of Prime Minister

Ismail El Azhari's visit to India, the programme of economic cooperation between the two countries as well as to recruit a number of technical and judicial personnel and teachers for service in Sudan. Eight Sudanese students joined the Aligarh Muslim University.

Sudan was one of the three African countries ever visited by Jawaharlal Nehru as Prime Minister of India, the other two being Egypt and Nigeria. This visit in 1957 and the discussions Nehru had with the Sudanese leaders helped to strengthen the economic ties with Sudan. India's top irrigation engineer Dr. A.N. Khosla, who was then the Vice-Chancellor of Roorkee University, was sent to Sudan to advise the government on the proper utilization of the water of the Nile. The Deputy Prime Minister of Sudan, Mirghani Hamza, was one of the distinguished invitees at the inauguration of the Atomic reactor in Trombay by Nehru. India offered a credit of Rs. 50 million to Sudan to help buy Indian engineering goods, industrial machinery, chemicals and pharmaceuticals, and other products. During the state visit of President Farik Ibrahim Abboud to India in May 1964 Nehru told the visiting Sudanese leader that India would be happy to give Sudan technical aid to start new industries and referred to the possibilities of India buying more Sudanese cotton.

Ghana got her independence nearly a year after Sudan. It became the first African member of the Commonwealth. Nehru hailed it as an event of great significance in resurgent Africa. From the birth of Ghana, India took upon itself the responsibility to provide economic and technical cooperation. An Indian financial expert who helped Ghana was admitted to the civil engineering course at the University of Roorkee. An exhibition of Indian industries was held in Accra in April 1956. An adviser on industrial development was sent to Ghana, while a number of Ghanaian Ministry came to India in its first year of independence. Prime Minister Kwame Nkrumah paid an official visit to India in December 1958. This helped further strengthen the close and friendly relations between the two countries. In 1958, Ghana approached India to assist in securing the services of engineers, doctors, architects, geologists, agricultural experts, material engineers, work superintendents, and science teachers. Twenty of such professionals were sent to Ghana in 1959.

Nigeria became independent on October 1, 1960. India sent a high-powered delegation led by the then Law Minister, A.L.K. Sen to participate in the celebration. India's economic cooperation programme with this important country of Africa started even before it became free. India's assistance in technical field was considerably expanded in the post-independence are with the loan of services of a large number of trained personnel from India. Cooperation was also extended in the military field. A Nigerian economic mission led by the country's Ministry of Finance visited India in June 1961 to benefit from India's experience in planning and also to seek increase trade with India. After visiting industrial establishments and research institutions in India, the mission identified a number of fields where it needed India's help in training the necessary manpower. Oil was on the top of its agenda, because Nigeria had just then struck rich deposits of oil. Agriculture, including irrigation, and railways were the other fields in which Nigeria wanted to benefit from India's experience. From 1962 onwards India helped to streamline Nigerian Airways. An Indian was made its general manager. Six captains, six senior pilots, one chief planning engineer and one chief inspector were recruited from India on a three-year contract to train Nigerians to man their airways.

Indo-Nigerian cooperation in the sphere of defence took shape during Nehru's time. India helped to set-up its Defence Academy by lending the services of eight senior officers. Fourteen Indian naval officers belonging to different branches were also sent to Nigeria to assist in the development of the Nigerian Navy. Some Nigerian naval officers came for training at Cochin. Prime Minister Nehru's visit to Nigeria in September 1962 could be taken as the high watermark of the growth Indo-Nigerian cooperation. The discussions brought out of the desire of the two countries to further expand cooperation between them. It was then proposed in Lagos that about 500 Indian defense services personnel would be employed in the service of Nigeria for reorganizing Nigerian defence services. A majority of them would be engaged in creating a nucleus of the Nigerian Air

Force and the remainder would serve the navy and army. Nigeria also needed Indian technical experts in the field of economic planning and education.

With the east African countries of Kenya, Uganda and Tanganyika, India has had flourishing exchanges from very early times. A part from trade this included professionals from India going to these countries to assist them, and students from these countries coming to India for higher studies. After independence of these countries in the early sixties, economic cooperation with India received a boost. Indian assistance in the reorganization of the East African Airways was notable.

Prime Minister encouraged a high-powered Indian industrialists' delegation to visit Ethiopia, Ghana, Kenya, Malawi, Nigeria, Zambia, the Sudan, Tanganyika and Uganda. Nehru's hope in the utility of such a visit was fully vindicated in the report submitted by the delegation to the Government of India in November 1954. The report enthusiastically noted that Indian businessmen could "purposefully collaborate and cooperate" in setting up joint industries in Africa. Emphasizing that the setting up of industries in Africa could be regarded as one of the tests of our domestic economic strength, the delegation suggested the creation of an appropriate agency for cooperation with African countries. The report referred to the possibility of setting up joint industrial ventures in different countries in such field as cotton textiles, sugar, cement, jute, and light engineering products. The report stressed: "The general investment climate in Africa is favorable and the facilities offered are reasonable." But it suggests that the Indian efforts that had to be made must match with the offers being received by these countries from other sources. "Indian machinery and capital equipment which is the main basis of our capital participation, has to be supplied on a competitive basis."

The report was appreciated by the Government of India and as a result, the future years saw the establishment of a large number of joint ventures in a number of African countries by countries like Pakistan and China. Today there are over hundred joint ventures in production, and several more on the anvil. The important countries which have cooperated with India in this field are Kenya, Mauritius, Nigeria, Tanzania and Zambia.

India's programme of economic and technical cooperation with the African countries is undoubtedly Nehru's brainchild. It certainly is a modest one. And, yet, as Nehru was never tired of pointing out it has vast scope for expansion. Given the fact that tremendous amount of political goodwill and understanding exists between the peoples and governments of India and Africa, it is but natural that the ideas of cooperation among developing countries and collective self-reliance, as ordained by non-alignment, are gaining firm ground. At the same time, denied adequate economic and financial backing by the developed countries, the developing countries are left with no option but to inculcate the spirit of partnership among themselves.

African countries are now getting to know the fact of India's experience in developing its own resources. The idea of sharing this experience has, in fact, become a two-way traffic. Sharing of experience in reality means pooling together of resources, know-how, production methods and markets. The complementarities in the economies of India and the countries of Africa assume a great relevance in this context.

It is well understood that this self-reliant approach is bound to open up a promising vista for the bulk of humanity living in Africa and India. This might not happen overnight, but constraints and bottlenecks disappear when there is a will on both sides to cooperate.

CONCLUSION

It is now axiomatic that interdependence is an economic compulsion and that for it to be acceptable, it has to be based on equality and free will. The UN Economic Commission for Africa had rightly pointed out: "South-South cooperation is being undertaken in a spirit of understanding and dignity, wholesomely devoid of the traditional dependence of the donor and recipient psychology of colonial relationship."

Nehru was a tireless advocate of economic cooperation on terms of equality between nations. His critics, particularly from the Western countries, had sought to dub his efforts of promoting international cooperation as veiled forms of Indian imperialism; fortunately, no African country was taken in by this. Constituting one-half of the non-aligned world, the African countries committed to promote cooperation among developing countries, do not see anything adverse in grasping the hand of mutual cooperation extended by India.

References

The Discovery of India (Calcutta: Signet Press, 1946) The Unity of India, Collected Writings, 1934-40, London: Lindsay Drummond, 1948).

Independence and After (Delhi: Ministry of Information and Broadcasting, Publications Division, 1949).

Speeches, September 1946 to May 1964 (Delhi: Government of India, Publications Division)

H.Y. Sharada Prasad and B. Nanda, *Selected Works of Jawaharlal Nehru* (First Series), Vols. 1-15, ed. M. Chalapathi Rau (Delhi: Orient Longman and NMML, 1972).

H.Y. Sharada Prasad and B. Nanda, *Selected Works of Jawaharlal Nehru* (Second Series), Vols 1-15, ed. M. Chalapathi Rau (Delhi: Orient Longman and NMML, 1984).

Asaf Ali, Aruna, *Private Face of a Public Person* (Delhi: NMML 1989).

Bhatia, Prem, *Indian Ordeal in Africa* (Delhi: Vikas, 1973)

Haksar, P.N. (ed.), *Nehru's Vision: Peace and Security in the Nuclear Age* (Delhi: Patriot Publishers, 1987).

Karanjia, R.K., *The Mind of Mr. Nehru* (London: Allen and Unwin, 1960).

Nand, B.R. (ed.), *Indian Foreign Policy: The Nehru Years* (Delhi: Vikas, 1976).

Yunus, Muhammad, *Persons, Passions and Politics* (Delhi: Vikas, 1980).

Zakaria, Rafiq (ed.), *A Study of Nehru* (Bombay: Times of India Publications, 1959).

Report of the Ministry of External Affairs, New Delhi, 1948-64.

17

Economic Philosophy of Jawaharlal Nehru and its Implications: An Appraisal

Ambrish Kumar Jha

Nehru's concern at the time of independence was the variety of national problems that India inherited from the British Rule. Correctives as devised by Nehru—planning, land reforms, and industrialization in a mixed economy framework—have been presented in this paper. Actually speaking, Nehru's economic philosophy was an amalgam of both Western thinking and Indian traditions and the prevailing conditions of the country. Problems that the country now faces are often attributed to the failures of Nehru's policies. This is an unwarranted criticism that one must brush aside.

I. INTRODUCTION

Pt. Jawaharlal Nehru was the uncrowned king of India, latter the Prime Minister of Indian Republic, for he hated monarchs, princes, potentates and prelates. In the political firmament of India, he shined as the only sun. He was the idol of intellectual India.

Of him Dr. Pattabhi Sitaramayya, an ex-Congress President said; "Pandit Nehru is the outstanding figure of the time, whose presence is universally courted and coveted, whose upraised figure is a warning to the nations of the world, whose place for international peace is the sermon on the Mount of a new Messiah. The world sees in him the successor of Mahatma Gandhi and the embodiment of Gandhiji's gospel of truth and non-violence, the Commonwealth discovers in him its saviour, and India recognizes him as its one leader."

Born in 1889 with a silver spoon in his mouth, in the midst of pomp, plenty and splendour, he was the only son of Pandit Motilal Nehru, a co-worker of Gandhiji. He got his early education at Harrow and higher education at Cambridge. He studied law at the Inner Temple and came back as a Barrister at Law and joined the Allahabad High Court where his father had a roaring practice. After some time, he left his practice and joined India's freedom movement on Gandhiji's appeal. Since 1929 it was he who had been practically conducting and controlling the Congress and its policy. He was sent to jail many times during India's freedom movement. On four or five occasions he got the highest honour of the presidentship of the Indian National Congress. If Gandhiji was the soul of the Congress, Nehruji was its body. If Gandhiji formulated principles and policies, Nehruji translated them into action, championed them and gave them a form, a shape, a logic which made them acceptable to all.

In the Congress session held on the bank of river Ravi in Lahore under the presidency of young Nehru in 1929 the Congress declared its goal of "Poorna Swaraja." It was complete departure from the previous Congress policy. This Congress session also decided to observe 26th January as Independence Day and to launch the Civil Disobedience Movement under the leadership of Gandhi. India got freedom on 15th August 1947. Pandit J. Nehru became the Prime Minister of Indian Republic.

If the initiation for economic freedom of India can be

said to have been the work of any one person, it was the work of Pandit Jawaharlal Nehru.

Indian economic thought in pre-independence period was influenced by many factors such as the mass poverty, Indian nationalism, anti-British sentiments, and contact with the West.

During the period of the nationalist movement, the Indian leaders attributed the mass poverty in India to the British rule. Naturally, they thought freedom from the colonial rule as the remedy. Economic theory in India during the nationalist movement was concerned with one main aim, that was to provide a momentum to the nationalist movement. Some of the leaders formulated certain economic theories to show that the British Government was exploiting the Indian masses in a number of ways.

Pandit Jawaharlal Nehru identified eradication of poverty, eradication of illiteracy, eradication of disease and scientific production, distribution and abolition of untouchability as our chief national problems. He thought that the above problems can be tackled through socialist line because distribution gets priority only in socialist agenda. After the First World War, he visited Russia and was deeply influenced by what he saw there. During freedom movement he came into contact with leader, he had seen the real condition of farmers in the slave India. After independence he became the policy-maker of the country because people trusted in his leadership.

In the present paper, Nehru's economic thoughts based on amalgamation of Western and Indian conditions can be classified and studied under the headings like Planning, Land Reform, Mixed Economy, Industrialization and other critical aspects.

II. NEHRU'S EARLY IDEAS ABOUT PLANNING

The Indian National Congress resolutions from 1929 emphasized the 'need to make revolutionary changes in the present economic structure of the society and to remove grave inequalities in order to remove poverty and ameliorate the condition of masses'.

The Government of India Act, 1935 introduced provincial autonomy which led to the formation of the Congress Government in eight provinces. In 1938, the Congress Working Committee appointed a group of experts headed by Pandit Jawaharlal Nehru and included economists, industrialists and representatioves of other professions. The Committee regarded the irreducible minimum income as Rs. 15 to 25 per capita per month. Over a ten year span, an increase of 200 to 300 per cent was recommended. Such an increase would (i) mean an improvement in nutrition—a balanced diet having calorific value of 2300 to 2400, (ii) double the then per capita consumption of cloth, and (iii) provide at least 100 sq. ft. housing space per capita. Along with this, important objectives were borne in mind: (a) Increase in agriculture and industrial production, (b) reduction of unemployment, (c) increase in per capita income, (d) liquidation of illiteracy, (e) increase in public utility services, (f) provision of medical facilities, and (g) increase in the average expectation of life.

With the outbreak of the Second World War many members of the National. Planning Committee including its Chairman were arrested. Later on, attempts were made to revive the Committee but failed.

Bombay Plan (1944)

The second attempt in planning was the Bombay Plan issued by a group of prominent industrialists. An outlay of Rs. 10,000 crore was recommended over fifteen year period. The objective was to double the per capita income by trebling the national income. The outlay was divided among different sectors as follows--Industry including power, Rs. 4,480 crore, agriculture, Rs. 1,240 crore, Commerce, Rs. 940 crore, education, housing, etc. Rs. 3,340 crore the sources of finances were tobe-External finance Rs. 2,600 crores (including Rs. 1000 crores of sterling balances and foreign borrowing Rs. 700 crore) and internal finance Rs. 7,400 crores (consisting of savings Rs. 4,000 crore and created money Rs. 3,400 crore).

It is intestring to note that this group of industrialists favoured, state control in the form of price fixing, dividend freeze, licensing and other instruments. State ownership had a place where the State finances an enterprise (shades of the present joint sector) and it was necessary for enforcing state control. A 'Pigovian' type of society, i.e., enlightened mixed economy was envisaged.

In 1944, a Planning and Development Department was set-up with a board of same names as in the past to assist it, consisting mainly of the secretaries of economic department. Departments of central government, Provinces and the Indian states were requested to prepare detailed plans. Training of technical personnel was to be accorded priority. A total resource gathering exercise of Rs. 1,200 crore was envisaged by the Centre and Provinces. In 1945, an Industrial Policy statement was issued, first of its kind in this field. It had some distinctive features:

1. The state would assume a positive role in development, a departure from the old *laissez-faire* policy. Special importance was attended to the iron and steel industry, the machine tool industry and the heavy engineering industries.
2. Industrialization should increase national wealth, provide more employment and make the country better prepared for defence.
3. Equitable distribution of wealth to be created.
4. Central control by the state of twenty industries like textiles, aircraft, ship-building, heavy engineering, cement and iron and steel.
5. State participation in basic industries like electro-chemicals, non-ferrous metals, prime movers, electrical machinery, etc.
6. Assistance to private industry through loans, research facilities, infrastructure base and other means.
7. Licensing of undertakings to prevent regional concentration and counteract the tendency for private investment to go where there are quick returns without the overall social objective in perspective. The fixing of targets was laid down.
8. Controls on the lines envisaged in the Bombay Plan.

Thus even in pre-independent India there was a large measure of agreement on the following principles:

(i) Centralized planning with the state playing an active part.
(ii) Licensing and controls.
(iii) Balanced economic growth with priority to basic industries.

In the wake of the traumatic shock of partition and the resultant holocaust, the Constituent Assembly embraced the doctrine of the welfare state to promote development on a large scale with the widest measure of social justice.

Pandit Nehru was a man of letters who had studied the history of world. He was well-known to Marxist background. Being a peasant leader he was fully aware of feudal ex-ploitation. His pre-independence thinking on planning and his belief in socialism combined with his intimate knowledge of not only world history but also of Indian socio-economic situation prevailing at that time envisioned him for post-independence planning.

III. NEHRU ON LAND REFORMS

During freedom movement, Nehru travelled throughout country. He saw the economic condition of peasants who were the pivot of Indian economy. He was convinced that the Indian farmers could become the agent for modernization of agriculture if they were enabled to do so. He recommended "land to the tillers." For that the first enabling act was land reforms that gave farmers entitlement to land. The era of land reforms started with legislation for abolition of intermediaries, which was undertaken between 1948 and 1954. Tenancy reforms were undertaken from the year 1953. The third phase of reform started in 1956 with the legislation for imposition of ceiling on existing holdings. Several programmes were launched by central government for uplift of rural poor and rural areas. He introduced Community Development Programme in the mid-1950 with a view to raising the awareness and development of village through an appropriate network of Community Development Programmes and extension services. The community development blocks were set-up in 1952 for integrated area development in the rural areas. The Block Development Officer (BDO) and Project officers in each block were responsible for co-ordinating programmes of road, building, school construction and the like for their areas after consulation with the Panchayati Raj bodies and the necessary agencies. The BDO was supported by Extension officers in agriculture, co-operation, animal husbandry, etc. There was provision for V.L.W. (Village Level Workers) post also who co-ordianted between peasants and blocks. The First Five Year Plan accorded the highest priority to agriculture, for betterment of agriculture Nehru's government initiated large investment in irrigation, power, rural roads, markets and communications and scientific research and technology.

IV. NEHRU ON MIXED ECONOMY

Pandit Jawaharlal Nehru was the architect of planning in India. He was the propounder of mixed economy principle in India. On the one hand, he was influenced by the planning strategies of the USSR, on the other hand, he was influenced by the Western model of development. Pandit Nehru and the Indian planners had operated the model through a mixed organizational structure of the advanced countries. He was influenced by J.M. Keynes' notion of state intervention also.

Like that of democratic socialism the term mixed economy was also a new philosophy that had been evolved and adopted in the Indian economic planning. Although Nehru gave more importance to the public sector for equitable development of the Indian economy, but he did not underrate the initiative and enterprise of the private sector. He considered that the public sector was to play a central role in the development of rural infrastructure and basic research and extension.

Some Indian economists disliked Nehruvian concept of mixed economy where he gave more importance to the public sector. On the issue of mixed economy, Dr. B.R. Shenoy emphasized again and again that private sector should be at the centre in economic development with abolition of all price and import control measures. He advocated free market economic policies where private businessmen could work successfully. To justify his argument he mentioned the remarkable progress of West Germany during 1948-53, within five years. The production of Germany after 1948 increased by 45.5 per cent—a phased programme of denationalization of public sector enterprises.

Another great economist P.R. Brahmananda also disliked excessive state interference in economic activities. He considered this issue as conflict between Nehruvian economic order and Gandhian economic order. To him, it was a clash between: "The force of normative ideology seeking to mould the behaviours of individual groups and institutions along a postulated socialist pattern and the force of natural propensities and interest of individual, groups and institutional, postulated as self-oriented and utilitarian in the science of economics."

He cited a number of examples to show the consequences of extension of state power in our economic activities. The motives behind the nationalization of major private banks were to utilize more of banks' resources for public sector, to enforce priority lendings on banks, to control allocation of credit from the bank and indirectly to reduce the proportion of lending to industry and to divert resource for other uses. Thus both the RBI and the Finance Ministry exert control over the operations of banks. This dual control over banks weakened the RBI's supervision mechanism. The origin of non-performing assets commences in big ways after nationalization. Politicians started clamoring for loan meals and later for waivers of loans and interest. The nationalized banking system was gradually getting ruined. Even the monetary policy goals of the RBI could not be implemented in the short period. It was only after 1992 that efforts were started for the rehabilitation of the damaged banking system after the Narasimaham Committee Report in the 1990s.

He claimed that government expenditure's share in GDP is to be kept at minimum in order to make reform measures successful. Government expenditure as a proportion of GDP was barely 10 per cent in 1950-51 and development expenditure was about 40 per cent of the total government expenditure. But due to the Fifth Pay Commission Report and the enlarged subsides in 1997-98, government expenditure had crossed 30 per cent of GDP, while development expenditure turned out just 50 per cent or even less. These statistical data for the two periods—1950-51 and 1997-98 reflect the very fact that the public sectors in Indian economy are not very much concerned with development aspect of the planning.

Nehru's concept of mixed economy was landmark in the history of economic development of India. The post-independent period was not bright. Mass poverty was prevailing in the Indian economy. Basic infrastructure was too poor. There was no sound agricultural and industrial base, economic power concentrated in a few hands. Private sector enterprises were not ready to come forward to invest in such sectors like basic infrastructure (education, road, electricity, irrigation) and basic key industries. That was the reason, he gave more importance to the public sector enterprises. He did not underrate the private sector enterprises. To my mind, Nehru did not stifle private sector enterprises, rather gave them same importance in the economic development of the country. If private sectors were in the core of economic development activities during post-independence period, economic situation would be another. Private sector enterprises want more profit. Under such circumstance capital would be accumlated in a few hands. The ditch between poor and rich would be broad. The goal of democratic socialism will not be attained. The small and marginal farmers and rural artisans did not get loans or credits from commercial bank till the nationalization in 1969. The public sector enterprises played significant role in the economic development our country. So the neo-liberal criticisms of Nehru's concept of mixed economy is not justified.

V. NEHRU ON INDUSTRIALIZATION

Pandit Jawaharlal Nehru visited Russia in 1928. He was deeply influenced by the Fledman model which was the basis of Russian economic development. Prof. P.C. Mahalanobis prepared a growth model with the consent of Pt. Nehru which was introduced in the Second Plan. This model is mathematical in nature and is based on the technique of operational research. Operational research is designed to make the most effective use of scarce resources to meet given ends. It involves observation, experiment, deduction and induction.

This strategy emphasized investment in heavy industries to achieve industrialization which was assumed to be the basic condition for rapid economic development. Pt. Jawaharlal Nehru was also of the view that the development of heavy industry was synonymous with industrialization. The core of the strategy adopted by the Indian planners for the Second Plan was rapid industrialization. It would be essential to devote major part of the development outlay to building basic heavy industry like steel and the engineering industry for making different types of machines, the multipurpose river valley projects for irrigation and power.

VI. JUSTIFICATION OF NEHRU'S ECONOMIC PHILOSOPHY

The policy-makers and the planners had justified this strategy on the following grounds:

(a) Diversification

Under the British rule, India was forced to concentrate on agriculture and on agro-based industries. Now there is a need of diversification from the point of view of production, employment and defence. Resources, therefore, should be applied more towards the development of industries rather than to agriculture.

(b) Reducing pressure on land

Industrialization would reduce the pressure of population on land by shifting the surplus agricultural population to industries.

(c) Development of other Sectors

Rapid industrialization was an essential condition for the development of not only agriculture but also for all other sectors in the country, such as urban sectors, trade and commerce, transportation, and banking, etc.

(d) Productivity

Productivity of labour is much higher in manufacturing than in agriculture.

(e) Capital formation

Investment in the heavy sectors will help the Indian economy to build up a large volume of capital stock and at a faster rate.

(f) Self-reliance

Heavy industries help to lay the foundation for a strong and self-reliant economy, partly through rapid expansion of all the sectors of the economy and partly by eliminating the dependence of the country on imports of machinery and equipment.

VII. IMPLICATIONS OF THE STRATEGY

The basic purpose of this strategy was to achieve self-sustained growth by diverting increasing proportion of investment into the establishment of machine building industries. Some of the important implications are mentioned here.

(a) Supply of Consumer Goods

The planners were clear that the growth of heavy industries would be limited by the growth of consumer goods in the household sector. Hence in Nehru-Mahalanobis model, there was active encouragement for cottage industries producing consumer goods.

(b) Small Scale Industries and Agriculture

Due importance was given to small scale industries and agriculture which were the sources of consumer goods.

(c) Place of Agriculture

The strategy of self-sustained growth based on heavy

industries had also considered the necessity of self-sufficient agriculture. Nehru stated, "We shall find that this industrial progress cannot be achieved without agricultural advance."

(d) Role of Public Sector

This strategy assigned a dominant role to the public sector. As investment in the heavy industries was very high and as the gestation period was too long and also with low profitability the government felt that heavy industries should be, by and large, in the public sector.

(e) Role of Private Sector

The development strategy also expected the private sector to develop and expand its activities in a large area of economic activity. The private sector was given an important place in the mixed economy of India.

(f) Role of Foreign Trade and Foreign Aid

The strategy emphasized that the creation of export surplus and export promotion should go hand in hand with rapid industrialization.

The 'heavy industries' investment strategy was hailed during the Second and Third Plans but had come in for considerable criticisms since then.

VIII. EMPLOYMENT OBJECTIVE

The Mahalanobis strategy considered the development of basic and heavy industries which came in conflict with the employment objective of our plans. The strategy adopted a policy of encouraging labour-intensive techniques in consumer goods industries along with the capital-intensive sector of heavy industries. Employment objective was not achieved during the successive plans. That is why some Indian economists like A.K. Dasgupta, Dr. P.R. Brahmananda, Dr. C.N. Vakil, and Professor Shenoy have criticized the Nehru-Mahalanobis model of heavy industries. This model put priority for heavy industry and related infrastructures, a low proportion of resources for agricultural sector, in order to make strong industrial base for Indian economy. This model pays little attention for the development of demand-generating sources like small scale industries producing light consumer goods. Professor A.K. Dasgupta supported at first the Mahalanobis strategy of making the industrial base for Indian economy and opined that demand to be generated in the market exogenously. Later on, he changed his view and wrote in his book entitled "*Phases of Capitalism and Economic Theory*" (1983). An expansion on industrialization of a kind which neglects employment, may show results in the initial stages, in terms of output per unit of labour employed. It may also lead to the formation of fixed capital in the form of building machinery. But the economy should find itself deficient in circulating capital such as raw materials and food. Professors Vakil and Brahmananda placed to the Planning Commission the wage goods model as an alternative planning strategy of Nehru-Mahalanobis model. Wage goods refers to basic needs of human beings. According to Dr. Brahmananda, wage goods are those goods, "which are necessary for the subsistence of population and for labour in order to perform with full capacity."

Assumptions of this model are:

(a) Wage goods are assumed to be exclusively Food.
(b) Labour can produce capital goods without the assistance of other factors.
(c) There is a mechanism by which average consumption on the farm can be kept constant subsequent to the transfer of the labour of the farm can be siphoned off to feed it while it would be engaged in producing goods.

In order to ensure full employment with stability this model places much importance on the interactions among the three economic variables, namely, supply of wage goods, rate of population growth, and level of investment. The interplay among these three variables would be such that the level of investment should be kept above the growth rate of population and substantial extent of inflow of wage goods, should be provided in order to overcome unemployment. But in India during the period 1990-91 to 1996-97, the growth rate of food production stood at 1.3 per cent. It would be substantially less than the population growth.

Professors Vakil and Brahmananda introduced in this model three innovative concepts: 'wage goods gap', 'consumption multiplier' and 'employable unit'. They measured unemployment in terms of wage goods and the demand for the unemployment is measured in terms of potentially available surplus workforce. The deficiency between the two is critical wage goods gap. This wage goods gap is to be abolished in order to ensure full employment with stability.

Professor Shenoy has also criticized Mahalanobis' heavy industry model. He had highlighted the fact that continuous negligence of agricultural sector by the Planning Commission would bring poverty in Indian economy in two ways. First by reducing per capita consumption of cereals, pulses, edible oil, cloth, etc., and secondly, by shifting of investment in the heavy and basic industries, it would reduce the level of employment.

Shenoy opined "Rupees one crore invested in agriculture may add to the Indian material product, annually, about Rs. 60 lakh of output, or over twice the addition from industries and the employment generated in industries, for the same amount of capital invested."

Professor Shenoy observed that the squeeze in plan outlay in two successive five year plans, the agricultural sector had been starved of credit and capital. The rate of interest on agricultural loan was very high and workers had been receiving lower rate of wage. The high cost of credit had made the farmers incapable of introducing New Agricultural Technology, thereby loosing the number of working days and the daily wage rate.

CONCLUSION

Post-independence period was gloomy in India. The socio-economic condition was very crucial. Our nation had to face several problems like mass poverty, mass unemployment, mass illiteracy, mass malnutrition, and refugee problem. India was predominantly an agricultural country. There was no industrial base. We had to import even a needle and knife from abroad then what to talk of heavy machine and tools. We had to repay a lot of foreign exchange for arm and garment. Agriculture was backbone of our country at that time. There was need of new technology and new equipment for reformation of agriculture. There was heavy pressure on agricultural sector due to the rising trend of population. How to develop a new born independent nation, was a question before the economists and policy-makers. Pandit Jawaharlal Nehru made up his mind to establish industrial base so that the major problems of India could have been solved. That was the reason that Pt. Nehru adopted the Mahalanobis heavy industry model. Finally, we may say that Nehru-Mahalanobis strategy took India to the position of the tenth most industrialized country of the world. It was the effort of Pt. Nehru that has made India a most advanced country of the world in the areas of Science and Technology, space and Atomic Research and Information Technology.

Some economists have criticized Nehru-Mahalanobis model of economic growth because it does not solve basic problems like mass poverty, mass unemployment, mass illiteracy and malnutrition of Indian economy. They have also criticized the Nehru's principle of mixed economy and insufficient attention to agriculture. To my mind, it may be true to some extent but Nehru cannot be blamed for slow growth. The real causes behind it are following:

(a) It is the outcome of parliamentary democracy.
(b) We have no work culture. We are best talkers rather doers. I may say that the failure of public sector in India should be taken as an administrative failure and lack of work culture in our employees.
(c) We are the best planners rather than implementers.

References

Jawaharlal Nehru (1962), *An Autobiogrphy*, Allied Publishers, New Delhi.
—— (1961), *The Discovery of India*, Asia Publishing House.

Brahmanand P.R. (1978), *Planning for a Futureless Economy.*

—— (1995), *Planning for a Wage Goods Economy.*

—— (1997), *50 Years of Free Indian Economy.*

Dasgupta, A.K. (1965), *Planning and Economic Growth.*

——(1963), *Phases of Capitalism and Economic Theory.*

Shenoy, B.R. (1968), *Indian Economy Policy (1968),* Indian Planning and Economic Development.

18

Economic Philosophy of Jawaharlal Nehru: An Agenda for Justice and Equality

NILIMA SAHAY, ARUN KUMAR AND POONAM

Nehruvian economic thinking needs to be addressed in a historical setting. Global economic thinking in tandem with the pre-independent years of Nehru's life influenced Nehru's economic philosophy. In the process, Nehruvian economic policies made a strong 'visible hand' of the state in India's development scenario. For economic justice, Nehru desired to have an activist state under which public sector had been assigned a special role. Politics of patronage played a key role in extending urban and rural support base of the Congress Party.

I. GLOBAL THINKING OF NEHRU

Any economic thinking which is bound to operate in a liberal democratic set-up may enshrine equity and justice. In other words, economic thought in a liberal democracy does not function in a vacuum, it must respond to the aspirations and material needs of the people. Nehruvian economic philosophy can be seen in a historical context. It was a product of a long process of interactions, compromises and the accommodation of diverse ideas and ideologies. Both 'time' and 'space' influenced Nehru in moulding his economic philosophy. Nehruvian economic thinking is a product of both global economic thinking as well as domestic politics. Globally, the ideological conflict between communism and capitalism as represented by two power blocks influenced the Nehruvian economic thinking. Domestically, Nehru as the leader of the Indian National Congress, which was a movement for national freedom, had to protect the interests of various social groups. In every policy issue, Nehru tried to maintain a balance between domestic and global compulsion by evolving a consensus with the nation.

Nehru on Capitalism

His views on capitalism are still very significant, private initiatives and acquisitiveness are the pivot around which a capitalist order clustures. Despite great opposition Nehru also recognized the contribution of capitalism.

He did not rule out profit entry into his free economy derived from the *laissez-faire* economy. After independence his efforts were concentrated on building up a new modernized India—a socialist pattern of society through democratic process. Jawaharlal Nehru had an inflicting faith in co-operation because to him co-operation help actively in peaceful economic change. Jawaharlal Nehru had pragmatic practices, intellectual and idealist approach to lead the country in the right direction. His ideas regarding agricultural development are very crucial even today in the age of globalization, green revolution and white revolution. To him a proper land policy is essential for agricultural process.

Planning Advisory Board

Nehru immediately set-up a Planning Advisory Board as soon as the Interim Government came in the picture in 1946. He formed economic programme committee on Congress. The Planning Commission was constituted in 1950.

Nehru as a Planner

Nehru was a planner long before he got the authority which could enable him to introduce planning in Indian economy.

Nehru on Development

Nehru's economic thought evolved during the nationalist movement in which the basic idea behind the Nehruvian economic philosophy was the attainment of a developmental interventionist state to modernize the backward society and the welfare of its social classes. Moreover, India's dominant policy-makers favoured the creation of a self-reliant economy and a powerful state. The bourgeosie class extended its support to the Congress for achieving an interventionist state, which, it felt, was essential for the development of the indigenous bourgeosie class. However, Nehru, on his part, projected the attainment of an interventionist state before the masses as an instrument for development and modernization. In fact, the state visualized by Nehru had the potential to function with relative autonomy *vis-à-vis* the interests of the dominant class and the industrial and business groups.

Nehru on Socio-economic and Political Justice

The Indian National Congress, as a movement for freedom, played an important role in moulding Nehru's economic thinking towards justice and equity. The multi-class, caste, regional and religious nature of the nationalist movement under Gandhi forced the Congress to arrive at a social consensus on its economic politics and programmes. The idea was to provide social, economic, and political justice and to ensure the dignity of the individual.

Nehru on State Intervention for Development

After independence, Nehruvian economic thinking assumed centrestage in Indian development strategy. The Nehruvian era can be considered as the foundational stage of institution-building in independent India. The allround presence of the development state and the experiment of democracy gave greater impetus to the development of political institution. These political institutions under the patronage of the developmental state provided a framework to accommodate the demands of new classes in a democratic way. The Congress transformed itself into a political party and emerged as a major political institution in India. The policies and strategies of the Party were geared towards building a self-reliant modern economy in which political freedom could be made meaningful for the masses. The Congress Party, which was the ruling party in its economic policies, argued for an interventionist state which sought to take an active role in the development process. The intention for strengthening such a state by the party was due to both domestic and global factors. Domestically, the Congress wanted to project its image as the inheritor of the multi-class, multi-caste mass movement and it needed the continued support of all sections of society. Globally, it needed the assistance of the Soviet Union for the reconstruction of Independent India, though India adopted a non-aligned path in the bipolarized cold war era.

Nehruvian Thinking before Independence

The post-independent Nehruvian economic strategy was influenced by the pressure emanating from the international system, domestic, political coalition and the influence of ideology. The dominant thinking among policy-makers of the newly independent nation states was the vital role the developmental state could play in institution building during the formative years of development. Mainly, two events had contributed to the strengthening of a strong developmental and interventionist state in their economic strategy in the post-Second World War Period. Firstly, the strong nationalist and 'anti-colonial nature' of the movement, the 'Great Depression' of the 1930s, the rise of 'Keynesian economic thinking' and the 'Second World War' revived the questions of the state, government policies, state-market relations, growth distributive justice, etc., secondly, the success of state planning in achieving rapid industrialization in the Soviet Union greatly influenced policy-makers in 1950s. Subsequently, in the 1940s and early 1950s 'development economics' emerged as a sub-discipline in analyzing the dominant role of the state in the economic development of the developing countries. The state assumed the role of a 'visible hand' in the nation-building process by acting as an agency for the welfare of the people.

Nehru on Mixed Economy

Nehru was influenced by the success of the Soviet experiment of centralized planning and by the emergence of 'developmentalism' as a new philosophy of economic policy. However, he argued that India must evolve a model of her own, which was based on democratic socialism and aimed at mixed economy and economic planning. Nehru, in fact, tried to place his economic agenda in the Congress Party forum. In January 1948, at the AICC's Economic Programme Committee which met under the Chairmanship of Nehru and proposed radical measures to bring about equitable distribution of the existing income and wealth and prevent the growth of disparities with the process of industrialization. The Industrial Policy Resolution of 1948 was another significant development in this direction. It emphasized, among other things, a progressively active role for the state in the development of industries coupled with a valuable role for private enterprises, properly directed and regulated.

Nehru on Public Sector

The Delhi Congress Session of 1951 declared that the Congress stood for progressive extension of public sector to various fields of economic activity. Further, the private sector was to function in close accord with the public sector for the fulfillment of common national objectives. On 21st December, 1954, Nehru said in the Lok Sabha that the objective of our economic policy should be a socialistic pattern of society. However, the official confirmation of the Congress Party's stand was made at the *Avadi* Session of the AICC in 1955. The *Avadi* Session adopted a resolution stating that the establishment of a 'socialistic pattern of society' was the Party's objective. And the Party reached a consensus regarding its policies and strategies based on this objective. The aim was to create a mixed economy, a mixed polity, and a mixed society. For instance, the political circumstance after independence forced Nehru to move towards left-oriented policies. Politically, the Congress Party under Nehru had to counter the 'Swatantra Party' for its pro-liberal, and market-oriented approach.

Nehru on Equity and Justice

The Nehruvian economic thinking based on equity and justice was, in fact, a synthesis of all the major ideological currents that were in existence within the Congress Party. These were the Gandhian philosophy of Sarvodaya, that advocates a self-sufficient village economy based on small scale industries. But the socialist doctrine as advocated by the Western educated congressman like Nehru who wanted heavy industrialization and the dominance of the public sector and the third approach advocated by Sardar Patel and Rajendra Prasad based on private capital and market economy, Nehru synthesized these three major ideological currents of the 1950s: the unrestrained free market capitalism, modified welfare capitalism, and the more radical communist model into his vision of economic development and political democracy. The underlying philosophy and ideology of Nehruvian economic thinking were to give more roles to the state in economic development and a subservient role to the market. Nehru believed that poverty and hunger in India can be removed by means of strengthening the role of the state. Towards this direction, Nehru geared towards centralized planning, commanding heights of public sector in the mixed economy and provision for public subsidies to various groups. Thus, Nehru gave the state an economic base, and powerful economic base and a powerful economic presence which ensured its autonomy and guarded it against blackmail and manipulation by organised interest. Nehru conceptualized planning as the first step towards the goal of a socialist society. But at the same time he regarded the domestic values of the capitalist society as indispensable for the full growth of a just society.

Nehru-Mahalanobis Strategy on Economic Justice

He therefore, tried to reconcile the virtues of these two extremes and arrived at a vision of a new society based on democratic socialism. The Second Five Year Plan laid the foundation for economic development known for its "Nehru-Mahalanobis" strategy. It envisaged a significant role for the public sector and stressed the need for heavy industrialization. The domestic and small scale industries were given protection for competition. The Industrial Policy Resolution of 1956 was another significant development in demarcating the role of public and private sector in Indian development. The basic objectives of the economic policy as explicated in the Industrial Policy Resolution of 1956 were the commanding heights of the public sector over the private sector, faster expansion of basic and key industries, prevention of concentration of economic powers in private hands, regional balance and promotion of small scale industry. Nehru thought that industrialization can bring social justice by removing poverty in India. In his view industrialization should address the poverty of the people. Industrial progress should be benefited by vast majority of the people and not a few industrialists and capitalists. Nehru says raising the standard of living of the masses must be the first priority in any scheme of Industrial advancement and not a subsidiary benefit that may follow from industrial reconstruction. It can be seen that the process of accommodation began with the formulation of the Second Five Year Plan and became fully established with the proclamation of the Industrial Policy Resolution 1956. Though, the Industrial Policy Resolution of 1956 set out some principles of Nehruvian Philosophy, it retained sufficient ambivalence to placate the uncommitted elements.

Nehru as the Founding Father of Modern India

Thus Nehruvian economic philosophy not only laid the foundation for economic modernization but also social and political modernization in India. The modernization process initiated by Nehru had some peculiar characteristics *vis-à-vis* those initiated in other newly independent countries of the decolonised era. It had a kind of relative autonomy both at the domestic level as well as global level. Domestically, it succeeds in bargaining with the traditionally upper and dominant castes and classes in the process of modernization.

It has been suggested that Nehru stood for the replacement of culturally rooted rationality by formal rationality for the replacement of the individuals as a part of communities, by the nation of individuals an unencumbered selves, for the replacement of collective, communitarian, affective, spiritual, orientation by individualistic calculative, constructarian values and finally, for the replacement of an undifferentiated value system by separate spheres of morality, art and science. In the economic realm, central planning and public sector were the major instruments of modernization.

II. SUMMING UP

To conclude, Nehruvian economic philosophy on economic justice and equity is the product of the compulsions of liberal democracy in India. However, the economic thinking was benefited by the Congress Party rather than the masses at large. The Congress could manage to develop a patronage politics which strengthened its base among various social groups in India. For instance, the Congress, when it came into power, developed an elaborate structure of patronage distribution in a multi-class coalition in independent India.

The elaborate network of patronage in the form of subsidies, credits and public sector envisaged within the political economy under the purview of the developmental state enabled the Party to co-opt and absorb diverse social groups. By influencing the distributive policies of the Government, the party could meet the demand of its social constituencies and this contributed to broaden its mass base. The Government's soft budget constraints and the provision of public subsidies to various sectors and the generation of employment through and expansive state sector, expanded the party support in different spheres of the society. For example, the provision of large input subsidies to the farm sector in the form of fertilizers, power, seeds, irrigation and support prices for farm products helped the party to ensure the support of the agricultural communities. Planned development was a crucial part of the legitimating ideology of the Congress in power, and planning as a domain outside politics, become an essential instrument for patronage politics. It helped to find areas for resource allocation and overall development of certain regions. The institution of development and planning and other development programmes, by extending active agencies for development of the society, provided new social and economic opportunities. The introduction of poverty alleviation programmes, the adoption of redistributive measures, the launching of employment generation schemes, the high expenditure on the poor, programmes intended to empower socially marginalized sections, rural development schemes, high allocation in social expenditure, distribution, of essential commodities through fair price shops to the poor, etc. The disbursement and distribution of resources to the intended and unintended beneficiaries were done through various level of government structures like the state governments and local institution like Panchayati Raj, most of which were dominated by the Congress Party. Moreover, an elaborate network of patronage created by the party through the programmes of development planning enabled it to bargain with various social strata in rural and urban areas for political support. Thus, the programme of development and planning can be seen as one of the three ways by which the Congress established its dominance and the progressive expansion of its social base. While acknowledging the public sector enterprises, it strengthened the role of the private sector in the economy. The wide ranging public sector provided job opportunities and recruitment to professionals and developed the patronage of bureaucracy committed to the Party. The provision of affirmative action policies in the public sector stand a testimony to the governments commitment to the deprived sections of the society and established its linkage with these groups. It is considered that the pressure to use public revenues as patronage not only stems from the heterogeneous nature of India's dominant classes but also originates in the need to maintain electoral support in a democratic polity. It has been argued that this strategy of consolidation depend on a dispersal of power and patronage than it did on ideological appeal or organizational loyalties.

REFERENCES

Rao, V.K.R.V. (1960), *Planning without Dogma: A Study of Nehru*, Rafique Zakaria. A Times of India Publication, Bombay.

Venkateshwaram, R.J. (1962), *The Impact of Jawaharlal Nehru on Indian Economy*, Oxford University Press, Calcutta; p. 15.

Nanda, B.R. (1961), *The Nehrus, Motilal and Jawaharlal* (Allen and Unwin Publication, London).

Prasad, Bimala (1972), Jawaharlal Nehru's Report on International Congress against Imperialism.

Rao, V.K.R.V. (1971), *The Nehru Legacy*, Popular Prakashan, Bombay.

Singh, S.R. and Shrivastava, M.P. (2004), *Socio-economic Ideas of Nehru and Globalization*, Anmol Publication, New Delhi.

Chakrabarty, Bidyut (1992), *Jawaharlal Nehru and Planning, 1938-41, India at the Crossroads*, Modern Asian Studies.

AICC (1948), Report of Economic Programme Committee, New Delhi: Industrial Policy Resolution, 1948, New Delhi, Ministry of Finance.

Kothari, Rajni (1976), *Democratic Policy and Social Change in India: Crisis and Opportunities*. New Delhi, Allied Publishers.

Rangneckar, D.K. (1975), "Industrial Policy", *The Economic Times*, Annual Number.

Pantham, Thomas (1995), *Gandhi, Nehru and Modernity* in Baxi and Parekt.

Jawaharlal Nehru (1962), *An Autobiography*, Allied Publishers, New Delhi.

Jawaharlal Nehru (1961), *The Discovery of India*, Asia Publishing House.

Gopal, S. (1975), Jawaharlal Nehru, *A Biography*, Volumes I, II and III, Oxford University Press.

19

Nehru—The Builder of Indian Economic Empire

L.S.N. Prasad and P. Vasudeva Rao

This article presents contradictions in Nehru's policy—higher and higher production but with a social motive. For higher production, Nehru, in an unequivocal term, pleaded for state intervention as well as the growth of the private sector. However, contradiction came to the surface through the mixed economy principle. Nehru was rather hesitant for nationalization though he was not averse to it. His industrial policies stated that new industries would even be set up in backward regions of the country by the public sector to subserve the social objectives. At the same time, encouragement to the private sector and the big businesses was to be given. As a result, both higher output and social aspects of economic planning remained a dream. Further, despite the rhetoric of a balance between agriculture and industry to be maintained, the sufferer was the agricultural sector in the midst of the drive for industrialization.

Jawaharlal Nehru, the hero of many Indians in which I am one among them, is the builder of modern India. His vision was the foundation of modern democracy, which has deep rooted in India. His method of dealing with public is different with another leaders. His image as India's outstanding leader, a spokesperson for the idea of national liberations and progress in the Asian continent. He was the creator of political system in the country and its foreign policy.

I. STATE INTERVENTION AND *LAISSEZ-FAIRE*

Nehru was an advocate of state intervention. He opposed too much freedom. In this the Carlyle definition of *laissez-faire* and his opinion made him to oppose the state intervention. It was, "brought the law of the jungle. Pig philosophy", Carlyle called it. The poor fellows had little to say in the matter of daily activities that Nehru believed. It was the successful manufacturers at the top who wanted no interfere with their success. So in the name of liberty and the rights of property they objected even to the compulsory sanitation of private houses and interference with the adulteration of goods."[1]

After the Second World War Nehru opposed the attempts of the advocates of uncontrolled private enterprise to present the *laissez-faire* principle as some sort of guarantee of democracy and individual freedom. The main functions of the state, among many others, were, in his opinion, the economic functions, which were to be geared to social objectives and social activities. The tasks that Nehru set before the state in this sphere were of a dual character. "...We must encourage production, and at the same time, the social motive," he said. He admitted that the combination of these two goals is rather contradictory, since this combination rested on the preservation of the private sector.

In the year 1960, Nehru mentioned that if the role of private sector increase in the economy they will become as monopolies, which retards the social equality. "If, by any step that we take, production goes down, then we are cutting at the root of our advance and progress. If, on the other hand, private monopolies are built up, then we are encouraging a process which will come in our way badly and be harmful now and later. It will take us away very far from any kind of progress towards socialism."[2] However, in an economically weak country, the interests of production, and not of justice must dominate over all others, he thought.

Without fear of exaggerating or overstating Nehru's views, one can say that there was only one objective economic goal he had proclaimed that was quite realistic, namely to build up a strong national economy. This economic progress was undoubtedly linked with the rising cultural, educational and even material standards of some strata of the population, and also with the elimination of general backwardness, but even then it failed to resolve the basic social conflicts. Nehru was fully aware of that and at times even gave a sober assessment of his economic policy.

His principal line in the economy was the active participation of the state in economic development. Besides the social motive, and besides his sympathies for socialism, Nehru also had other purely economic considerations in favor of state intervention in the economy.

II. ROLE OF THE PRIVATE SECTOR

In Nehru's view, the private sector has no ability or resources to strengthen the economy. Even if it has ability and it has resources but it just has not strength or capacity to solve the situation by itself. It is a patent fact that you just cannot do it. Nehru addressed these words to the industrialists of the country back in 1950. The following year Nehru raised the same problem again: "But in this country and in countries like India where private enterprise, howsoever you may encourage it, is limited in scope and resources, the state must inevitably come in.[3]

Being aware that the private sector could not possibly achieve national reconstruction with its own resources alone, Nehru had come to the idea of socialism much earlier and under the influence of other factors. However, his conception of socialism had undergone marked changes that brought him closer to national reformism in the Afro-Asian countries.

Central to Nehru's economic policy was his desire to avoid the extremes of free private enterprise or total nationalization. He refused to adopt both the principles of the Soviet economic system and the unlimited freedom of private enterprise, which, in his opinion, did not exist anywhere in the world. "It is inevitable that those countries, which do not want either of the two extremes, must find a middle way. In that middle way, there is bound to be more emphasis on some factors than on others but obviously a middle way or a mixed economy, if you like to call it,[4] that, is inevitable."

III. THE ECONOMIC IDEOLOGY OF NEHRU— THE MIXED ECONOMY

Nehru's economic course did not remain the same all the time. Its principal landmarks were two resolutions on economic policy (1948 and 1956) and the five-year development plans. However, this course retained the basic principles of mixed economy. The idea of Nehru's mixed economy concept was that the public sector should develop not at the expense of the private sector, and not to its detriment. He also opined that the public sector was to take shape not through nationalization of private sector.

"Now we have been following a policy which is normally called a policy of 'mixed' economy, "Nehru explained. About his idea of mixed Economy was, "We encourage private enterprise and, at the same time, we widen the activities of the state in these matters."[5] The mixed economy played an important role both in the private and public sectors. Each sector had its own sphere of activity, and there was no strictly defined demarcation line between them. In Nehru's view, the strategic sector (the sphere of the predominant activity of the state) must constantly be expanding, while the non-strategic sector (private initiative) must narrow down. As an exception to the rule, Nehru allowed private capital invading the strategic sector.[6]

Conflict between Private and Public Sectors

Nehru singled out two principles of mixed economy, or two criteria of the coexistence of the private and the public sectors: the greatest possible increase in production with all the available means, and prevention of the aggregation of wealth and economic power in the hands of private individuals.[7] The two sectors must function in close coordination with each other, strictly in accordance with the national plans of economic development.

Nehru took a different view at different times about relations between the two sectors. In 1953, for example, he said that he did not see any ground for conflict between them. However, that was at a time when the public sector had not yet been developed in full. After some time, Nehru said, "now there is conflict between the private sector and the growing public sector, but I'm sure that too will be resolved peacefully and cooperatively."[8]

Role of Public Sector in the Mixed Economy

According to Nehru, the public sector was to be the leading sector in the future system of the mixed economy Towards, the end of his life Nehru came out against turning the mixed economy into a tool for strengthening the positions of private capital. "We have a private sector and a public sector, the public sector, being the more important, dominates the economic policy," he said in the Lok Sabha in December 1963. "Otherwise, there is no point in having a public sector to help the private sector."[9] The state would either possess or control the key centers of the national economy. Thus Nehru was strongly in favor of rigid control over the banks and the insurance business in the years of the struggle for independence and did not rule out the possibility of nationalizing the banks after India had, become an independent country.

Nationalization of Means of Production

Nehru was slow with nationalization, encouraged private capital, and fostered illusions about resolving class contradictions through cooperation and reconciliation between the social antagonists. In a speech in the Constituent Assembly on April 7, 1948, Nehru linked the industrial policy he had sponsored with the idea of compromise, and said: "That brings us to the transitional stage of economy. Call it what you like mixed economy or something else. Gradually we arrive at a stage when the center of gravity of the whole economy has shifted. Now, I rather doubt whether it is possible without a conflict or without repeated conflicts to bring about these changes, because people who are used to possessing certain interests or certain ideas do not easily accept new ideas."[10]

Here Nehru not only identified the mixed economy with the interim period, but also clearly expressed its contradictory and controversial character that sometimes he tended to forget. When the Second Five Year Plan was under debate, which among other things dealt with the role the private sector was currently playing, Nehru spoke about his belief that in the final analysis all the basic means of production would become national property.

The public sector was growing, but private capital was also strengthening its positions. All the enterprises that had been set-up in any sphere of industry belonged to the private sector and were not subject to nationalization. Private capital could even gain access to the key branches of industry, although that was done only in exceptional cases. This state of affairs was not the result of Nehru's backing away from his ideal in the pursuance of the economic policy. Speaking about the steady expansion of the public sector at the time when the Third Five Year Plan was being drawn up in 1960, Nehru said: "... It does not necessarily mean that the private sector is eliminated even at a much later stage. It does not mean that thing at all. I do not know and I am not a prophet, enough to say that will happen twenty, thirty or forty years later. But I can well imagine the private sector functioning but naturally in limited ways."[11]

This means that much money was paid without immediate and direct economic effect, i.e., without raising the level of production. Nehru thought it undesirable. He considered that at times too much importance was attached to the acquisition by the state of existing enterprises at a time when it was much more urgent to build new enterprises. Nehru criticised the Indian Communists and Socialists for their ill-advised and rash appeals for nationalization. "If nationalization adds to production, we shall have nationalization at every step. If it does not, let us see how to bring it about in order not to impede production."[12]

However, the way out proposed by Nehru was not a search for ways and means that would enable nationalization with the least possible loss, but the investment of government funds in new industries or in the areas in which private capital did not invest due to the low rate of profit and its slow return on it. Calling for the building of heavy industry in India, Nehru pointed out that this mission held little attraction for private capital and rested solely on the government's shoulders.

All these things taken together prompted Nehru to make the conclusion that the government should not "in this age of changing technology pay to take possession of any old plant unless it happens to serve some strategic purpose."[13] In spite of Nehru's policy of coexistence of the two sectors and the guarantees given to private capital, his policy for consolidating the economic positions of the state met with stiff resistance from the right-wing forces which saw in it a threat to free enterprise.

Nehru attributed an important place to the private sector in the system of the mixed economy. This sector included all land in the country, i.e., its agriculture, "possibly" (in his words) the entire cottage industry, and also small and medium-sized enterprises, and even some of the big industrial establishments. These contradictions ought to be resolved by subjecting. Of course, he realized that the private sector could not be controlled as much as the public sector. However, his idea was to strengthen this control and not to confine it to making profit. He thought it necessary to extend control to the key economic positions in the private sector. One of the ways of bringing pressure to bear upon private enterprise was state aid. Nehru insisted that such aid would be possible after the government had set-up a controlling mechanism.

Their sole reason being a lust for economic power and not the promise of high profits. "I think it is highly objectionable that economic power should be in the hands of a small group of persons, however able or good they might be," he said. "Such a thing must be prevented."[14]

IV. SOCIALISTIC PATTERN OF THE SOCIETY

Back in 1955, Nehru called upon the Indian business community not to fear "a socialistic pattern of society." He requested them to adjust to this ideal and to serve India at a profit to themselves.[15] The Indian capitalists had every reason to believe in his sincerity. Nehru's arguments about the benefits of socialism did not prevent them from enriching themselves. In 1956, reiterating the importance of the role played by the private sector, Nehru remarked that gradually this sector would fade away and that the government would have from time to time to readjust its policy first.[16] However, up to the end of his life, the private sector did not fare any worse than before. The ideas of the gradual exclusion of the private sector faded away. At the same time the encouragement it got was taken as a matter of course, and this soon began to yield tangible results. The committee report delivered by Prof. Mahalanobis, who had played a prominent role in the drafting of the Second Five Year Plan, said that the Government's policy was responsible for the growth of the private sector and especially big business.

It is clear that Nerhu's critics on the Right viewed his plans of industrialization and of creating a strong public sector and his ideals of socialism as something very un-Indian. They pointed out that in spite of the impressive achievements in different spheres, the main goals set in the plans had remained unfulfilled. This referred not only to the social aspects of planning but also to the growth rate of industrial production.

V. NEHRU'S VIEWS ON CORRELATION OF INDUSTRY AND AGRICULTURE

Nehru's views on the correlation of industry and agriculture somewhat changed when he became the Prime Minister. During the First Five Year Plan period the emphasis was on the development of agriculture. "We came to the conclusion, rightly or wrongly, that in the First Five-Year Plan, the most important thing was the agricultural front," Nehru said in 1954. "But, essentially, we realized that food shortage was the big problem and we concentrated on that, we did that because we felt that unless we had a strong food basis, our industrial efforts might well be bogged down."[17] At the same time, Nehru pointed out that India must industrialize as quickly as possible, that she could not raise the living standard of her population or even retain her independence without building heavy industry which must be both owned and controlled by the state.[18] During the Second Five Year Plan period, priority went to the development of industry, especially heavy industry, and this meant considerable growth of the public sector. In his statements made in the 1950s Nehru tried to put across the idea that industrialization provided not for the expanding manufacture of consumer goods, no matter how important and useful this might be, but for the creation of the key branches of heavy industry that would give rise to other types of industry without which the country's independence was in jeopardy.[19]

And yet the balance between industry and agriculture that Nehru had spoken about was upset. The achievements of agriculture in the First Five Year Plan period had apparently been grossly exaggerated; the poor harvests that followed were evidence of that. Starting from the second half of 1963, Nehru again changed his line of argument on the correlation of industry and farming. This time he laid stress on the special role played by farming in the creation of a healthy national economy, which he regarded not only as a source of food-stuff and raw materials, but also as a major source of revenue in an agrarian country: "I am for industry, I am all for steel plants, heavy industries and all that, but I do say agriculture is far more important than industry. Because, it is out of the success of agriculture that industry comes. If you fail in agriculture, you have little to stand upon. Where do you get the wherewithal to have industry? It is out of the surplus from agricultural production that you build your industries and therefore it has become of the utmost importance that agriculture should flourish and should produce the goods and surpluses needed for industrial growth."[20] In August 1963, Nehru said that "...our strategy of economic development is essentially modernization of agriculture and the training of our rural masses in the use of new tools and new methods."[21]

Agriculture had been badly neglected in India, in the hope that harvests would grow all on their own without any great effort being made by the peasants. It stands to reason that the policy of industrialization was not entirely forgotten. Nehru continued to criticize the opponents of heavy industry and of the public sector. However, here too, there was an apparent shift of emphasis. In effect, Nehru admitted that in his search for accelerated economic development the onesided growth of industry to the detriment of agriculture had carried him away, thus forgetting the need to balance all the branches of the economy as the first commandment of planning. Nehru was not the only statesman in developing countries to have fallen into this error. It was typical of many leaders of the newly independent countries who betrayed a noble impatience in the achievement of genuine independence and social progress. But in politics cold calculation is rated higher than noble sentiment.

Nehru was right linking the reverses in agriculture with the setbacks in the agrarian reform. "After 15 years of independence, our programme of land reform has not been fully implemented for various reasons, and because of various pressures," he said in 1963. The slogan that the land should be turned over to those who till it, a slogan that figured in Nehru's statements and in the documents of the Indian National Congress on agrarian policy remained on paper only, just like the plans for the elimination of poverty in India. Millions of peasants were in effect deprived of all incentives to work on land. This shows that their problems had not been solved, that they were losing faith in the future and were indifferent to government measures.

In effect, modernization of agriculture, in changing the world outlook of the peasant, in introducing him to new farming methods in order to wrench him away from age long backwardness Nehru saw the key strategy of India's economic development. However, he tended to forget that such modernization could not be achieved only through propaganda, through technical know-how or even through capital investment. He ignored the social aspect of modernization: to resolve the class contradictions in the countryside. But the social climate was not favorable in this respect. Modernization, which widely benefited the capitalist elements in the countryside, bypassed the bulk of the peasantry, down-trodden, poverty-stricken and landless.

CONCLUSION

This paper is outlined about the contribution of Nehru for the development of Indian economy. Because of him, we have an excellent basic industries. In spite of liberal policy followed by the governments from 1991 onwards, the contribution of Nehru to the development of our economy may not fade away.

Notes and References

1. *Jawaharlal Nehru Speeches,* Publications Divion, Ministry of Information and Broadcosting, Government of India, 1970, Vol. 3, p. 69.
2. *Ibid.,* Vol., p. 81.
3. *Ibid.,* p. 589,
4. *Jawaharlal Nehru Speeches,* Vol. 4, p. 70.
5. *Ibid.,* p. 45.
6. *Jawaharlal Nehru Speeches,* Vol. 3, p. 6.
7. *Ibid.,* pp. 278-79.
8. *Jawaharlal Nehru Speeches,* Vol. 4. p. 12.
9. *Jawaharlal Nehru Speeches,* Vol. 5, p. 47.
10. *Ibid.,* p. 78.
11. *Jawaharlal Nehru Speeches,* Vol. 3, p. 588.
12. *Ibid.,* p. 488.
13. *Ibid.,* p. 508.
14. *Jawaharlal Nehru Speeches,* Vol. 4, p. 89.
15. M. Brecher (1959), *Nehru: Apolitical Biography,* Oxford University Press, London, p. 531.
16. *Jawaharlal Nehru Speeches,* Vol. 3, p. 102.
17. *Jawaharlal Nehru Speeches,* Vol. 4, p. 523.
18. S. Abid Hussain (1962), *The Way of Gandhi and Nehru,* Asia Publishing House, Bombay, p. 6.
19. Jawaharlal Nehru (1960), *India Today and Tomorrow,* Indian Council of Cultural Relations, New Delhi, p. 39.
20. R.K. Karanjia: *The Mind of Mr. Nehru,* George Allen and Unwin Ltd., London, p. 60.
21. *Ibid.*

20

Nehru: A Visionary for Democracy and Development

S.K. Karimulla and A. Ranga Reddy

As Nehru is rightly considered as the founder of parliamentary form of democracy and economic development through the vehicle of economic planning, this paper aims at concentrating largely on Nehruvian economic ideas like mixed economy, socialistic pattern of society, etc., Democracy and development are interdependent and have the potentiality of curing all the ills of the economy as well as improving societal welfare.

I. ORIGIN OF PARLIAMENTARY SYSTEM

The institution of Parliament being the greatest political invention of man, the Parliament should reflect the will of the people of the country as a whole. Parliamentary democracy will fail, unless we learn to work together in national interest. Democracy without discipline leads to *mobocracy* and chaos, and discipline without 'democracy leads to slavery'. In the 14th Century, Parliament began to present petitions (bills) to the king, which with his assent would become law.

Legislative Assembly of Britain and of other governments modeled after it. The British Parliament consists of the Monarch, the House of Lords and the House of Commons, and its roots to the Union (C.1300) of the Great Council of the Kings Court, two bodies that treated with and advised the King. In the 14th century, Parliament was split into two houses—with the lords spiritual and temporal debating in one and the Knights and burgesses in the other. Roberts Walpole was the first party leader to Head the Government, as Prime Minister (1721-42). Rules of parliamentary procedure originated in Britain in the 16th and 17th centuries and were subsequently adopted by legislatures around the world. Roberts' Rules of order, codified in 1876 by the U.S. General Henry M. Robert (1837-1923) and regularly refined and enlarged, is the standard set of rules used by legislatures in the U.S. Generally accepted rules, procedures and practices used in the governance of deliberative assemblies. They are intended to maintain decorum, ascertain the will of the majority, preserve the rights of the minority, and facilitate the orderly transaction of business. Nehru, the Prime Minister of India laid solid foundation for democracy and development in India.

II. A SHORT BIOGRAPHY OF JAWAHARLAL NEHRU

Nehru was born in November 14, 1889, Allahabad and died on May 27, 1964, New Delhi. He was the First Prime Minister of India (1947-64), son of Independence, advocate Motilal Nehru (1861-1931). Nehru was educated at home and in Britain and became a lawyer in 1912. More interested in politics than law, he was impressed by Mohandas K. Gandhi's approach to India's independence. His close association with the Indian National Congress began in 1919; in 1929 he became its President, presiding over the historic Lahore Session that proclaimed complete independence as India's political goal. He was imprisoned nine times between 1921 and 1945 for his political activity. When India was granted limited self-government in 1935, the Congress Party under Nehru refused to form coalition governments with the Muslim League in some provinces; the hardening of relations between Hindus and Muslims that followed ultimately led to the partition of India and the creation of Pakistan. Shortly before Gandhi's assassination in 1948, Nehru became the first Prime Minister of independent India. He attempted a foreign policy of non-alignment during the cold war, drawing harsh criticism if he appeared to favour either camp. During his tenure, India had to face aggressions of troops on several occassions by Pakistan over the Kashmir region and a war with China over the Brahmaputra River Valley. He wrested Goa from Portuguese. Domestically, he promoted democracy, socialism, secularism and unity, adapting modern values to Indian conditions. His daughter Indira Gandhi became the Prime Minister two years after his death.

III. VITAL ECONOMIC ISSUES

In agriculture, large scale state intervention in the shape of extinguishing or modifying rights in property, controlling farm practice and regimenting the peoples' way of life from a prior considerations may be ever disastrous. Talk of a socialist pattern of society has been very much in the air. Nehru couples it with the welfare state as a twin objective which Congress Party has accepted. Of course, *Sarvodaya* group was against Socialism as a goal. Nehru has discounted the importance of the Communist, Communal and Praja Socialist Parties. He realizes that there can be no socialism on the basis of a pauper economy in which production is the key to progress. For elimination of inequality social ownership or control of the principal means of production is not an inescapable necessity. On the contrary, from the point of view of rapidly increasing production without adapting totalitarian coercion, there is everything to be said for an enlightened policy to encouraging private industry. Maulana Azad gave cogent reasons why nationalsation is no panacea, and British experience seem fully to bear this out. But a far more potent reason which was weighted with countries bred in—the democratic tradition against going in for socialism or for a socialistic pattern is their rooted faith in liberty as the very life breath of democracy. We in India who have accepted the democratic way of life cannot afford to jeopardise that supreme value.

1. Move to Socialistic Pattern of Society

Britain had welfare state without socialism and doing very well on it. Nehru had painstakingly sought to explain that they are not thinking of that kind of socialism at all that they contemplate something which will be as distinct from the Marxist-Leninist conception of socialism as from capitalism. Nehru's instincts are essentially democratic. He realizes that socialism of his dream cannot be realized in a day. He knows that means are no less important than ends. If confronted with the choice between socialism and democracy, we have no doubt he would prefer the latter any day.

The Hindu in November 1958 wrote that our failure to reach the Plans' food targets shows that not enough was invested in agriculture. Industrialization is not an end in itself. What should be aimed at is the reconstruction of the whole country from the village up. Today, we have roads and railways which link the big towns, we have business and industry and education mainly concentrating in the towns. But the purchasing power of the villager does not rise. The villagers want schools, bridges, markets, improved tools and machines, fertilizers as well as irrigation and electricity.

2. Mixed Economic System

Mixed economy is an inescapable consequence of the political and economic character of the country. *The role of the state should be that of a catalyst. It should not become an octopus that seeks to control every thing.*

Our plans have failed so far mainly in this latter aspect. There has been too much dependence and Central Government direction and too little of local initiative and inspiration. Neither the progress of agriculture, which is so vital for the solution of the food problem nor the diversification of industry which is essential for providing employment, will be possible unless the impulse for improvement and organization comes from the bottom, from the village and district level.

3. Rainbow of Secularism

Nehru felt that secularism did not mean something

opposed to religion or "a state where religion as such is discouraged. It means freedom of religion and conscience, including freedom for those who may have no religion." And it means a "State which honours all faiths equally and gives them equal opportunities and does not allow itself to be attached to one faith or religion."

Delhi is the eternal city, as the ruins of its forerunners-Indraprastha and Hastinapur—testify. It is the heart of India only a nit -wit can regard it as belonging to the Hindus or Sikhs alone. From Kanyakumari to Kashmir and from Gujarat to Assam, all Hindus, Muslims, Sikhas, Parsis, Christians and Jews who people this vast sub-continent and have adopted it as their dear motherland have an equal right to it. No one has the right to say it belongs to the majority only and that the minority can remain only as the underdogs. Whoever serves it with the purest devotion must have the first claim.

IV. KASHMIR AND INDIA

On the eve of Independence, All India Congress Committees (AICC) stand as declared in its resolution of June 15, 1947 was that "the people of the States must have a dominating voice in any decisions regarding them." In contrast, Mohammad Ali Jinnah asserted on July 30, that the ruler would decide which of the two States to accede to" or to remain independent. When a dispute arose with Pakistan over Kashmir's accession to India on October 26, 1947 following a tribal raid from Pakistan, Nehru said repeatedly the people would nonetheless, decide the issue in plebiscite. The international agreement that was used by V.K. Krishna Menon's words on the modalities of a plebiscite in the form of two resolutions of the UN Commission for India and Pakistan (UNCIP) dated August 13, 1948 and January, 5, 1949. Shaik M. Abdullah, Prime Minister (from 1947 till 1952) had a strong disapproval of plebiscite. On August 8, 1953 Shaik Abdullah was sacked from the office of Prime Minister of Jammu and Kashmir and put him behind the bars. Nehru felt that why would they live in a country where the Jan Sangh (presently Bharatiya Janata Party) and the Rashtriya

Swayamsevak Sangh are constantly beleaguering them. Nehru was always preaching the Mission of Secular democracy.

At present, Kashmir is an integral part of Indian Union on the basis of 'Accession' and as a symbol of Indian Secularism. Bharatiya Janata Party demanded that Kashmir is an integral part of India by removing article 370. Even today, Kashmir is a burning problem that has swallowed lot of wealth, men and energy. We are looking for amicable solution in this decade.

V. THE KAMARAJ PLAN

In August 1963, an attempt was indeed undertaken to enhance the party influence over the government through, what came to be known as "the Kamaraj Plan." The idea was to revert back government Ministers to Party positions after certain tenure and *vice versa*. Jawaharlal Nehru sympathized this theory, but hardly put his weight behind its implementation. Instead, his colleagues like Morarji Desai alleged that he used the Kamaraj Plan to remove all possible contenders "from the path of his daughter, Indira Gandhi." Besides, the Kamaraj Plan created a new dispossessed group within the Congress who had been deprived of their Ministerial positions. This increased intra-party factional squabbles. The spirit of the Kamaraj Plan was thus greatly lost.

VI. DEMOCRACY AND DEVELOPMENT

Development involves investment. It naturally involves savings—both private and public. Both are necessary. He would not like to spend a large part of resources in making more and more weapons. The industrial background has to grow, which means that we should provide for this process of development all the more. In planning, you must have clear social imperatives. In a democratic country like India, we cannot think of any social objective which does not touch the vast masses of the people. We want to produce more and more wealth and also have it properly distributed. We should continue with democracy, functioning in as wide a measure as is possible, even though the shadow of war and other troubles have hovered over us. Democracy is a complicated way of functioning and sometimes it involves delays. I think we should get rid of these delays. India is not merely a land of mountains, rivers, forests, cities, towns; it is a mass of human beings, many of them struggling for a bare pittance. We have to have perspective planning, that is, we must plan for the next 15 years or 20 years.

Ever since we become free, we have been absorbed in this major war against poverty, ignorance, illiteracy and all that. The democracy we profess and practice has not substantially grown in most countries. We established the democracy largely taken from the British and partly from the American practice.

VII. CONCLUSION

Nehru—a multifaceted personality—had introduced Parliamentary Democracy and Five Year Plans for development which became solid and strong roots for fast development. Villages were founded as 'engine of growth' for all-round development. Mixed economy was considered as a competitive boon system! Secularism was treated in Constitution and in practice, as a backbone. Even under globalization era, Kashmir is even today become a bone of contention for both countries. Democracy and development were interdependent for curing all ills, and pushing economy for welfare of all.

Notes and References

Britannica (2005), Britannica Ready reference Encyclopedia, New Delhi, Vol. 7, pp. 84, 218.

Parthasarathy (1978), A Hundred years of *The Hindu*, the Epic Story of Indian Nationalism, Kasturi and Sons Ltd., Madras, pp. 703-14.

S. Gopal (1980), *Jawaharlal Nehru: An Anthology* (Ed. Vol) OUP, Delhi, pp. 327-33.

The Hindustan Times (1948), January 18.

A.G. Noorani (1999), How and why Nehru and Abdullah fell out, *Economic and Political Weekly*, pp. 268-72.

Suranjan Das (2001), The Nehru years of Indian Politics, Edinburgh Papers, *Centre for South Asian Studies*, No. 16.

Publication Division, GoI (1983), Jawaharlal Nehru's Speeches, 1963-64, Vol. V, 49.

21

Nehru and the Policy of Mixed Economy

ASHISH N. PANDYA

Section 1 delineates how some world events like the creation of the socialist Soviet state, Great Depression of the 1930s, Keynesian economic philosophies and influences helped to create roadmap for India's economic development engineered by the country's first Prime Minister, Jawaharlal Nehru. We move from the ideas of mixed economy presented in section 2 to the ISI strategy of industrialization in the third section. However, this inward-oriented policy created the problem of debt accumulation—both internal and external. The paper concludes that a rethinking on the mixed economy is considered necessary.

INTRODUCTION

Jawaharlal Nehru had his school and college education in England where he also studied law. With the prevalent intellectual ethos in England in those eventful years of the first quarter of the 20th Century, it is not surprising at all that he evolved into a sound liberal socialist like many of his contemporary scholars. He had an abiding commitment to democracy and all the fine values that are associated with it. While he had genuine differences with Mahatma Gandhi on the economic philosophy and policy, his faith in democracy was further strengthened as he worked in close collaboration with him during the freedom struggle that eventually emancipated India from the British rule in August 1947.

I. EARLY INFLUENCES

Nehru witnessed some very significant events in the world history—the First World War followed by the Bolshevick Revolution in October 1917 that established the first Communist Government in the U.S.S.R. The capitalist world under the leadership of England was thrown in the Great Depression in the late 1920s that lasted for four years and posed a great threat to the very survival of the capitalist system. The capitalist world could regain its pre-1929 level of economic activity only in 1939 when another major catastrophe, the Second World War, struck it. At the end of the War that witnessed the atomic holocaust, England emerged as a debtor country while America ascended as a major creditor nation of the world. John Maynard Keynes, by far the most influential economist of the 20th Century, held the view that capitalism was inherently unstable especially as it enters the stage of high level of income and employment. Analyzing the nature of the economic crisis and the narrowly conceived trade policies, he wrote, "We have here an extreme example of the disharmony of general and political interest. Each nation, in an effort to improve its relative position, takes measures injurious to the absolute prosperity of its neighbours, and since its example is not confined to itself, it suffers more from similar action by its neighbours then it gains by such action itself. Practically all the remedies popularly advocated today are of this internecine character. Competitive wage-reduction, competitive tariffs, competitive liquidation of foreign assets, competitive currency deflation, competitive contraction of new developments, all are of this beggar-my-neighbour description. A modern capitalist is a fair-weather sailor. As soon as a storm arises, he abandons the duty of navigation and even sinks the boat which might carry him to safety by this haste to push his neighbours off and himself in."

Under the impact of Keynes' ideas, state intervention in the economic affairs of a country, now came to be regarded, not as a necessary evil, but as a positive good. If a communist economy in which all means of production are owned, controlled and managed by the state and in which private initiative and enterprise have no worthwhile role to play, is not a desirable arrangement, a completely *laissez faire* economy in which all business decisions regarding investment and production are taken by private individuals, would also not be acceptable it violates the acceptable norms of equity and human dignity. Keeping this serious dilemma of the real world situation in mind, Nehru gave the concept of the mixed economy with a view to harness the scarce resources of India for the overall betterment of India's population, whose vast proportion lived under abysmal economic and social conditions.

II. WHY MIXED ECONOMY?

By the middle of the 20th century, India had to choose a strategy that would ensure rapid economic development, as also rapid industrialization commensurate with its vast resources. Therefore, in order to sustain a fast rate of industrial production in future, it was thought advisable to create a strong foundation of heavy and basic industries like iron and steel, coal, aluminum, electrical equipment, etc. With the rate of savings below 10 per cent per year, private sector found it extremely difficult to raise necessary risk capital from the seriously underdeveloped capital markets of India. Under the British colonial rule, India could develop only consumer goods industries—predominantly cotton textile and jute textile in which she enjoyed considerable natural advantage in the form of availability of cheap raw materials; the only exception was the steel mill established by the doyen of Indian industrialization – Jamshedji Tata—in 1907 (Tata died in 1904 but prepared the ground work for this great business enterprise) which under the stiff British competition could become profitable only after 17 long years in 1924. Again with low per capita income and expenditure, demand for goods and services was also so small so as not to enthuse private sector industrialists to come forward with highly capital intensive basic industries for which the gestation period is quite long.

Under these circumstances, Nehru chalked out a middle path—reserving heavy capital goods industry for the public sector and leaving the consumer goods industries for the private sector that had already come forward with the setting up of the textile and jute mills in Mumbai, Kolkata and Ahmedabad right from 1850s in the wake of the setting up of the railways during the British rule in India.

The manner in which the industrial revolution worked in the capitalist countries of the West brought to the fore serious contradictions of that system—vast and growing inequality of income and wealth as well as degradation of human beings to mere factory workers, leaving hardly any scope of human ingenuity. This created disillusionment among the masses who were completely uprooted from their moorings. Nehru wrote, "Communism comes in the wake of this disillusionment and offers some kind of faith and some kind of discipline. To some extent, it fills a vacuum. It succeeds in some measure by giving content to man's life. But inspite of its apparent success, it fails partly because of its rigidity but, even more so, because it ignores certain essential needs of human nature.

There is much talk in communism of the contradictions of capitalist society and there is truth in that analysis. But we see the growing contradictions within the rigid framework of communism itself. Its suppression of individual freedom brings about powerful reactions. Its contempt for what might be called the moral and spiritual side of life not only ignores something that is basic in man but also deprives human behaviour of standards and values. Its unfortunate association with violence encourages a certain evil tendency in human beings."

"I have the greatest admiration for many of the achievements of the Soviet Union. Among these great achievements is the value attached to a child and the common man. Their systems of education and health are probably the best in the world. But it is said, and rightly, that there is suppression of individual freedom there. And yet the spread of education in all its forms is itself a tremendous liberating force which ultimately will not tolerate that suppression of freedom. This again is another contradiction. Unfortunately communism became too closely associated with the necessity for violence and thus the idea which it placed before the world became a tainted one. Means distorted ends. We see the powerful influence of wrong means and methods (Nehru, 1958)."

And let us now read a few lines by a philosopher in Nehru, *"This argument leads to the Vedantic conception that everything,* whether sentient or insentient, finds a place in the organic whole; that everything has a spark of what might be called the divine impulse or the basic energy or life force which pervades the Universe. This leads to metaphysical regions which tend to take us away from the problems of life which face us. I suppose that any line of thought sufficiently pursued leads us in some measure to metaphysics. Even science today is almost on the verge of all manner of imponderables. I do not propose to discuss these metaphysical aspects, but this very argument indicates how the mind searches for something basic underlying the physical world. If we really believed in this all pervading concept of the principle of life, it might help us to get rid of some of our narrowness of race, cast or class and make us more tolerant and understanding in our approaches to life's problems."

III. RATIONALE FOR IMPORT SUBSTITUTION POLICY

Closely linked to the issue of mixed economy versus *laisez-faire* policy is the one associated with the foreign trade policy. While the International Monetary Fund and the World Bank, from their inception, strongly pleaded for the outward-oriented free trade policy (or the export promotion policy), most of the poor underdeveloped countries right from the 1950s pursued an inward-looking foreign trade policy (or the import substitution policy). In other words, guided by the export pessimism hypothesis advocated by economists like Nurkse, Prebisch and Singer, Nehru also threw his weight in favour of this argument. Thus, while the few highly developed industrialized economies of the world pursued the export promotion policy gradually reducing import duties on manufactured goods under the GATT arrangements, the vast majority of the developing countries worked with the import (restricting) substitution policy. And there was a rationale for this in those days when the colonised countries were just becoming free from the economic exploitation of a century or even longer, their mistrust for the economic policies recommended by the IMF and the World Bank in whose decision-making these poor countries had very little voice, was just palpable. Explaining this great ideological divide between the export promotion strategy and the import substitution strategy, it is observed, "The first reason for the separation of many economies from the international system derived from the widespread conviction that an alternative set of economic rules or even a different logic applied to developing countries. The differences concerned the appropriate degree of exposure to the international economy and the desirability of domestic financial stability... A difference in understanding about the operation of the international economy and the associated conviction that the other side was acting out of a fundamentally political logic, profoundly handicapped the IMF in its relations with many developing country members. Many influential analysts, however, believed that poorer countries would be damaged by exposures to the international system, that emerging manufacturers would be destroyed and that the export of a limited number of commodities would create an untolerable dependence. Access to capital flows would be difficult or impossible."

"Some analysts went further than Singer and Prebisch and asserted that the entire process of development was a political struggle. According to this view, developed countries, in order to be able to appropriate for themselves a greater share of the world's resources, had used the theory of neoclassical economies as an ideological instrument. Their insistence on comparative advantage and the mutuality of gains from trade constituted a duplicitous and hypocritical masking of their own exploitative interests. Import substitution strategies, on the other hand, might provide an economic basis for the assertion of sovereignty and political independence, as well as self-enrichment by developing countries. If this analysis was valid, the demand for speedy balance of payments adjustment looked like another weapon of developed countries to hold down developing countries below their optimum growth path."

Some Unfavourable Effects

With the scarcity of savings in India, the Government of India had to resort to public borrowing year after year. The large part of public borrowing was subscribed to by the financial institutions like the nationalized commercial banks, Life Insurance Corporation, and others. The Reserve Bank of India went on increasing the Statutory Liquidity Ratio and the Cash Reserve Ratio. As a result of this, together with other measures like concessional lending to the priority sectors, the banks experienced shortage of loanable funds, lending to increase in the lending rates by them, adversely affecting the investment climate in the Indian economy.

Again, with emphasis on the development of heavy industries, demand for imports from abroad went on rising year after year. At the same time, export performance did not improve significantly. As a result of this policy, India had persistent deficit in its balance of trade and deficit in its current account of the balance of payments. India had to resort to external borrowing from the multilateral financial institutions and a few friendly countries. All this cumulatively led to increasing burden of both—the internal debt as well as external debt.

CONCLUSION

While the policy of mixed economy was a sound economic idea in the 1950s and the 1960s, it certainly required some sound rethinking and consequent modifications in some of the basic economic polices like the fiscal and the monetary policies. No country in the world can hope to secure rapid industrial development with high interest rates and similarly no economy can afford to have persistent balance of payments deficits and consequent increase in external debt. Sooner than later, such an economy would be downgraded by the international rating agencies, making it difficult for it to borrow further and eventually leading to the foreign exchange crisis.

In 1966, when India devalued her rupee, there was an opportunity to open up the economy to some extent. Similarly, once the industrial growth slowed down considerably after 1975, there was an opportunity to look at the desirability of continuing with the loss-making public sector units and allowing entry of the private sector into some more industries. While some of the public sector units like the oil refineries and others have done quite well, many others proved to be cost inefficient, draining away scarce resources of our developing economy. Some of the crucial heavy and basic industries could never have been developed in the fifties and the sixties except by the public sector as these units required huge lumpy investment with a long gestation period.

And finally taking into account the serious financial crisis in the U.S.A. whose correct magnitude is still known, it is time to look into the policy of leaving all sensitive financial decisions to the mortgage bankers and the investment bankers as a part of the unbridled globalization. Keeping such anxiety like this in mind, George Soros said, "Because of the failures of socialism, communism, we have come to believe in market fundamentalism, that markets are perfect; everything will be taken care of by markets. And markets are not perfect. And this time we have to recognize that, because we are facing a very serious economic disruption, now we should not go back to a very highly regulated economy because the regulators are imperfect. They are also human and what is worse, they are bureaucratic. So you have to find the right kind of balance between allowing the markets to do their work, while recognizing that they are imperfect. You need authorities that keep the market under screwing and some degree of control."

References

Keynes, J. M. (1931), *"The World's Economic Crisis and the Way to Escape"*, Jalley Steward Lecture.

Nehru, Jawaharlal, A note published in *A.I.C.C. Economic Review*, August 15, 1958 reprinted in *Selected Speeches*, Vol. 4, 1957-63.

Nehru, Jawaharlal, *ibid*.

James Harold (1996), *International Monetary Cooperation since Bretton Woods*. International Monetary Fund and Oxford University Press.

Soros George, "Interview to the New York Review of Books", May 15, 2008, on his recently released book, *The New Paradigm for Financial Markets: The Credit Crash of 2008 and What it Means*, from an article by C.P. Chandrashekhar in *Frontline* May 23, 2008.

Index